CHICHESTER
IN THE 1960s

CHICHESTER
IN THE 1960S

ALAN H.J. GREEN

The History Press

DEDICATED TO THE MEMORY OF:

John Birch (1929–2012), organist of Chichester Cathedral 1958–80
and
Peter Iden (1945–2012), celebrated Chichester artist

Much-missed friends who contributed so much to the artistic life of this city they loved,
and also contributed material for this book which, sadly, they were not to see in print.

Front Cover

Change: Buses reversing in Tower Street in 1956. At that time buses terminated in West Street
and the necessary reversing caused much congestion. By the 1960s this problem had been
removed with the opening of a proper bus station in Southgate, which was fortunate as the
rapid increase in car ownership in that decade would have meant that West Street would
have been gridlocked for most of the day.

Culture: One of the most distinguished Cicestrians in the 1960s, Bernard Price Price was a
writer, broadcaster, art connoisseur and antiques expert. Here he is seen opening the new
headquarters for the 12th Chichester Scout Group in 1969.

Back Cover

Conservation: Chichester became the subject of a study into conservation in 1968 but, sadly,
only after the east side of Somerstown had been unnecessarily destroyed in 1964.

First published 2015

The History Press
The Mill, Brimscombe Port
Stroud, Gloucestershire, GL5 2QG
www.thehistorypress.co.uk

British Library Cataloguing in Publication Data.
A catalogue record for this book is available from the British Library.

ISBN 978 0 7509 6141 7

Typesetting and origination by The History Press
Printed in Great Britain

Contents

About the Author

ALAN H.J. GREEN was born and educated in Chichester and observed the changes to his city in the 1960s at first hand.

He writes and lectures widely on his long-held interest in Chichester's history and the art and architecture of Georgian Britain. He is chairman of the Chichester Conservation Area Advisory Committee, on which he represents the Georgian Group, and serves on the committees of both Chichester Local History Society and the Sussex Industrial Archaeology Society. Alan H.J. Green is author of a number of local titles including *Chichester: St John's Chapel and the New Town* and *The Buildings of Georgian Chichester*. He lives in Chichester.

Acknowledgements

Researching a work of this size and complexity would not be possible without considerable assistance from a large number of organisations and individuals. Acknowledging that assistance brings with it the risk of omission, and if I have committed this crime I apologise unreservedly and assure the *umilee* that this was owing to ever-increasing senior moments rather than a cavalier attitude to their contribution.

I must begin with the ever-patient staff of West Sussex Record Office (WSRO), where the bulk of the research was carried out, and who supplied scans of photographs and permission to publish them. I also thank the staff of Chichester Library where I accessed the all-important microfilms of the *Chichester Observer*. I must thank the town clerk, Rodney Duggua, and Clare Adams of Chichester City Council for granting me access to the council's archive and permission to reproduce their photographs of civic occasions. Similarly Prof. Clive Behagg, vice chancellor, and Janet Carter, archivist, of the University of Chichester kindly supplied photographs and information about the building of the Chapel of the Ascension of the former Bishop Otter College and gave permission for their reproduction here for which I am most grateful. Martin Hayes, County Local Studies Librarian of West Sussex County Council Library Service, kindly supplied information about the new Chichester Library and the photograph of the much-vaunted computerised ticketing system in use.

Producing this book has made for a pleasurable stroll down memory lane – and not only for me, for it has been my privilege to be able to stir the memories of many other Cicestrians and raid their photograph albums, thus adding contemporary anecdotal and photographic evidence to the story. These include Anne Scicluna, John Templeton, Chris Butler, Garry Long, David Stuckey, Allan and

Pat Ware, Linda Wilkinson, Richard Pailthorpe, Martin Philmore, Gerry Adams, Geoffrey Claridge, Eve Willard and the late John Birch and Peter Iden.

It is a local historian's dream to discover rich seams of previously unpublished photographs to illustrate his tome and I have been particularly fortunate to be given access to two such collections. The first was that of John Iden, who as a young man was a very keen photographer, meticulously cataloguing and dating each negative. When a building was threatened with demolition, off John went to record it. The second collection was that of Rod Funnell who, as an architect practicing in the city in the 1960s (he designed the new library), took progress pictures of the projects with which he was involved. To both these gents I am extremely grateful. Once again John Templeton has kindly granted me permission to reproduce more of his superb – and now famous – 1960s slides, most notably those of the Big Freeze of 1962/63.

I am also grateful to Terry Carlysle who has a nose for sniffing out Chichester snippets and artefacts on the Internet, and making eBay purchases on my behalf via the good offices of her daughter Felicity, who is skilled in the art of virtual auctions, which I am not.

I have attempted to record many of Chichester's organisations, institutions and businesses of the period and in this have received valuable help from people involved, namely Allan and Pat Ware (St John Ambulance Brigade and Girl Guides), Michael Merritt (12th Chichester Scouts) Mick Bleach (Bleaches Coaches) Gerald Brockhurst (Everymans Coaches), Pam Jones (Granada Cinema), Vera Abraham and Sue Marchant (Jessie Younghusband School) and Rachael Morriarty and Eileen Brown (Bishop Luffa School). In many cases this has resulted in unearthing yet more unpublished photographs as well as forgotten artefacts.

The controversial development of the East Broyle Estate spanned the decade and I am grateful to Ian Creswick for access to the deeds of his East Broyle house and to his son Richard who, when on a work experience placement at WSRO, helped me with the research into this convoluted project; to Graham Brooks and Michael Merritt who provided some early photographs of the development and to Ken Rimell and the *Chichester Observer* for permission to publish the two aerial photographs.

To all these I express my deep-felt thanks for their time, support and – above all – generosity.

LIST OF ILLUSTRATIONS

27. Stride & Son notice of auction of East Broyle Farm, 1959
28. No. 74 Norwich Road when new in 1968
29. No through road! East end of Norwich Road today
30. Aerial view across East Broyle Estate looking west, 1975
31. View across East Broyle Estate looking north, 1975
32. Extract from 1960 Ordnance Survey of St John's Street
33. South end of St John's Street, 1966
34. Basin Road looking south, 1962
35. Town map of 1966 showing revised alignments of ring road
36. Nos 32–35 Southgate and Bedford Hotel, 1960
37. Orchard Street seen from North Walls, 1965
38. East end of Franklin Place being demolished, 1967
39. Northgate car park under construction, 1961
40. Demolition of Halsted's ironfoundry, 1960
41. Cover of Chichester conservation area study report, 1968
42. Nos 48–57 George Street, Somerstown, 1963
43. East side of Broyle Road, Somerstown, 1963
44. Another view of Broyle Road, Somerstown, 1963
45. Demolition of Waggon & Horses, Somerstown, 1964
46. View across Somerstown during demolition, 1964
47. Eastgate Square, 1960
48. Eastgate Square, 1964, with Sharp Garland's shop being demolished
49. Sharp Garland's shop being demolished, 1964
50. View of the cathedral from Westgate Fields, 1960
51. Chichester College under construction, 1964
52. Westgate 'bottleneck' looking west, 1962
53. Last look at the view of the cathedral from Westgate Fields, 1962
54. Southgate end of the ring road under construction, 1965
55. Buildings on the west side of Southgate awaiting demolition, 1963
56. Westgate in July 1962
57. Nos 16–40 Orchard Street, 1961
58. West Street with demolition of Westgate in background, 1963
59. Another view of Westgate demolition, 1963
60. Old theatre on South Street when it was Lewis's furniture shop
61. Model of Chichester Festival Theatre
62. Festival Theatre under construction, 1961
63. Festival Theatre, 1967
64. Interior of Festival Theatre, 1962
65. Cover of First Season Festival Theatre programme, 1962
66. Postcard with commemorative postmark for first Festival Theatre season, 1962

INTRODUCTION

The 1960s, often lauded as the 'greatest' era of the twentieth century, are generally remembered as either a time of welcome liberation from the straight-laced propriety of the first half of the century or an era of great destruction when the hearts were ripped out of our towns and cities in the name of progress. Either way it was a decade of great change – change that was felt right across the land, and even sleepy Chichester was provided with many threats and challenges thereby, as well as gaining some welcome new assets.

It has to be admitted at the outset that Chichester (pronounced by its natives as *Chiddester*) has always been something of a backwater, never acquiring a fast, direct road or railway link of its own to London and not being en route from London to anywhere more important either. This meant (and still means) lengthy journey times which may be the major reason why it has not undergone the exponential growth of other south coast towns but instead remained pleasantly small. In 1961 its population was 20,118 and it had only risen to 21,170 by 1970; at the time of writing it is some 25,000 but Chichester is now being threatened with unwelcome rapid expansion to satiate the national demand for more housing.

In the 1960s Chichester was still very much a market town. Wednesday was market day, with beast and traders' markets taking place at the Cattle Market site in Market Road. At this time cattle were still being driven through the streets from the station by colourful drovers. Chichester was also still a garrison town; the large barracks at the top of The Broyle had been home to the Royal Sussex Regiment since 1881, but they relocated to Canterbury in 1960 and, after a gap, the barracks became home to the Royal Military Police (the Recaps) who took up residence in 1964 and entered fully into the life of the city.

Chichester has always been regarded by its younger residents as a dead town where 'nothing ever happens', and in the 1960s the young had go to Portsmouth or Brighton (or, even worse, Bognor) for their thrills. Chichester was seen by them to be anything but 'swinging'. However, the spirit of the 1960s did not entirely pass Chichester by; the city did provide some refuge for the young in its new coffee bars and the jazz club at Fishbourne. Celebrities from the world of rock and roll would appear from time to time, most notably when some of the Rolling Stones were tried here for drugs offences in 1967, an event that emptied out the local girls' schools whose pupils took the morning off to scream outside the courthouse.

Chichester, as with all cathedral cities, has long had artistic associations, but the opening of Chichester Festival Theatre in 1962 set it on the road of being the city of culture that it is today. That a national theatre could be built – and thrive – in such a one-horse town as Chichester baffled the pundits, but built it was, and it attracted no less a personage than Sir Laurence Olivier as its first director. It remains a popular draw to the city.

Chichester did suffer at the hands of 1960s developers but this was checked sharply by a public backlash over some particularly brutal destruction that took place in 1964 and, three years later, its being adopted by the Minister of Housing and local government as a subject for a conservation study.

Sixties Chichester was a city with tremendous civic pride which engendered great loyalty amongst its citizens, many of whom served it in all sorts of ways. Indeed it was striking how, in the course of the research, the same well-known Chichester names kept cropping up in different connections.

Having been born in 1950, the 1960s were my formative years and I witnessed at first hand how the decade shaped (and, perhaps more importantly, failed to reshape) the City of Chichester. With the eye of an observant schoolboy I watched eagerly all that was going on around me, rejoicing in the constant activity at the railway shunting yard, enjoying the hard winter of 1962/63 and not noticing any particular inconvenience, observing the building of the Festival Theatre and lamenting the running down and final, unnecessary destruction of the east side of Somerstown.

Chichester has been well served by local historians over the years and so some subjects – the building of the Festival Theatre and the fate of Somerstown for example – have already been covered in much detail elsewhere. Where this is the case such subjects have still been included but covered less exhaustively so as to permit more space to be devoted to those that have not; the stories of the creation of the museum, swimming pool and new library, for example, being told here for the first time and in detail.

It is often a moot point as to when a decade actually begins. Technically it should be with the '1' year – i.e. 1961 – and run to 1970, but here I will include all nine of the 'sixties' years and, now and again, drift back into the late 1950s and forwards into the early 1970s in order to provide a more complete picture. Consider it to be a long decade, as in 'the long eighteenth century'.

I did not set out to cover every single aspect of Chichester life in the 1960s, to have done so would have been – for me – an insurmountable task. The choice of what has been included is entirely mine, and naturally (even self-indulgently) I have veered towards those subjects which most interested me or touched me personally in some way during the era in question. To those who have bought the book only to find their pet subject omitted, I apologise.

In this work, documentary research has been backed up by personal memories to produce an account which is primarily evidential, but spiced with memoirs[*] of the city during the 1960s, hopefully providing some nostalgia along with some long-forgotten facts about Chichester in the Swinging Sixties.

Alan H.J. Green
Chichester, 2015

---

[*] Memoirs, especially when recalled in advancing years, can be notoriously unreliable hence the order of priority.

ONE

PRELUDE: THE SWINGING SIXTIES

'If you can remember the 1960s you weren't really there' runs an oft quoted, but seemingly unattributed, maxim about the decade that brought an explosion of youth culture: summers of sex, drugs and rock and roll, long hair, free love, the cult of the hippy and, particularly, liberation. As a result of this the sixties have become almost venerated, ushering in, as they did, some of the most significant social changes of the twentieth century – 'The old order changeth, yielding place to the new', as King Arthur lamented from his death-barge in Tennyson's *Morte d'Arthur*.

It was an explosion that was waiting to happen. Post-war austerity meant that rationing had continued into the 1950s with 'make do and mend' remaining the order of the day. The Festival of Britain had been held in 1951 and was intended to inject a spirit of optimism into a jaded nation. Chichester took part, in its provincial way, staging its own celebrations over the months of May to October 1951 and in the programme the mayor, Russell Purchase, describing the times as 'difficult days', urged Cicestrians* to participate in the projects and activities that had been arranged. Unfortunately the hope of a prosperous new age was slow in coming and the 1950s are irretrievably tinged with an air of dowdiness.

Youth rebellion was a theme that ran throughout the 1960s, sometimes reflected in almost tribal warfare. The most significant manifestation of this was in the 'Mods and Rockers' skirmishes. 'Mods' rode motor-scooters and 'Rockers' fast motorbikes and each was wedded to different varieties of popular music and clothing. In the summer of 1964 swarms of Mods and Rockers descended upon south coast seaside resorts and engaged in pitched battles in which knives were used. In Sussex, Brighton was particularly affected in this respect but I remember

* 'Cicestrian' is the term for those who were born and brought up in Chichester.

1. The cover of the programme for Chichester's Festival of Britain celebrations. (Author's collection)

seeing such swarms gathering on the green at Littlehampton one Sunday after-noon that year. The family beat a hasty retreat to the station before any trouble broke out.

THE POLITICS

In 1960 Harold Macmillan's Conservative government were in power, headed by a prime minister well remembered for his famous epithet 'The British people have never had it so good.' Not everyone shared this view however and, unbe-known to him at the time, 'Supermac's' days were numbered in the land. Within a few years he was to be brought down by a series of scandals involving his gov-ernment ministers.

The first part of the M1 – Motorway One – from London to Birmingham had opened in November 1959 under the Minister of Transport, Ernest Marples, whose family construction company – Marples Ridgeway – just happened to have built it. In 1961 Marples commissioned the infamous Beeching Report on the future of British Railways; it was published in March 1963 and set out to prune Britain's rail network from 21,900 route miles to 16,900 and close 2,363 stations.[1] The future of transport was seen by the government as being in roads not railways; car ownership was increasing rapidly, offering freedom from a life dictated by bus and railway timetables, and a powerful road lobby was emerging to influence parliamentary decisions in this direction. The brief post-war golden age of rail and coach travel was rapidly coming to an end.

Whilst the Beeching Report was being got ready for the printers, the whole country was plunged into chaos by sub-arctic conditions that maintained a heavy covering of snow from Boxing Day 1962 until March 1963. Even the sea froze, and all this took place in an era when comparatively few had central heating – especially here in provincial Chichester – so the 'Winter of 1962/3' became legendary. The wartime spirit was revived to keep the country going.

In 1963 a notorious scandal broke involving John Profumo, the Secretary of State for War, who was exposed as having a steamy affair with a 19-year-old model, Christine Keeler, whose favours were also being sought by the Assistant Soviet Naval Attaché in London. After lying about the affair in the Commons, Profumo resigned in June 1963. The following September Macmillan resigned as prime minister in the face of personal illness and rising public scorn about scandals, and he was replaced by Sir Alec Douglas-Home, whose tenure was to be short-lived; Labour came into power, but with only a small majority, in October 1964 under Harold Wilson, a man who, apart from sharing the same Christian name, was as different from Old Etonian Harold Macmillan as a grammar-school boy could be. The country had felt a need for change – the old order had to go and the first Labour government for thirteen years was elected.[2] Meetings between grandees in exclusive London clubs were replaced by beer and sandwiches at No. 10.

In November 1963 the world was shocked by the assassination of American President John F. Kennedy, one of those events so momentous that everyone remembers where they were at the time – I do; I was in bed, aged 14, with pneumonia. The ease with which Kennedy was able to be picked off by a sniper as he rode in an open car ushered in a new age of security consciousness that was to get steadily more rigorous and invasive as the century wore on.

Another general election was called in 1966 under which Labour increased its majority, something that was necessary to ensure that new legislation could be passed. Harold Wilson won the election with a majority of ninety-seven over the Conservatives, led by Edward Heath, and the Liberals under Joe Grimmond. However, the influence of the trades unions grew and strikes over pay and conditions became commonplace; everyone wanted that bit more out of life and Wilson's social contract – an unofficial agreement with the unions – failed to curb the unrest.

One major plank of the Labour manifesto was the concept of universal comprehensive (i.e. non-selective) secondary education. A few new comprehensive schools had been opened in London under the previous Conservative government as an experiment in doing away with the stigma of failing the Eleven-plus examination, the examination whose passing was necessary to gain a place at a grammar school. Under Labour's policy all grammar and secondary modern schools would be converted to comprehensives and much progress was to be made with this in the 1970s, resulting in grammar schools becoming a rarity. In West Sussex all grammar schools were to be completely eliminated, but in neighbouring Kent and Surrey many survived.

The year 1968 was marred by civil rights demonstrations in Befast which marked the restart of 'the Troubles' and the infamous 'rivers of blood' speech made in Birmingham on 20 April by the right-wing Conservative MP Enoch Powell, who advocated an end to immigration in a speech which polarised the nation.[3] The following year, 1969, the politically charged 'space race' between the USA and Russia saw the first man land on the moon in July; America won the race.

At home Harold Wilson's policies, which included devaluing the pound in 1967, failed to get the country back on its feet after what he described as 'thirteen wasted years' and he was ousted by Edward Heath's Conservative government in the 1970 general election. Edward Heath had the task of leading the country into the 1970s, which, as it happened, were to prove no less turbulent.

THE CHANGING FACE OF THE TOWNSCAPE

From the early 1960s, in some parts of the country crooked developers were brib-
ing corrupt councillors into condemning areas of quite serviceable Georgian
and Victorian housing, after which said developers were permitted to reap the
benefit of the sites. Investigations into such suspected practices eventually resulted
in the famous trials of two men, the millionaire developer-architect John Poulson
and Councillor T. Dan Smith who was the Labour leader of Newcastle City
Council between 1960 and 1964. The trials finally took place in 1973 and both
men were detained at Her Majesty's Pleasure having been convicted of corruption.[4] Unfortunately massive redevelopment – whether driven by criminal activity
or not – had swept across the country throughout the 1960s, changing the face
of many towns and cities; even historic Bath, now a World Heritage Site, was
badly affected. In larger cities, under the aegis of slum clearance, poorer families
were re-housed in faceless tower blocks whose shiny novelty quickly gave rise to
unexpected social problems. The London Borough of Croydon was redeveloped
into a business centre with a massing of ugly, high-rise office buildings (several by
Mr Poulson himself) irretrievably altering its character.

Much 1960s architecture can best be described as tacky, both in construction and
appearance, and the wholesale destruction of older buildings that were in the way
can only be described as philistinism. The Town and Country Planning Act had
come into force in 1947 and buildings deemed to be of historic and architectural
importance had begun to be listed in 1950, but neither of these constraints seemed
to be allowed get in the way of this 'progress'. There were lessons to be learned but,
unfortunately, they were not to be learned until it was far too late for many places.
Chichester, as we shall see, got off comparatively lightly in this respect.[*]

It is against this backdrop that the history of Chichester in the Swinging Sixties
has to be set.

Notes

1   *The Reshaping of British Railways* produced by the British Railways Board under the chairmanship of Dr Richard Beeching – who had come from the chemical industry. (Published by
HMSO, 1963.)

2   Burke, J., *An illustrated History of England* (London, HarperCollins, 1985).

3   Obituary of Enoch Powell, *The Daily Telegraph*, 9 February 1998.

4   Obituary of T. Dan Smith, *The Independent*, 31 July 1993.

[*]   1964 was the year when destruction was at its height in Chichester, and the effects were
indeed dire but could have been much worse – see Chapter Four.

TWO

ROUND AND ABOUT
THE TOWN HALL

Throughout the 1960s Chichester was administered by a mayor and Corporation, as it had been since medieval times. Known as 'Chichester City Council' (but often shortened to 'the Corporation') this body displayed all the civic pride which came with such an ancient foundation, and its elected members, many of them Cicestrians, all lived in the city they sought to serve. This was local government at its most local – and none the worse for that.

2. Civic pride: civic duty. The procession to the cenotaph on Remembrance Day, 1962. The two mayor's constables, carrying staves, precede the macebearer who escorts the mayor, Cllr John Selsby, who is followed by the mayor's chaplain and then the members of the council. They are seen in St Pancras passing the end of New Park Road. The building in the background is the former Elizabeth Jonston's Girls School which by this time had undergone a gender change to become an annexe of the Central Junior Boys' School in New Park Road. It was demolished in 1966 as was the large shed behind it which was Farr's Depository. (Chichester City Council)

CHICHESTER CITY COUNCIL

Chichester City Council still exists but, as we shall see, now reduced to parish council status. The Chichester City Council of the 1960s was a very different body, it was responsible for providing virtually all public services within the city boundary – planning, highways, sewerage, refuse collection, water supply*, housing, parks, markets – you name it, the city council did it. It also managed Chichester Harbour and owned Dell Quay. Indeed, Chichester City Council was equivalent – but on a much smaller scale – to one of those 'unitary authorities' that have recently been created; current perceived wisdom being that it is probably better to have all functions under one large umbrella rather than several smaller ones – what goes around comes around as they say. The rural area outside the city boundary was administered by Chichester Rural District Council whose offices were at Pallant House, the building that is now Pallant House Gallery.

In the 1960s, membership of the council comprised eighteen elected councillors and six aldermen from whose ranks were chosen the mayor and deputy mayor.[1] Councillors were elected by the citizens of Chichester to serve a term of three years and a constant stream of endings-of-terms plus the occasional death and resignation meant that at least one municipal election needed to be held every year from 1959 to 1970 to elect new councillors. The main elections were held on the second Thursday of May, but interim ones would be called if necessary.

Before the Second World War those who stood for election as councillors did so on their own ticket and were not put forward or sponsored by a political party, candidates conducted their own campaigns and stood solely because they wanted to serve their town. However, after the war party politics began to enter local government and in the 1950s Chichester City Council became infected, but some candidates still stood on an independent ticket. However, when the one and only Labour councillor lost his seat, the Conservative members dropped their political labels and re-registered as independents. In the May 1957 campaign the *Chichester Observer* carried the headline 'IND. RATEPAYERS ON WARPATH AGAIN' and reported that two candidates would be standing on the Independent Ratepayers ticket, who, if elected, would bring their total numbers to five.

In May 1960 there was a particularly high number of candidates – eleven – for the six vacant seats and the candidates, who include some prominent Chichester names, and the votes they polled were as follows:[2]

(E) William Brookes, civil servant		795
(E) John M Selsby, electrical engineer		707

---

* Water supply was transferred to Portsmouth Water Company in 1963.

(E) Robert Owen Stewart, Air Ministry employee	581
(S) William Chiverton, engineer	747
(S) Reginald Dray, company director	344
(S) John Sanctuary, machinist	478
(S) Robert Stephens, tobacconist and confectioner	867
(W) Alfred Brinsmead, manufacturer's agent	671
(W) John Gilbert, bank clerk	777
(W) Jeremy Goodyer-Pink, soft drink manufacturer	614
(W) Gordon Douglas, licensed victualler	487

Those elected on 12 May 1960 were Messrs Brookes and Selsby to the east ward, Stephens and Chiverton to the south and Gilbert and Brinsmead to the west. It is noticeable that the eleven candidates were all male. J.M. Selsby, the electrical contractor, traded from a shop in Westgate and Robert (Bob) Stephens ran the famous confectionery and tobacconist shop by the entrance to Priory Park, a shop well known to thousands of past Chichester children. Both these men, plus John Gilbert and William Brookes elected at the same time, were to go on to hold the office of Mayor of Chichester, but for John Gilbert this was not to occur until 1971, beyond the era of this account. However, that appointment was to be an

3. *The mayor-making ceremony of 1960 in the Assembly Room with Cllr William Pope receiving the civic insignia. To the left is Eric Banks, the town clerk. The impressive seventeenth-century mace lies on the table. (Chichester City Council)*

historic one as he was the first Roman Catholic Mayor of Chichester since the Reformation*. Until the recommendations of the Second Vatican Council were ratified in 1965, a Catholic mayor would have been impossible since Catholics were forbidden, by their own canon law, from participating in Protestant services; a Catholic mayor would not have been able to attend his own important civic services in the cathedral**.

At this time the city council had reverted to a largely apolitical existence, but that all changed in the election of May 1962.

For the 1962 election the Liberal party put forward a candidate, Mervyn Cutten, a well-respected Cicestrian (and, as it happens, local historian) for the south ward and his campaign leaflet urged voters to 'put life into local government' by going Liberal. Cutten topped the polls with 962 votes, the next highest number of votes going to William Pope, whose campaign slogan was 'Vote for Pope, the Ratepayers' Hope', with 674.[3] The following year Labour put up a candidate as did the Liberals, and the Liberal was elected. This caused the *Chichester Observer* to publish its report on the election results under the headline *Will Party Politics Come Back Again?* :

> … for three or four years all has been quiet politically but what will happen now that there are two Liberals? Is there likely to be a revival of the events following election of the first Socialist ten years ago? The Liberals say there will definitely be no party line in the Council Chamber …
>
> … the Chairman of the Conservative Constituency Organisation, Barry Rose, declared that he 'could not imagine Conservatives standing quietly by and allowing Liberals to obtain control without opposition'.[4]

At the 1965 municipal election the Liberals held seven seats and the Conservatives again expressed concern, Mr Rose telling the *Chichester Observer* that the Conservatives would not stand by indefinitely and saying:

---

* Told to the author by Anne Scicluna, John Gilbert's daughter. Anne is both a city and a district councillor and has thrice been Mayor of Chichester, thus maintaining the family tradition.

** Chichester High School for Boys, which I attended in the 1960s, was not a church school so its morning assemblies, although religious, were non-denominational. However, prior to Vatican II, Catholic boys were forbidden by the same dogma from attending the main assembly – but even after it they only attended on Fridays, and for the rest of the week they had their own services conducted by a Catholic member of staff.

YOUR LIBERAL CANDIDATE

MERVYN CUTTEN is

★ 46 years of age and is employed as a bedding manager at a Chichester furniture store. He resides in the South Ward and is already well known to many electors.

★ keen to see public opinion developed and made more effective in local government. To this end he is anxious to establish a permanent means of meeting the South Ward electors.

★ particularly interested in the City. He was responsible for the " Changing Chichester " exhibition which he organised last year.

★ anxious to see Chichester developing more quickly. Too much emphasis is placed on preserving that which is old. That which is worthwhile should be preserved but our sights must be set on the future.

37, Whyke Lane,
Chichester.
May, 1962.

To the electors of the South Ward

Ladies and Gentlemen,

It is with much pleasure that I present myself to you as the first Liberal candidate at the Chichester City Council elections for very many years.

I stand as a Liberal because I feel that every elector is entitled to know a candidate's politics as these must play some part in a Councillor's approach to local affairs. If by standing as a Liberal I can help to break down the apathy which exists at local elections I shall feel that something worthwhile has been achieved.

This month over 2,200 Liberals will be seeking election to local authorities in England and Wales. This is half as many again as last year. Since 1959 the number of Liberal councillors in the country has trebled. Everywhere they are bringing a breath of fresh air into the Council Chamber and furthermore they keep the electors informed of what is going on.

I have already met many of you—and I hope to meet many more in the course of the next few days. If you have any points you would like to raise please ring me at Chichester 4027 (evenings), or call at the above address, and I shall be only too pleased to discuss them with you.

Yours sincerely,
MERVYN CUTTEN.

Put some LIFE into local government

— GO LIBERAL !

VOTE CUTTEN

Printed by Chaffer and Son, Chichester, and published by P. F. Weston, 6, Ettrick Ciose, Chichester.

4. Mervyn Cutten's campaign leaflet for the 1962 city council election in which he sets out his party-political stall. (WSRO)

The problem is that the City will shortly have (if we do not enter the fray) a Liberal-controlled council while we believe the majority of Chichester is, in fact, Conservative minded.[5]

The rest, as they say, is history. From then on party politics returned to the manifestos, although some continued to stand as 'Independent Ratepayers', and from 1970 the political allegiances of council candidates began to be recorded in the minute books. With the benefit of hindsight, one has to wonder whether we might have lost something through the politicisation [sic] of local government. Was it not better when there was no voting along party lines because there were no party lines to toe?

There were only three wards then, east, south and west, and of these west was by far the largest, including as it did Parklands and Summersdale. West Ward was getting larger as a result of expansion in both Parklands and Summersdale, and in May 1965 the Corporation, who had been considering the creation of a fourth (north) ward, decided to defer any such decision for a year[6] – which they did every year after that, to the end that creation of the North Ward did not happen until after local government reorganisation in 1974.

Although the election of councillors was by the citizens of Chichester, the election of mayor and his deputy was not; these important offices were elected by councillors themselves. Mayoral elections, followed by the mayor-making ceremony, took place in the last week in May, as they had done since 1947. Mayors were elected to serve a term of one year, but at this period it was usual for them to be re-elected at the end of the first year to serve a second term. Once elected, the mayor nominated his deputy. The holders of these offices through the 1960s were:

	Mayor	**Deputy**
1959–61	William Pope,	George Welch
1961–63	John Selsby,	Harry Ball
1963–65	William Brookes,	Alfred Brinsmead
1965–67	Harry Bell,	Samuel Watson
1967–69	Robert Stephens,	David Thomas
1969	Samuel Watson	James Seddon
1970	Thomas Siggs	Arthur Ingram

The mayor's salary – or 'remuneration' as it was called – was £700 per annum in 1964 increasing to £800 in 1967 and £850 in 1970. Some senior councillors were elected from within as aldermen, and there were typically up to six of these, three of whom would be appointed as returning officers. Aldermen could not

5. Cllr Harry Bell being made Mayor of Chichester in May 1965, here signing the declaration of acceptance under the watchful eye of Eric Banks, the town clerk dressed in his wig and bands. Harry Bell served as mayor for two years at the end of which, in 1967, he was elected an alderman. (Chichester City Council)

hold a council seat and so, on such elevation, further municipal elections had to be held to elect a replacement councillor.[7] It seems to have been customary for ex mayors to be put forward as aldermen but this was not always the case and, as they were only elected for six years, it was not seen as a life peerage. The elections for aldermen took place at the same time as the mayoral election*, as did the appointment of one councillor to the office of bailiff.

As has been mentioned, civic pride in Chichester ran – and indeed still runs – very deep, and many great Chichester families served the city they loved in many ways, including as councillors. One such was Bassil Shippam (the singular spelling of whose name alone commands attention) who in March 1962 was awarded the Freedom of Chichester 'in recognition of his services to the City' and he was presented with a pair of Georgian silver candlesticks.

In May 1963 one of the most revered of all members of Chichester City Council died. That man was Alderman Thomas Jesse Eastland. Thomas Eastland, always known by his second name Jesse, kept the Wheatsheaf in Oving Road with his wife, Alice. He had been a railwayman, but serious injuries

---

* When Chichester City Council became a parish council in 1974, the office of alderman died out.

sustained in a shunting accident had forced a career change and he entered the licensed trade. He was a man of strong socialist principles but when local government became politicised he refused to allow his views to affect his civic life and always stood as an independent.[8] The minutes of the council meeting of 22 May contain a lengthy tribute to the man who was first elected to Chichester City Council in 1932, becoming an alderman in November 1939 and mayor in 1947. In addition to his civic duties, Jesse Eastland was a magistrate, the founder of Chichester Trades Council, vice president of Chichester Amateur Athletics Club, vice chairman of Chichester Licensed Victuallers' Association and chairman of the Chichester and District Allotment Society. He was awarded the MBE for services as vice chairman of the West Sussex Employment Committee and was given the Freedom of the City in 1959.[9]

On the day of his funeral the full council processed in solemn state to Southgate Methodist Church with the mayoral mace draped in black crepe.[10]

In an election in July 1963 three candidates were put forward for election as alderman to replace Jesse Eastland, namely William Brookes, Maurice Evans and J.M. Selsby. Selsby was elected to serve until May 1964 (i.e. the next mayoral election) and so in October there was a municipal election to find a new East Ward councillor to replace him, won by William Brookes. Electioneering then was incessant.

ENTER THE FAIR SEX

As we have seen, Chichester City Council was predominantly male in its make up but Alice Eastland, wife of Jesse, managed to buck the trend back in 1925 when she was elected as the first female councillor. Against the odds she went on to become the first female Mayor of Chichester in 1953, progressing – naturally – to become the first female alderman in 1961, from which office she retired in May 1967. She had been joined in the 1930s by Miss Jessie Younghusband but their career paths were not to be followed by other women until the 1960s when, possibly inspired by the equal rights movement, more stood for election. In 1960 Mrs Macadam features in the list and in July 1964 Kathleen Smith was elected in place of William Pope who had been made an alderman. Kathleen Smith would, in due course, go on to became mayor. When Councillor Alfred Brinsmead died in October 1964 his wife Gladys was elected in his place, bringing the number of lady councillors to four. In January 1969 Councillor Richard Butler died and his wife, Elsie, was elected in his place, becoming the fifth female councillor. Interestingly in the role calls of attendees in the minute book the ladies are always designated

6. *Cllr Alice Eastland, the first female Mayor of Chichester, seen here presenting Bishop George Bell with a silver inkstand to mark his gaining the freedom of the city on 10 June 1954. She served on Chichester City Council from 1925 to 1967. (Chichester City Council)*

'Cllr Mrs …'.[11] In the decades to come women were, of course, to play an increasing role in both local and national government.

THE COMMITTEES

As well as attending all meetings of the full council, the elected members all had to serve on various committees in which they were given a degree of choice. It was at these committee meetings that, as well as mundane day-to-day matters, policies were formulated for ratification by the full council. The list of committees that existed in 1964 gave plenty of scope for members to opt for some truly riveting meetings. These were:

Cemeteries, Parks and Gardens
Civil Defence
Establishments
Finance and General Purposes
Harbour

Highways
Markets
Public Health and Housing
Sewerage and Waterworks
Town Planning and Buildings

The council maintained a separate account for monies obtained from rates, and every March they would calculate the charge to this account for the coming year and the rate, which would be charged against citizens' dwellings to fund it. This was probably the measure against which most citizens judged the efficacy of their council. Between 1963 and 1967 the rates rose from 9s in the pound to 11s 3d.[12] Naturally ways of saving money on services were constantly being examined, but in October 1968 it was resolved that charging for the use of public conveniences (by the famous 'penny-in-the-slot') would be *dropped* within the city, a public-spirited initiative which could actually reduce income!*

THE TOWN CLERK

In any town council the most important officer was the town clerk, around whom the council revolved. It was always his name that appeared on statutory documentation, rather than the mayor's. In Chichester, as a symbol of his importance, he always wore a Georgian-style wig, gown and bands at civic functions**. For the first half of the 1960s the town clerk was the much-loved Eric Banks who had been appointed to the post in 1936 and remained in office for thirty years. A very dapper man, he was highly efficient at his job and always courteous, even when he had to take a firm line with either a member of the public, a councillor or a member of Corporation staff.

On 28 April 1961 a banquet was held to mark the silver jubilee of Eric Banks' appointment as town clerk at which he and his wife were presented with gifts. He continued in office for a further five years until he retired in January 1966. That month the full council resolved unanimously that:

> … the Council tender to Mr Eric Banks their sincere appreciation of the courteous, efficient and admirable manner in which he has discharged the important duties of Town Clerk of Chichester during the period of thirty years from 1936 to 1966, and invite him to accept a pair of Georgian silver candlesticks as mark of their esteem.

---

* In 2012, Chichester District Council came under severe public criticism for proposing to close public conveniences and/or reintroduce charging in order to reduce expenditure! Some closures occurred but, to date, charges have not been introduced at the survivors. *Sic transit.*

** The custom lives on – the city council still has a town clerk who dons wig and gown for civic events.

DINNER IN HONOUR
OF THE
TOWN CLERK OF CHICHESTER
(ERIC BANKS, ESQ.)

on the occasion of the

Silver Jubilee of his Appointment

as Town Clerk

1st April, 1936

The Assembly Room   Friday, 28th April
Chichester   1961

7. *The menu for a dinner in honour of the silver jubilee of the appointment of Eric Banks as town clerk. The function was held at the Assembly Room on 28 April 1961 – the grace was sung by the Cathedral Choir. (Chichester City Council)*

8. *Eric Banks being presented with a pair of Georgian silver candlesticks by the Mayor of Chichester, Cllr Harry Bell, on his retirement as town clerk on 5 January 1966. (Chichester City Council)*

Georgian silver candlesticks seem to have been the preferred retirement gift for senior dignitaries! In retirement Eric Banks continued to live and serve in the city, being heavily involved with the cathedral where he was always to be seen on sidesman duty in the choir. Eric Banks was replaced as town clerk the following February by Mr George Heather who served in that office for the rest of the 1960s.

Mention must be made here of the ceremonial office of macebearer. Just as the town clerk donned his wig and gown for civic duties, the mayor and Corporation would also dress up in robes, and the mayor would sport his chain of office and be led in procession by his macebearer. From March 1942 this duty had been performed by W.C. Walter, who retired in 1965, at which time he was paid an annual fee of £5. The council, as a token of their esteem, decided to present him with a piece of silver costing not more than 10 guineas. In the event Mr Walter opted for a watch and Mr S.F. Parker replaced him as macebearer with no increase in remuneration – but he was equipped with a new hat.[13]

THE MUNICIPAL BUILDINGS

The city council's main offices were at No. 61 North Street, a much-extended Georgian house named Greyfriars, but the 1731 Council House, a bit further down the same street, which also housed the mayor's parlour, was used for meetings of the council and civic functions. Other important public buildings owned by the Corporation included the Assembly Room at the rear of the Council House, the Market House (popularly, but erroneously, termed the 'Butter Market'), the Market Cross and Eastgate Hall.

9. *The Chichester City Council offices at Greyfriars, No. 61 North Street, seen here in the 1950s. The building still stands unlike the medieval church of St Peter the Less, seen in the background, which was demolished in 1957. Its site was redeveloped in the 1960s as a Co-op department store, the building now occupied by Lakeland Plastics. (Chichester City Council)*

10. *The interior of the Council Chamber in 1961. The chandelier had been bought for 12 guineas in 1799 and survives to this day, unlike the four flying-saucer-like lights which (fortunately) were removed in a later redecoration scheme. (Chichester City Council)*

THE CITIZENS ADVICE BUREAU

Back in 1947 the council had agreed in principle to set up a Citizens Advice Bureau. This was in response to a national initiative to provide places where members of the public could call in to seek confidential free advice on all matters to do with life in general. The idea was that the advisors would be trained volunteers so, once set up, the bureaux would cost very little to run. Nothing happened in Chichester though and after constant deferrals the idea was dropped in 1958, councillors opining that such a facility was 'not necessary'. In 1964 the town clerk, Eric Banks, took up the cause once again having received a letter from Sir Harold Bramwell, chairman of the National Citizens' Advice Bureau Committee, asking that Chichester City Council reconsider their previous stance. In a lengthy memorandum to the Finance and General Purposes Committee meeting of 18 September 1964, Eric Banks set out the case for a Citizens Advice Bureau, citing the past record of progress – or rather lack of it. The committee agreed and resolved to set up a meeting of interested bodies to explore the matter. This resulted in a public meeting at the

Council Chamber on 11 December 1964 at which the idea was enthusiastically taken up, and a committee involving local voluntary bodies was established. The Citizens Advice Bureau was taken forward as a joint venture with both Chichester and Midhurst Rural District Councils, all of whom made grants towards the project, and the bureau opened at Bell House in Chapel Street in June 1965.[14]

Relocated to Theatre Lane after the wholesale, and ill-advised, redevelopment of Chapel Street in the 1970s, the 'CAB' still provides a very useful and valued service to citizens.

MUNICIPAL PUBLICATIONS

Conscious of Chichester's importance as a tourist destination on account of its rich history, the city council issued a number of publications for sale. One of these was a guidebook, loftily subtitled *The Sole Official Guide – issued by the Corporation of Chichester.* This was a constantly evolving publication of long-standing and in the 1960s its editor was the renowned antiquarian Francis Steer, the county archivist, who provided a scholarly perambulation around the city for discerning visitors as well as much useful information about services for residents. The seventeenth edition of the guide emerged in 1963 and ran to seventy-two pages plus an advertising appendix of twenty-eight pages and a fold-out map at the rear. It was pocket sized and its limp green cover bore just the city crest and the wording 'CITY OF CHICHESTER' in gold. It cost 2s 6d. As a token of gratitude for his services in producing this edition – which he seems to have done free of charge – Francis Steer was given a cheque for 50 guineas by the city council.[15] The eighteenth edition appeared in June 1967 with seventy-four pages and no advertising supplement, and a revised version of this edition was issued in 1972 when it cost 15p. Decimal currency had been introduced in 1971 and perhaps this was used as a smokescreen to hide the price rise to 3s – in old money!

Perhaps the most significant of the council's publications were the Chichester Papers, a series of monographs on the city's history, the first of which, entitled *Bishop Edward Story and the Chichester City Cross,* appeared in 1955. This was written by that same Francis Steer who was to become general editor of the series, and whose name indeed appears on many of them as author. At their meeting of 25 September 1961, the Finance and General Purposes Committee voted to pay Francis Steer 50 guineas 'as a token of the Council's great appreciation of the eminent services rendered by him as general editor of the series'. By 1963 the number of titles had risen to thirty-one and the town clerk, Eric Banks, reported in a memo in February that year that the outlay on producing the Chichester Papers amounted to £2,854 at the end of January and sales had netted £1,400. He explained that the value

THE CITY OF

CHICHESTER

*The Sole Official Guide
issued by
The Corporation of Chichester*

17th Edition

The Chichester City Council

1963

11. (Left) The flyleaf of the 17th edition of
The City of Chichester Guidebook *which
contained a mine of information for both residents
and visitors alike, as is witnessed by the contents
page (below). (Author's collection)*

CONTENTS

12. *The cover of* Chichester Paper *31,
published in 1963, on the subject of Chichester's
vanished needle industry. It was written by Francis
Steer who was also general editor of the whole
series. The design of the paper cover is very dull
by today's standards and was in a single colour
chosen from a drab range of grey, green, pale
blue, brown and crimson. This did, however, give
substance to the allegation that you can't judge a
book by its cover! (Author's collection)*

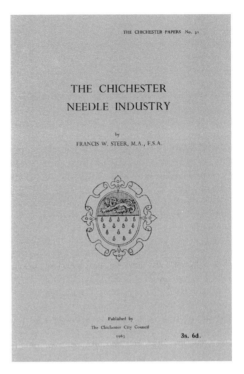

THE CHICHESTER PAPERS No. 31

THE CHICHESTER
NEEDLE INDUSTRY

by
FRANCIS W. STEER, M.A., F.S.A.

Published by
The Chichester City Council
1963   3s. 6d.

of the stock in hand exceeded the differences in these two figures and predicted higher sales when the bookstall in the new museum opened.[16]

The Chichester Papers were slim booklets, which typically carried a centre spread of black and white photographic plates, but they were not cheap. No. 31, to which the town clerk referred (*The Chichester Needle Industry*), had just fourteen pages of text and four of photographs and was priced at 3*s* 6*d* which compared unfavourably with *The City of Chichester Guidebook*, but for his money the purchaser received an impeccably researched monograph on a subject hitherto unexplored. They were all printed by Moore and Tillyer at their works in St John's Street.

No. 50, *Chichester: the Roman Town* by John Holmes, duly appeared in 1965 but was published by West Sussex County Council rather than the city council although the rather unexciting cover design was identical to those that had gone before. Publication of future Chichester Papers stayed with West Sussex County Council but their production slowed markedly for there was a gap of two years before the next one, No. 51 (*The Eric Gill Memorial Collection* by Noel Osborne), came out in 1967. This had twenty-six pages of text and four of plates and was priced at 6*s*. What was to have been the very last one appeared in 1968 as No. 52 (*The John Edes House, West Street, Chichester* by Francis Steer) but, after a gap of four years, the city council produced No. 53 *The Council House, Chichester*. Although written by Francis Steer it bore no resemblance to its predecessors; instead of being printed it was a duplicated, typewritten A5-sized booklet with no illustrations and had a rather apologetic air about it. That really was the end of the venture.[*]

---

[*] In 2011 Chichester Local History Society revived the tradition and published the first of a series of New Chichester Papers under the general editorship of Prof. Paul Foster of the University of Chichester.

Despite long being out of print, the fifty-three Chichester Papers still provide a rich seam of scholarly research into often esoteric areas of the city's history and are frequently the starting point for new researchers. They stand as a tribute to both the vision of Eric Banks, the town clerk, and the meticulous work of Francis Steer, the county archivist.

TWINNING WITH THE CITY OF CHARTRES

One effect of the aftermath of the Second World War was the desire to forge better relationships within Europe and this was reflected from the early 1950s in a number of twinning initiatives between British towns and cities with places of similar status on the Continent. Chichester was twinned with the French cathedral city of Chatres in 1959, an event marked by the attachment of the city seal to the *Deed of Jumbelage* that brought it all about on 28 February. Throughout the 1960s the Chartres Twinning Committee arranged joint activities, including exchange visits not only between dignitaries but also parties of schoolchildren. At the end of October 1960 the mayor and his macebearer visited Chartres to attend the celebrations of the 700th anniversary of the founding of their cathedral. Fortunately for the poor macebearer his travel expenses were reimbursed by the council. The venture was supported by a group known as the 'Friends of Chartres' whose membership rose from eighty-three in 1963 to 392 in 1965.[17] As a result of the influx in French visitors, the city council decided to produce a French version of their visitors' leaflet, which was published in January 1966.

Proposals for celebrations to mark the tenth anniversary of the twinning in 1969 fell by the wayside on account of 'other commitments' (curiously the minutes do not record the nature of these 'commitments') so they were deferred to 1970 and took place in Chartres over three days in May of that year. At the jollifications the proposal to rename the ring road across Westgate Fields *Avenue de Chartres* was floated and, it was reported, the proposal was 'well received'.[18] One can only imagine that the French contingent had not actually seen the bleak dual carriageway that was to be associated with their fair city. Had they done so they might not have been quite so enthusiastic.

CHANGE IN THE AIR

Much of the council's time from 1966 onwards was taken up with the business of reorganisation – both local and national. On 31 May 1966, Harold Wilson's Labour government set up a Royal Commission under the chairmanship of

Sir John Maud (soon to become Lord Redcliffe-Maud) to examine the structure of local government in England and make recommendations for improvements. The commission were empowered to visit the offices of any council to examine their records. Both Chichester City and Rural District Councils as well as West Sussex County Council were in the commission's sights.

Whilst the city council co-operated fully with the inquiry (not that they had any option!) they disagreed strongly with the proposals that West Sussex County Council were submitting to the commission. At the meeting of the full council on 23 November 1966 Councillor Heald, seconded by Councillor Thomas, moved that:

> The Council, having considered the draft proposals to be submitted to the Royal Commission on Local Government by the West Sussex County Council:
> (i) condemns the proposal for the total destruction of local self government in the County, which would be completely unacceptable to the citizens of Chichester.
> (ii) points out that the proposals do not fall within the Commission's terms of reference, which require them to recommend authorities and boundaries which will sustain a viable system of local democracy: and
> (iii) reaffirms its support for the constructive evidence given to the Commission by the Town Clerk on behalf of the Council in his letter dated 27 October .

The motion was carried, so the proverbial gloves were well and truly off. It was seen, rightly, that under the commission's recommendations larger authorities were being proposed which would abolish small, truly local councils such as Chichester's.[19]

An interim version of what became known as 'The Maud Report' appeared in October 1967[20] and was debated at length by the mayor and Corporation, who disagreed with most of it. The council resolved to send a deputation to Parliament in April 1969 to air its views, but the untimely death of the city's Conservative MP, Walter Loveys, who was to receive them, put paid to the visit. Instead a report giving the city's views was sent to the Non-County Boroughs Committee, a body whose uninspiring title should not have encouraged much hope.

The final version of the Maud Report was published in June 1969 and recommended, as expected, the creation of fifty-eight unitary authorities and three metropolitan areas; its findings were endorsed by Prime Minister Harold Wilson, who proposed to introduce the reforms in the next Parliament.[21] In the event, the Maud Report was not to be implemented, for in 1970 Labour were ousted from office by Edward Heath's Conservative government who immediately dismissed it and started planning their own local government reforms, which would be on a two-tier system. However, these reforms, which were introduced in April 1974, still brought about the demise of Chichester City Council in the form in which it

13. Civic pride lived on beyond 1974. In January 2001 the 500th anniversary of the Market Cross was marked by a re-enactment of the dedication ceremony. Here the Mayor of Chichester, Cllr David Siggs, preceded by his macebearer, heads down North Street en route from the Council House to the cathedral. In contrast to the 1962 procession (see page 22) the two mayor's constables heading the procession have been replaced by two firemen in ceremonial uniform including brass helmets and axes. The fire brigade have the freedom of the city. (Author's collection)

had been throughout the 1960s. Most of its responsibilities were transferred to the new Chichester District Council with a few others (e.g. highways and street lighting) going to West Sussex County Council.

Under the new regime Chichester would cease to have a Corporation and was not even entitled to parish status since its population, at 20,600, was above the ruling figure of 20,000. As such it was set to lose its ancient powers and privileges. Eventually, after a vigorous campaign, parish status was granted and so the traditional office of Mayor of Chichester, and the civic insignia that go with it, continues unbroken.[22]

From then on local government of Chichester became, and at the time of writing still is, a three-tier affair with many decisions on the city being taken in district and county committees by members who do not live in, or properly understand, it.

Notes

1 WSRO C/32, Chichester City Council minute book, 1954–65.
2 *Ibid.*
3 *Chichester Observer*, 24 April and 18 May 1962.
4 *Ibid.*, 17 May 1963.
5 *Ibid.*, 21 May 1965.
6 WSRO C/32, op. cit., 17 May 1965.
7 WSRO C/32, op. cit.
8 Edward Brown, *Chichester 1950s*, p. 55 (Chichester, EB Publications, 1996).
9 WSRO C/32, op. cit.
10 *Chichester Observer*, 17 May 1963.
11 WSRO C/33, Chichester City Council minute book, 1965–74.
12 WSRO C/32 and C/33, op. cit.
13 WSRO C/32 and C/33, op. cit.
14 WSRO C/32 and C/33, op. cit.
15 *Ibid.*
16 *Ibid.*
17 WSRO C/32 and C/33, op. cit.
18 WSRO CD/4, minutes of Chichester City Council Finance and General Purposes Committee, 1966–74.
19 WSRO C/33, op. cit.
20 Report on the Management of Local Government Committee.
21 Royal Commission on Local Government: Report Vol. 1, HMSO, 1969.
22 Scicluna, A., *Chichester's Struggle for Parish Status under Local Government Reorganisation Chichester History No. 29*, pp. 2–9 (Chichester Local History Society, 2013).

THREE

PLANNING A CITY
FOR THE SIXTIES

The radical 1960s approach to town planning was fuelled by the rise of modernism coupled to the mantra of slum-clearance and the exponential rise in road traffic. This last tenet required congestion to be 'designed out' by means of road widenings and new ring roads.

Inevitably these ideas were to be visited on Chichester, even if not always taken up, but the seeds for its 1960s modernisation were actually sown back in 1949 – they just took rather a long time to sprout. Mercifully this lengthy germination period meant that the damage being inflicted upon Chichester by 1960s' thinking was curtailed when early public backlash against demolition managed to bring about a change in the Corporation's thinking.

THE VISION FOR THE FUTURE –
THE SHARP REPORT

Back in 1947 Chichester City Council had engaged a town planner, Dr Thomas Sharp, to advise them on 'the preservation and re-planning of this ancient city'. The driver for this had been the famous Town and Country Planning Act of 1947 which, *inter alia*, transferred the statutory responsibility for planning from Corporations to county councils. West Sussex County Council took over responsibility for the planning of the City of Chichester from the Corporation and duly met its obligation under the Act to prepare development plans for all the areas under its jurisdiction. This had to be done in consultation with what the Act referred to as 'county district councils' and Sharp's report, published in January 1949, provided the Corporation's input to the consultative process that resulted in both a development plan and a town plan for the City of Chichester.

14. The cover of Thomas Sharp's report entitled Georgian City. *Despite its benign title and fine line-drawing of Nos 4–6 East Pallant, Sharp's report was anything but a plan for conserving the Georgian city. However, his ideas formed the basis for the town planning of Chichester in the 1960s. (Author's collection)*

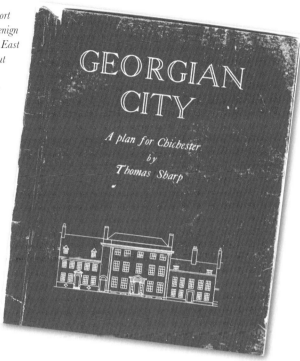

The Sharp Report was entitled *Georgian City* (beguilingly sub-titled on its flyleaf *A plan for the preservation and improvement of Chichester*) and in ending his foreword to it the mayor, Alderman Jesse Eastland, said:

> The City Council has therefore decided that it is proper to put Dr Sharp's propos-
> als before the public, whose concern the city is, and before the authorities, namely
> West Sussex County Council and the Ministry of Town and Country Planning,
> who have the statutory authority for planning it.[1]

In the municipal election of May 1949, Leslie Evershed Martin, a man who was to launch the Festival Theatre project ten years later, pronounced in his manifesto unequivocal support for Dr Sharp's plan:

> I think this is brilliantly conceived and worthy of the Author and the City. As soon
> as each part of the plan can be put into operation it will be thoroughly considered
> and amended where necessary. At last we can see in the near future the provision
> of the much needed baths, proper conveniences, and full use of new and existing
> car parks. I am determined to resist to the utmost any attempts by outside planners
> to spoil this City of ours. Public opinion must be heard. Your vote will assure this.

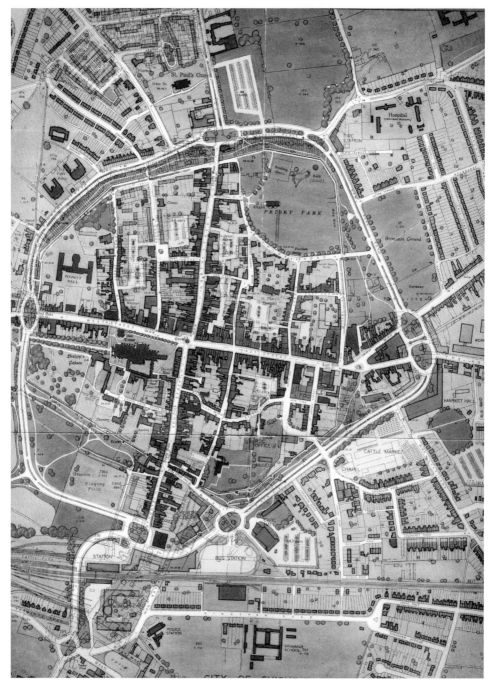

15. The master plan from Thomas Sharp's report which includes a ring road cutting across Westgate Fields, the redevelopment of Somerstown and a car park on the Sloe Fair Field. These ideas were to be implemented in the 1960s. (Author's collection)

The plan was indeed adopted, but the interpretation that Dr Sharp had placed on 'preservation' is somewhat wide of that which is understood in today's conservation-conscious times: amongst its radical proposals was the demolition of 700 houses deemed to be slums, the creation of a ring road, destruction of the water meadows, the building of a swimming pool and a theatre and creating a transport interchange next to a rebuilt railway station. Many of his ideas where to influence the changes that came about in the 1960s, but not without some pain: Sharp's report will be cited many times in the course of this work.

PLANNING FOR CHICHESTER

The county council soon delegated planning powers for the City of Chichester back to the Corporation but retained a strategic planning role, and the agreement setting out the delegation was regularly reviewed. The delegation included giving the Corporation the power to issue Article 4 Directions* unless they were unwilling so to do, when the county would resume that right.[2]

The Corporation's Town Planning and Buildings Committee met at least twice a month to determine planning applications, and in the early 1960s was chaired by Cllr Geoffrey Marwood, who just happened to be my chemistry master at Chichester High School for Boys. I had absolutely no idea that he shot off after school to perform this extra-curricular duty!

In October 1960 the secretary of the Royal Fine Arts Commission felt moved to write to the town clerk on the vexed subject of high-rise buildings, saying:

> In the opinion of the Commission, high blocks of buildings within the immediate neighbourhood of the old city would seriously damage its architectural character and it is hoped that their introduction would be strongly discouraged.

The county planning officer expressed the hope that the Corporation would agree. They did, and thankfully to this day no tower block of either flats or offices has ever dared raise an ugly head to scar the city's skyline.

---

* Some items under the Town and Country Planning (General Development Order) 1950, were classed as 'permitted development' for non-listed buildings – the use of colour and the form of windows and doors being examples. Article 4 of the Order allowed, in special cases, the planning authority to issue a Direction removing certain permitted development rights from designated areas, meaning that planning permission there would be needed to – say – change windows and doors. It did require councils to have the will to introduce Article 4 Directions, which they often lacked – and sadly many still do.

The Town Planning and Buildings Committee had their work cut out for, in addition to myriad alterations and extensions to the city's building stock, they had some fairly major schemes on their hands, some of which we will encounter here and in later chapters. To assist them the Corporation engaged several times in the fifties and sixties the eminent architect Sir Hugh Casson to provide advice.[3] Sir Hugh Casson had risen to fame as director of architecture for the Festival of Britain, so his views carried considerable clout. In 1976 he was elected president of the Royal Academy but by then his involvement with Chichester had ceased.

It is a natural reaction to be highly critical of what happened in the city during the 1960s, especially in that *annus horribilis* of 1964 which, *inter alia*, saw the whole-sale destruction of the east side of Somerstown as we shall see in Chapter Four, but a detailed study of the minute books of the Town Planning and Buildings Committee reveal – perhaps surprisingly – that they could in fact be quite demanding and planning applications were regularly rejected for not being of the standard required or being detrimental to the historic townscape that they in actual fact wished to conserve.

In January 1963 the Planning Committee began to take a tough line with chain stores (or 'multiple retailers' as they were then known) over the poor quality of design of their shopfronts and signage. This was reported on the front page of the *Chichester Observer* in an interview with the committee's vice chairman, Cllr Foote, which caused the local Chamber of Commerce to launch a counter attack.[4] At the same time the committee received a postcard from a Mr D. Grant, who sent his congratulations on their work in preserving the character of Chichester and their 'struggle with aggressive commercial philistines'. The committee rallied around and passed a motion of confidence in Cllr Foote and the public stand that had been taken on this issue. Following this attack the town clerk set out the council's declared planning policy, which was as follows:

(1) To preserve as far as humanly possible the old buildings which give the City its distinctive character, especially if they are capable of repair and restoration to meet modern requirements.
(2) Where new buildings are erected, to secure that they are of the right design appropriate to their surroundings and genuine, i.e. not merely a reproduction of an historical style, and
(3) To enforce control in all cases of planning contraventions.[5]

On this last point, in March 1963 planning officers reported twenty-two cases of unauthorised signs which should have been subject to planning consent and ten cases where inappropriate signs needed to be removed. The offending owners were written to and asked to take the requisite action. The following year the city centre became an area of special control for advertising.

It is in the light of their declared policy that we should examine some of the more significant planning decisions that were taken in the 1960s and thus judge – objectively – the Corporation's wisdom and degree of adherence to its creed.

BUILDINGS IN THE WAY OF TRAFFIC

Since the dawn of the horseless carriage, Chichester's cramped city centre had been host to much traffic congestion. Until the Chichester bypass opened in 1939, the main A27 trunk road passed right through its centre, using East and West streets, and obstructions such as the Market Cross and the 'bottleneck' at Westgate exacerbated congestion. However, although the bypass syphoned off east-west through traffic, that heading north-south was not catered for, so much traffic was still clogging up the city in the early 1960s.

Whilst moving the Market Cross – a scheduled ancient monument – in order to ease traffic flows was clearly not an option, that of increasing the space around it was, and Sharp went so far as to suggest that frontages around the Cross should

16. The way things used to be. Lennards' shoe shop at No. 1 East Street and No. 88 North Street seen in 1915. It survived another forty-five years before developing the symptoms of age that doomed it. Note the proliferation of Edwardian advertising marring its elegant façade – something from which we would recoil today. (Author's collection)

17. *Lennards' shoe shop seen supported by raking shores in February 1960 whilst a Bedford pantechnicon picks its way cautiously past the Market Cross and into East Street. (Courtesy of Ken Green)*

18. *Nos 1 and 2 South Street had been the famous Barrett's bookshop which closed in 1959. When this photograph was taken in May 1963 it was the city centre office of the Festival Theatre. (Courtesy of John Iden)*

be 'set back a little – some 25 feet or so'. In the early 1960s two opportunities came the Corporation's way to do just that when adjacent ancient buildings began to show signs of distress.

The first of these was Lennards' shoe shop that occupied a prime site on the corner of North and East streets. It was a four-storey building that, in common with several others around this time, began to develop worrying cracks in its façade. One of the causes of this phenomenon was undoubtedly vibration from increasingly heavy vehicles which reacted unfavourably with the shallow foundations that were a feature of so many Georgian buildings. In 1959 raking shores had to be erected against the teetering façade which further impeded traffic flows.

In January 1960 the owners of the Lennards' building, the trustees of St Mary's Hospital, wrote to the Corporation advising that they were considering rebuilding it, and later that same month the city surveyor reported that two more shores were needed to keep the building standing. The tenants, Lennards, negotiated to take over the now-empty Jay's ironmonger's shop at Nos 7 and 8 East Street whilst the premises were rebuilt. As the building had been declared dangerous, demolition was scheduled to commence within fourteen days. The Corporation persuaded the St Mary's Trustees to engage Sir Hugh Casson for the design of their new building. This they duly did, and Casson's design for the replacement building will be discussed in Chapter Nine. During the planning process urgent consideration was given to setting back the façade to permit an easing of the passage around the Cross. In the event this did not happen for vehicular traffic, but pedestrian flow was increased by supporting the corner of the new building on a column with the shop entrance recessed behind it.[6] There seems in all this to have been no consideration given at all to saving the historic building, which is surprising given its contribution to the setting of the Cross.

Diagonally opposite Lennards' shoe shop, on the corner of South and West streets, was another Chichester institution, Barrett's bookshop. This had closed in 1959 and it was bought by the Corporation who intended to demolish the building, use part of the site to widen the street and then sell on the remainder to a developer. Russell and Bromley, who had a shoe shop next door at No. 3 South Street, straightaway expressed an interest in acquiring the site to build a new, larger shop. This eventually came to fruition (all reading this book will be aware of Russell and Bromley's shop) but it took a very long time to do so.

In March 1960 Chichester Festival Theatre Trust were granted a lease of the ground floor for use as a display and fundraising centre whilst Hugh Casson was engaged to advise on the rebuilding. This he did in October 1961 with a design similar to his Lennards building but with a ground-floor arcade, however nothing was done about implementing his ideas and the Law of Delay set in. A condition report made in 1964 indicted that demolition would endanger the party

19. Nos 25, 25A and 26 North Street occupied by Jacob's Library and Chitty's cycle shop, were decidedly dilapidated in March 1964 and doomed to disappear from the street scene. Jacob's Library at No. 25 has already closed down. The narrow entrance to Crane Street is seen in the foreground. (Courtesy of John Iden)

wall with Russell and Bromley's existing shop at No. 3, and by December 1965 the new ring road across Westgate Fields had opened so the Finance and General Purposes Committee decided that the expenditure of £700 on road widening at the Cross was no longer justified; this element of the scheme disappeared.[7]

The buildings were listed but ministerial objections to their demolition were withdrawn on account of their structural condition; however, despite removal of this obstacle, the indecision continued. In August 1968 the Corporation explored new options for the beleaguered buildings, one of which was to refurbish (which was recommended by Casson), so common sense seemed to have prevailed at last. Sadly this was thwarted in July 1969 when the city surveyor reported that the condition of the building had now 'deteriorated considerably' needing raking shores – a common feature of 1960s Chichester – to be installed against its eastern façade. In April 1970 the building was sold to Russell and Bromley for £24,000 and its new owners went on to demolish it, along with their own No. 3, to build the present shop.[8]

As the city centre has been pedestrianised for over thirty-five years it is difficult to imagine a time when traffic thronged the four main streets and filtered off into myriad narrow side streets. One such was Crane Street that ran between North and Chapel streets, a narrow, one-way thoroughfare that was seen to be in need of widening – but this could only be achieved at the unfortunate expense of demolition of ancient buildings.

Nos 25–26 North Street was a typical Georgian re-fronting of the seventeenth-century timber-framed building. In the 1960s it was two shops; at No. 25 was Jacob's Library, a newsagent who sold 'interesting' magazines from high shelves, whilst Nos 25A and 26 formed Chitty's cycle shop. In fact cycles were only part of the business as Mr Chitty also sold electrical appliances and his famous home-made honey. Amongst the services he provided was that of charging accumulators

20. Oh no – not again! Raking shores go up against Doman's shop at No. 24 North Street in November 1965, but this time the building survived; the shores were to stabilise it whilst Nos 25–26 next door, seen here shrouded in scaffolding, were demolished. (Courtesy of John Iden)

used by those not on mains electricity to power their radios, or 'wirelesses' as they were then known. As a young boy I regularly took an old lady's accumulator to Chitty's for its weekly recharge, carrying the heavy glass container, with sulphuric acid sloshing around inside, next to my bare legs. By 1961 the building was in a run-down state and its owners had approached the Corporation suggesting that it be demolished and any land not needed to widen Crane Street be sold off and the profits shared.

This had appeal for the Corporation but, as always, things did not happen quickly and the building continued to deteriorate whilst the district valuer negotiated terms for the sale. He also had to arrange the vacation of No. 1 Crane Street (a property already acquired by the Corporation) which was to be demolished at the same time. All was finally agreed in September 1964 and demolition took place the following year.[9] Another historic building had been sacrificed to the great god Motor Car. A new building, named Sussex House, was built on the site extending back along the now-widened Crane Street.

A further – and much publicised – demolition, that of Sharp Garland's shop in Eastgate Square whose speedy execution carried further overtones of road widening, was a feature of 1964, Chichester's *annus horribilis*, and will be considered, along with Somerstown, in Chapter Four.

A FEW PLANNING BATTLES

The 'modernisation' of any ancient town centre inevitably involves the loss of historic buildings, but it is the expectation that a responsible planning authority would maintain a balance between permitting the change necessary to meet modern needs and conserving historic character. Naturally it was – and still is

– both cheaper and easier for a developer to demolish and rebuild rather than conserve and adapt an old building, and in 1960s Chichester there was much pressure by developers for the former course of action.

Of the city's four main streets East Street has suffered the greatest loss of historic buildings, a process which actually started at the end of the nineteenth century when the former Swan Inn, which had become a furniture emporium, was rebuilt following a disastrous fire. The new building – a bank – was a typical Victorian display of taste overtaken by money, being out of scale with its surroundings, of alien material and of vulgar design.

We will look at just four cases which show that between 1960 and 1964 the Planning Committee were taking an increasingly hardening stance against demolitions, imposing Building Protection Orders and being highly critical of poor modern design – at least in the four main streets.

A long-lost and much-lamented Chichester business is the legendary ironmonger's shop of T.E. Jay whose premises consisted of two former Georgian houses on the north side of East Street and a rambling collection of outbuildings behind. In May 1959 Thomas Jay signalled his intention to close the business and leave Chichester, but wished to turn the premises into a shopping mall – something that Chichester did not yet have. This proposal was refused planning permission in December 1959, so Tom Jay sold the site to Tesco instead.[10]

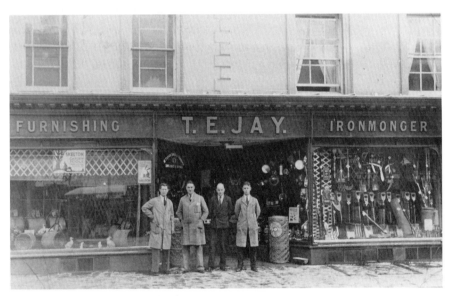

21. The famous ironmonger's shop of T.E. Jay at Nos 7 and 8 East Street pictured in 1958. It closed down the following year and its redevelopment sparked a lively battle for the Planning Committee. (Chichester City Council)

Tesco duly submitted an application in November 1960 to demolish Nos 7 and 8 and build a new supermarket on the site but this was refused, the committee opining that the design was 'detrimental to the amenities of the City' and had insufficient rear access. Tesco submitted a preliminary enquiry for a redesign in January 1961 but were promptly informed that the committee were not prepared to approve it. A further inquiry in May received a similar rebuff and Tesco were invited to submit yet another revised design which could be sent to the Georgian Group for its informed comment. Further rejections occurred in June and July 1961, and on the latter occasion the applicant was informed that:

> … the Committee requires for this site a building which, having regard to its scale and design and quality, is in harmony with the general street picture as explained to [your] architect.

An official planning application was made in August 1961 but when this was again refused on the grounds of the design and materials being 'detrimental', Tesco decided to build the shop anyway and at the same time take the matter to appeal. A hearing was held on 29 March 1962 and the appeal was allowed in July, much to the Corporation's chagrin.[11] The *Chichester Observer* reported the outcome under the banner headline 'Tesco wins planning battle', referring to the frontage that had been built without planning permission, which would not now have to be pulled down. It quoted the planning inspector as having stated that 'the criticisms levelled at the elevation are not so material as to justify rectification'. Speaking on behalf of Tesco, William Root QC pointed out that Tesco had tried for ten months to obtain planning permission for the £100,000 supermarket and that since there appeared to be no chance of agreement with Chichester City Council Tesco had completed the building in order to avoid losing many thousands of pounds in trading.[12] This marked the approach that many of the multiples were taking with local authorities when due procedure got in the way of generating profits.

Although the Planning Committee had not seen fit to oppose the principle of demolition of Nos 7 and 8 East Street in 1960 they did dig their heels in over No. 64 North Street (St Peter's House) two years later. St Peter's House was next door to the tiny medieval church of St Peter the Less, which had closed in 1953 and been demolished in 1957, an act of vandalism we would find shocking today. Its site and churchyard were eventually redeveloped as a department store for the Co-operative Society. St Peter's House was a large and attractive stuccoed Georgian house that came into a developer's sights in 1962, but planning permission to demolish and redevelop it was refused that December. The Corporation had a Building Preservation Order made on the house to prevent demolition but

22. *The end result – Tesco's new supermarket at Nos 7 and 8 East Street. Note the advertisements plastered over the windows for Green Shield Stamps, the precursor of toady's loyalty cards, issued to entice increased spending. (WSRO)*

23. *A view of North Street in the 1950s. Beyond The Old Cross is No. 64 North Street, St Peter's House, which was the subject of a (lost) planning battle in 1964/65 and beyond that the church of St Peter the Less which was demolished in 1957. The sites of both buildings and the churchyard were redeveloped in the 1960s, altering this vista. Note the lamp post on the west side of the street which was of the mercury-vapour type which imparted a bluish aura to the city's night-time scene. (Author's collection)*

24. *Nos 19–20 East Street pictured in March 1964 when it was occupied by Hepworths, the gentlemen's outfitter. It was required for an extension to Marks & Spencer, whose shop is just visible to the left. To the right of the picture is the National Provincial Bank, which was built in 1927 on the site of the birthplace of William Collins, the poet. (Courtesy of John Iden)*

its owners objected, stating that the building had been made unstable as a result of the demolition work next door.

Under two unsuccessful planning appeals by the owners, the Building Preservation Order was upheld, but in October 1964 their agents, Whitehead and Whitehead, sought consent under the terms of the order to demolish because the building was 'unsafe'. The Corporation dithered over purchasing the building, and when negotiations stalled in February 1965 the architect Stanley Roth declared that, as its condition had deteriorated even further, the owners were now at liberty to demolish it on the grounds of public safety. He duly instructed a demolition contractor to 'raze the building to the ground' but the replacement that eventually rose on the site did little to enhance the street scene. As a nod to history it was named St Peter's House.[13]

Another demolition that was vigorously opposed by the Planning Committee was for Nos 19 and 20 East Street. This Georgian building housed the shop of Hepworths, the gentlemen's outfitter, and in July 1963 Marks and Spencer made a planning application to demolish it in order to extend their shop on to its site. Marks and Spencer's shop was next door at Nos 16–18, a twentieth-century building in a style strongly suggestive of Edwin Lutyens[*], whose owners saw the need to expand both laterally in East Street and backwards into St Martin's Street. Messrs Hepworth were – apparently – very keen to sell their premises for this purpose.

Once again the Corporation refused planning consent and applied for a Building Preservation Order. The owners went to appeal, and in March 1964, following a Local Inquiry, the planning inspector announced that Nos 19 and 20 East Street could be demolished on condition that its replacement was not to be a continuation of the neo-Lutyens pile next door. What emerged was a weak

[*] There is no evidence to attribute this building to Lutyens but it does bear many of his hallmarks.

imitation of the doomed original; Marks and Spencer annexed the eastern half and Hepworths moved back into the other.[14]

A study of the Planning Committee minute books for the period shows that as a result of this hardening of attitude fourteen battles were fought to conserve rather than demolish historic buildings of which eight were won, including No. 12 North Street (extension of Woolworths into Bartholomew's old shop) the Fleece Inn in East Street and the Old Theatre in South Street. As well as Tesco, new buildings whose design came in for severe criticism included Lloyds Bank and Stocklund House in East Street, and Metropolitan House at Northgate.

THE CHAPEL STREET COMPREHENSIVE DEVELOPMENT AREA

The aforementioned demolition of Nos 25–26 North Street and the associated widening of Crane Street was tied into a long-running proposal for the total redevelopment of the Chapel Street area. Poor Chapel Street was the Cinderella of the city's back lanes: badly damaged by a bombing raid in 1943 and pillaged in the 1950s to provide rear access to premises in North Street, its undoubted earlier charm had waned considerably by 1960.

Indeed, when Thomas Sharp looked at it in 1947 much of its historic interest was already lost. Describing it as having 'fallen on evil days', Sharp went on to opine:

> The southern end of Chapel Street has a somewhat woebegone appearance – as indeed it might have since it was bombed during the War. And whilst war has blasted it, the advance of commerce has blighted it – the advance of the rearguard of commerce, for it is the back part of North Street shops, extending here, that have done most of the damage. It will be difficult to oust these commercial intrusions now and recover the old character of this once attractive lane.

Recovery of character was a challenge to which the Corporation did not rise, and so unloved had Chapel Street become that photographers routinely ignored it, unlike nearby Tower Street, which was also wiped away in the 1950s and '60s. Chapel Street is now only a memory in the minds of Cicestrians of a certain age; the Corporation's changing attitude to demolition did not seem to apply here.

In 1966 the city surveyor presented to the Finance and General Purposes Committee a revised plan for redevelopment of the land between North and Chapel streets for shopping and office use, and it was agreed to purchase No. 15 Chapel Street and some adjacent land with a frontage of 82ft for £17,075 to start if off.

West Sussex County Council, in their strategic planning role, submitted their proposals to make Chapel Street a Comprehensive Development Area – or 'CDA' for short – in June 1967, proposals which would go to public consultation. The idea, which would destroy virtually everything that was left of Chapel and Crane streets, proceeded apace with regular updates to the plan, in which a new GPO telephone exchange would feature large along with a supermarket. Once again Sir High Casson was engaged by the Corporation, this time as consultant architect for the CDA. Based upon Casson's master plan, Compulsory Purchase Orders were served on the doomed properties in December 1968, which attracted forty objections.[15] As a result a public inquiry was scheduled for June 1969 but, owing to continuing indecision and expressions of much ire from the Chichester Civic Society*, it was not held until 7–17 July 1970.[16] The outcome indeed led to the destruction of what was left of 'old' Chapel Street, save for three cottages and the Providence Chapel, but at least the supermarket did not materialise. However, none of that was to happen until the mid-1970s and is thus beyond the era of this book. Ironically Crane Street ended up becoming pedestrianized, so its widening and the associated demolition of buildings had all been in vain.

25. The west end of Crane Street in July 1966. The timber-clad building is that of Mason's Motor Factors whose sales included tyres. The wall in the foreground is to the garden of No. 18 Chapel Street which extended back into Crane Street. (Courtesy of Rod Funnell)

* The Chichester Civic Society was founded in 1945 and was concerned with, *inter alia*, the history of the city. It had its own excavations committee who carried out archaeological investigations on demolition sites. They also reviewed development proposals and frequently campaigned to save old buildings. The society was disbanded in 1980.

26. *Crane Street looking east in late 1966. The rubble in the right foreground is from the Mason's building. In the background is Sussex House, which was built on the site of Nos 25–26 East Street and 1–6 Crane Street. The corner shop with the canted front was Epicure, Chichester's first 'official' delicatessen. On the north side of Crane Street the three houses nearest the camera and the garden of No. 18 Chapel Street would perish in 1975 when redevelopment of Crane Street was completed. (Courtesy of Rod Funnell)*

FULFILLING THE HOUSING NEED – THE EAST BROYLE ESTATE

In the 1950s new housing had been provided – as suggested by Sharp – by extending the Parklands Estate to the west of the city, a development that had been started in 1934, but the housing need was still growing, so when East Broyle Farm came up for sale in 1959 it offered the ideal site where several hundred new houses could be built to meet the housing need for several years to come. This was to be the biggest housing development in Chichester in the 1960s.

The East Broyle Estate, as it was to become known, had a difficult birth and its evolution involved a continuous nine-year battle between the city council and the London developer – with the odd disagreement with the county council thrown in for good measure.

East Broyle Farm was a huge estate of some 72 acres situated on rising ground between St Paul's Road, the Midhurst railway line and Broyle Road. It was put on the market by the Henty family with outline planning consent for residential development. The sale particulars (see Fig. 27) show that the site was expected to

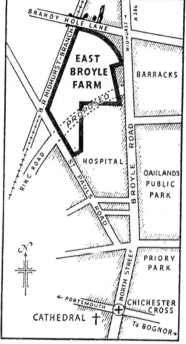

By direction of the Trustees of R. I. Henty, deceased.

CITY OF CHICHESTER

OFFER OF

FREEHOLD RESIDENTIAL BUILDING LAND

72 ACRES

With Outline Planning Consent

Including Provision for Open Space

Comprising

EAST BROYLE FARM

in the N.W. sector of the City, having access from
Midhurst Road A.286, Brandy Hole Lane and long
frontage to St. Paul's Road and proposed extension
of the Ring Road.

VACANT POSSESSION OF THE LAND.

FOR SALE BY AUCTION
as a whole early in 1960
(unless previously sold).

JOINT AUCTIONEERS :

STRIDE & SON,

SOUTHDOWN HOUSE, ST. JOHN STREET, CHICHESTER (CHICHESTER 2626), AND

KNIGHT, FRANK & RUTLEY,

20, HANOVER SQUARE, W.1.   (MAY 3771.)

27. Notice of the forthcoming sale by auction of East Broyle Farm. (Author's collection)

be served by an extension of the ring road that had been proposed by Sharp. East
Broyle Farm was bought by the Romford Finance and Development Company
of London and conveyed to them on 2 March 1960.[17]

The outline planning consent had been granted in February 1959, and when
in October of that year Stride & Son announced the forthcoming auction, the
Corporation's Finance and General Purposes Committee were recommended
to consider buying it, but this did not come to pass and the development of this
housing estate was to proceed as a private venture.

The county planning officer leapt in feet first and produced a layout for the new
estate in December 1959, which caused much ire in the Corporation, which not

only had not been involved in the exercise but felt that the proposed density was in excess of what they felt appropriate. As such the Planning Committee wrote to the owner's agent to advise them that this plan had 'no validity whatever'.

After their purchase of East Broyle Farm, the Romford Finance and Development Company quickly submitted their first planning application, which was considered at the Planning Committee's meeting on 27 April 1960. This was rejected as it did not contain enough detail and the developer was asked to try again. This they duly did the following September, but it was again refused, on grounds including that both the layout and design of the houses fell below the standard required, and the fact that development of the whole site in one go would result in too rapid use of the land available for new housing and leave no provision for the future expansion of the city*.

The county planning officer, apparently not having learned from his previous faux pas, tabled another proposal in December 1960, this time for 264 flats contained in six eleven-storey blocks – an unbelievably audacious suggestion considering his earlier agreement with the Royal Fine Arts Commission about how inappropriate high-rise buildings would be in Chichester! Although the developer was invited to inspect this proposal nothing more is heard about it – it was obviously quickly forgotten – *laus Deo*. [18]

In March 1961 the developer announced his intention to lodge an appeal (the first of many) against the Corporation's refusal of planning permission but offered to adjourn it on the condition that the Corporation compulsorily purchase land near The Wellington public house to enable the principal road for the estate to connect with Broyle Road. If no such agreement was reached by 30 March the appeal would proceed. Undaunted, the Planning Committee took a firm stand, resolving to inform the developer's solicitors that:

> ... the Committee has grave doubts as to whether the elevations submitted can be brought up to the standard of design required for this most important site and it must not be assumed that the Committee will approve any amended plans. They [the developer] should employ a fully qualified architect to prepare layout and design elements of the buildings.

The aspersions cast upon the developer's architect must have stung, and in July 1961 the committee was able to approve a revised application which covered the

---

* This was actually quite far sighted for 1960 – they seem to have distinguished between housing *need* and housing *demand* – and shows an awareness of the fact that building hundreds of new homes would encourage people outside of Chichester to move to the area and thus deny locals who needed a bigger or better dwelling.

road system and a first building phase of thirty-eight dwellings at the south end of the site, but approval was conditioned by a warning shot:

> ... it must not be assumed that the Committee would necessarily give approval to this type of development for the remainder of the area proposed to be developed by the applicant.

The developer's next move was to submit a programme whereby the building of 298 houses would be spread across six unequal phases, commencing in July 1961 and ending in June 1966. Although the vast majority of the houses would be to standard designs, thirty-one plots were to be offered for sale for the building of individually designed properties. This proposal was rejected as the Corporation wished the phasing to be spread evenly over a period of not less than ten years in order to limit the rate of growth.[19]

28. No. 74 Norwich Road when new in 1968. Michael Merritt, who provided this photograph, is the boy on the right-hand side. To the right of the picture is the solitary shrub presented to each household by the developer. (Courtesy of Michael Merritt)

Study of the sale particulars in Fig. 27 on page 59 will reveal the wording 'including provision for open space' and this open space was set aside adjacent to St Paul's Road and either side of the main road into the site. In December 1963 the committee roundly rejected the developer's proposal to develop the open space areas on the grounds of being contrary to the County Development Plan and also that sufficient land had already been allocated to meet demand for housing within the plan's period. Furthermore it would 'affect detrimentally the visual amenities of the locality on one of the principal approach roads to the City'. The developer quickly lodged an appeal against this decision with a hearing set for 11 June 1964.[20]

The appeal went ahead and the minister decided that the land should remain as open ground and be purchased by either the city or county councils. As neither council was prepared to buy the land, the Corporation decided that they would, after all, allow low-density development upon it, but the resultant planning application for this attracted thirty-four objections, including one from the county council. Refusal brought about another appeal from the developer and a public inquiry was held on 7 September 1966 at which the appeal was dismissed. In summing up his verdict the minister wrote:

> [The development] would be undesirable as it would leave a growing neighbourhood with no public space ... as a result residents would have to go elsewhere for that kind of enjoyment [physical recreation] and in doing so would be compelled to cross one or other of two main roads, a practice that would be particularly dangerous for children ... there are no physical reasons why the site should not make a satisfactory public open space.

In November 1967 the Corporation resolved to tell the developer that, subject to conveyance to them of the open land in consideration of a covenant, they would maintain it as an amenity space.[21] Much later, in 1992, the open land was to become registered as a village green and thus be endowed with a better measure of protection.

The Highway Committee meanwhile got involved over the names of the new roads. The ideas for the principal road being called The Mead, The Spurs or The Cloisters were all rejected, and instead the Corporation preferred it to be regarded as an extension of Sherborne Road, with other roads being named after cathedral cities. This last was agreed, but the principal road also followed the cathedral theme becoming Norwich Road. Approval was given to all the estate roads being adopted by the Corporation as public highways in September 1964.[22]

The Corporation diligently attempted to acquire the parcel of land next to The Wellington needed to connect Norwich Road with Broyle Road, but the

29. *No Through Road! The east end of Norwich Road today. The road seems determined to continue on its way to Broyle Road, but beyond the gates it has been blocked off by the Nuffield Hospital. (Author's collection)*

solicitor acting for the landowner advised that his client was unwilling to sell unless the Corporation bought the whole site. In the end the road link through to Broyle Road never materialised, and two houses were built across the intended alignment of Norwich Road, which in the 1970s made way for the Sherburne (now Nuffield) Hospital. However, pedestrian and cycle access on to Broyle Road was afforded by means of a path alongside The Wellington.

When the design of housing for the north-west side of Norwich Road (plots 260–74) was submitted in September 1969, it was savagely condemned by the committee, who were clearly far from impressed with the appearance of the emerging estate:

> Having regard to the size of the East Broyle Estate, the number of houses already built, and the prominence of this site near the main entrance and adjoining the principal approach road the proposed designs are below the standard required and would lack sufficient variety … further repetition will reduce the standard of amenity by increasing beyond acceptable limits, the already monotonous character …

The first East Broyle houses had Crittall steel windows, but for the 1970s builds a change was made to timber, metal windows having gone out of favour. Interestingly the title deeds to all the properties contain a restrictive covenant that the purchaser will not:

… use the said land or any building erected thereon for any trade profession business or manufacture nor for any purpose other than that of a private dwelling house with or without a motor garage for use only in connection with the occupation of such dwelling house.[23]

Whether this restrictive covenant banning trade was the cause of there never being any shops on the East Broyle Estate (something that was seen as essential on the 1940s Whyke and 1950s Parklands Estates to provide a focal point for the community) is a moot point, but no such facility was ever provided.

Construction of the East Broyle Estate continued well into the 1970s and eventually comprised 412 detached houses, and the honour of making the very first planning application for an extension goes to the then-owner of No. 9 Worcester Road, who did so in November 1967.

30. A superb aerial view across the East Broyle Estate, looking west, taken in January 1975. The line of trees running north-south near the top of the picture is the Midhurst railway line, beyond which can be seen the Old Broyle and Whitehouse Farm. Adjacent to the railway, houses are still under construction in Exeter Road. The road curving across the centre is Worcester Road and its white appearance, shared by the other roads, is owing to its concrete construction which was later to be surfaced with blacktop. From this view it is apparent how low was the density of the East Broyle development, something that would be envied today. The road in the foreground is Broyle Road and the shabby-looking building on the waste ground is a former static water tank that was used by the city engineer as a store for pipes and valves. That site has long since been redeveloped and beyond it is Broyle Close, a small development of very typical 1960s flat-roofed houses. (Chichester Observer, courtesy of Ken Rimell)

31. Another January 1975 view, this time from Worcester Road looking north towards houses under construction in Exeter Road. It can be seen that the detailing of these later houses had changed with timber rather than steel windows. Next to the telegraph pole is a Ford Classic, a car which today would be regarded as a 1960s icon. The corrugated-iron huts behind it are the site offices. (Chichester Observer, *courtesy of Ken Rimell*)

MORE HOUSING – LITTLE BREACH

The November 1965 review of the Town Map concluded that residential use could be made of four more greenfield, sites:

- New Park Road recreation ground
- Open space on the Orlits Estate in St James's
- The former Oliver Whitby School playing field at the south end of Sherborne Road
- Open space north of Boys' garage, Fishbourne Road[24]

None of these were to be developed in the 1960s, but in 1965 the city council proposed to acquire and develop for housing the area to the south of East Broyle Farm, known as Little West Breach Field. The Public Health and Housing Committee submitted an outline planning application for 165 houses and an associated new road which was approved on 5 October 1966.[25]

The intention was to build low-cost (what would now be termed 'affordable') houses for sale, aimed particularly at first-time buyers but with some retained for renting to hospital staff. The development used government funding that was only available where industrialised building systems were employed, in this case kit-built timber-framed houses. It was the first project of its kind.[26]

It was first intended to name the estate St Mary's but the postmaster objected as it might get confused with a development of the same name in Boxgrove, so it became instead Little Breach.[27]

Road and sewer works commenced in early 1967 and a show home was erected by the contractor Quickbuild, which opened in July 1967, and building of the first phase of timber-framed housing commenced. In February 1968 planning permission was granted for the second phase which was to build sixty-eight houses and a shop.

The shop proposal arose from the compulsory purchase order that had been served on Mr Gordon Hill who owned a shop at No. 53 Broyle Road, part of whose site was required for road widening. The Corporation offered Mr Hill a 99-year lease on a site for a new shop in Little Breach but negotiations on this dragged on until July 1970 when contracts on the compulsory purchase were exchanged and Hill's old shop in Broyle Road was demolished.[28] Sadly for the residents, a shop on Little Breach never materialised.

In July 1968 the Public Health and Housing Committee were told that all 103 houses built for sale had been sold, 70 to former council tenants and 33 to applicants on the waiting list. The development was obviously a success. By November 1968 all the road and sewer works were complete and a contract was awarded to Guildway for building the second phase of sixty-eight timber-framed houses. Two of the houses were to be two-bedroomed and sell for £3,750, whilst the remainder would be three-bedroomed and cost £4,025. Garages were available for an extra £200.[29] Little Breach eventually comprised 171 houses. As with East Broyle, vehicular access on to Broyle Road was not provided, albeit the possibility was explored in 1970, so all traffic – including pedestrians – has to come in from St Paul's Road. Little Breach had a physical junction at its north end with Norwich Road of the East Broyle Estate, but a temporary barrier was erected at the junction to prevent Little Breach construction traffic gaining access via the 'other' estate, a barrier which gave the impression of a 'them and us' divide.

... AND MORE OFFICES

Chichester's commercial growth demanded office space as well as retail outlets and several of the main-street redevelopments included an element of office space. Some new office space was provided on greenfield sites and two of these were in Newtown, a Georgian development of the former Blackfriars site.

The Newtown development plots on the corner of East Street and St John's Street were never built on, becoming instead a garden of a house opposite it in East Street, and then later a car park.[30]

A planning application to build three shops with two floors of offices over it was approved in August 1964 but subsequent revised schemes were refused as being 'below standard' and did not win the Planning Committee's approbation until September 1965. The scheme was for the bland, system-built block known as Stocklund House, but its construction was considerably delayed in March 1966 when the mandatory archaeological dig unearthed scores of skeletons of erstwhile friars who had to be re-interred in the cemetery.[31] Moral: redeveloping a burial ground comes with a high price tag!

Also discussed by the Planning Committee in September 1965 was a proposal for another office building, this time at the south end of St John's Street. A terrace of three fine Regency houses had been built on the west side of the street in the 1820s (now numbered 11 to 13) but the building plots south and west of No. 11 were not developed and became instead an exceedingly large garden to No. 11.

Planning permission for the office block was at first refused but a revised version was approved in December 1965 for the construction of a three-storey office

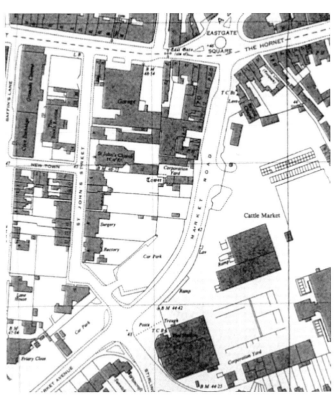

32. An extract from the 1960 Ordnance Survey showing St John's Street and the large garden at No. 11. A house had been built on this garden to the west in the 1950s but the rest remained undeveloped. The vacant site on the corner of St John's and East streets, which was to be developed as Stocklund House in 1966, can also be seen. (© Crown Copyright, 1960)

33. *A view that has changed. The south end of St John's Street in July 1966 seen from Market Avenue. The building on the right is No. 11 St John's Street and a flint-and-brick wall extends south from there enclosing the garden. The surveyor's ranging rod leaning against the wall indicates that something was about to happen. An office block was built adjoining No. 11 in 1966 and later a new road was cut through to the south of it into the Friary Lane car park. (Courtesy of Rod Funnell)*

block to be built next to No. 11. Construction was delayed and in February 1967 the architectural practice of E.G. Nash and partners offered to sell part of the garden of No. 11 to the Corporation within five years – for a nominal cost – to enable them to build a new link road to the car park in Friary Lane, subject to planning approval being granted for a revised, four storey, office block. This approval was given in March 1967 and construction went ahead.[32] The link road was opened in 1971.[33]

The largest 1960s office block in the city was Metropolitan House, built in a prominent position on the site of the former Elms Hotel at Northgate. This was the subject of another battle-royal between the Planning Committee and the developer whose constant revisions to the drawings met with equally constant refusals. The first refusal came in October 1963 when parallel applications for a six-storey office block over a filling station and garage and a stand-alone five-storey office block were both rejected. A public inquiry following an appeal against this decision, set for 24 September 1964, was called off when a further application had been negotiated and approved. A revised scheme for a four-storey block was passed in November 1965. This was for the typically charmless 1960s system-built monolith that was actually built but, in August 1967, the city surveyor reported that Metropolitan House had not been built in accordance with the approved drawings and felt that the town clerk should issue an enforcement notice. However, following discussions, the developer agreed to amend offending aspects of the executed works so the enforcement was not made. The completed building was made even more prominent by the completion of the Northgate Gyratory System in 1974, and it can hardly be regarded as an asset to the city.

The Ring Road

Traffic congestion had become such a notable feature of Chichester by the late 1940s that Thomas Sharp proposed a dual-carriageway ring road round the city to deflect north-south through traffic away from the centre and distribute local traffic to the four main gates. Three of the four segments of the ring would be created from exiting thoroughfares. In Orchard Street and Franklin Place all houses (some of his 700 'slums') would be demolished to make way for the widened road, whilst beyond Eastgate Square a gyratory system would be created linking the Hornet and St Pancras, after which the ring road would cross the Cattle Market and use Market Road/Avenue to Southgate where two huge roundabouts would be created. The fourth, and most controversial, segment involved driving a new dual carriageway across Westgate Fields to link Southgate with Westgate and this we will look at in Chapter Four.[34]

Sharp's ring-road proposal would have cut off the section of Basin Road north of the railway, so he proposed that all its houses – yet more of his 700 'slums' – would be demolished to make way for a new health centre. Although this part of the ring road was later to be realigned, leaving Basin Road as a thoroughfare, the twenty cottages on its west side were condemned as slums in October 1962. Conveniently perhaps, their site was later used to widen Basin Road as part of the Southgate Circulatory System. The *Chichester Observer*, under a headline 'Slumland Area Basin Road', reported on this event stating that, as a result of a public inquiry held in May of that year, the ministry inspector, Miss D.R. Lane, had considered the possibility of reconditioning the houses but found that their condition could not justify it, so a compulsory purchase order was sought.[35]

However, despite this early condemnation, the compulsory purchase order was not confirmed until December 1964, by which time some of the cottages had become a refuge for vagrants. Demolition finally commenced in March 1965 but there arose a strange stay of execution for Nos 2 and 4 at the north end of the terrace. No. 2 housed the surgery of Dr M.A. Bernays, whose practice served some 1,300 patients in the vicinity, and as he was experiencing difficulty in finding new premises he requested that he be allowed to stay put until the site was needed. To this West Sussex County Council eventually agreed, so No. 2

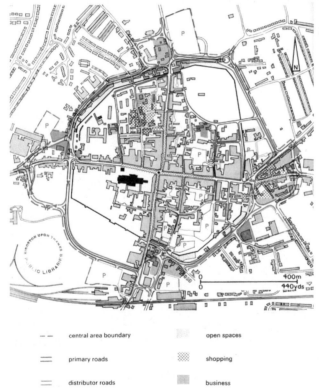

central area boundary

primary roads

distributor roads

service roads and areas

P   public car parks

traffic-free areas

open spaces

shopping

business

residential

civic, cultural and special

34. *Basin Road looking south in October 1962. These houses, Nos 2–40 (evens) were condemned that year and demolished under slum clearance. They would have been destroyed under Sharp's ring-road proposals which did not happen; however, completion of the ring road with Southgate Gyratory System and the widening of Basin Road eventually did take up their sites. (Courtesy of John Iden)*

35. *The town map of 1966, which showed a revised alignment for the ring road, save for the section across Westgate Fields which had already been built. An improvement over Thomas Sharp's original proposal, it nonetheless would still have brought about the destruction of houses in Orchard Street and Franklin Place. It also shows the proposed pedestrian precinct in the town centre. (West Sussex County Council)*

along with No. 4 next door (retained as a barrier) were allowed to remain in splendid isolation for a few years. In return Dr Bernays had to fund the cost of the eventual demolition.[36]

The county council updated the town centre map in 1966, which, along with the revised Development Plan, was submitted for ministerial approval. This showed a revised alignment for the three segments of the ring road not yet built, which, with the exception of the Westgate bypass, was largely what was to come to pass, but fortunately with less destruction than Sharp's original proposal. The new alignment involved a revised circulatory system at Southgate on which work started in 1971. West Sussex County Council compulsorily purchased Nos 32 to 35 Southgate in order to create the new link road to Market Avenue along with the northern part of the bus station forecourt needed to complete the loop. Basin Road was widened on its eastern side, swallowing the site of the former cottages although those on the west side were reprieved. The Southgate Circulatory System opened in 1972.[37]

The northern segments of the ring used Orchard Street and Franklin Place. Orchard Street was upgraded by the Minister of Transport to a Class I road in October 1965 and the task for improving it passed to the county council. A further-revised scheme for Orchard Street which spared virtually all the houses

36. A view of Southgate that was radically altered in 1971. The buildings between the 'Mason's Garage' sign and the Bedford Hotel – Nos 32–35 – were demolished that year to make way for the Southgate Circulatory System with its new link through to Market Avenue. The Bedford Hotel has since ceased to be, although its buildings remain, converted into twenty-first-century apartments. (WSRO)

37. *Houses on the north side of Orchard Street seen from North Walls in November 1965. This view was made possible by the demolition – under the aegis of slum clearance – of Nos 154–172 (evens) on the south side which has created the gap in the foreground. Under Sharp's proposals all the houses in Orchard Street would have been demolished to make way for a dual-carriageway ring road but this did not come to pass. This view is no longer possible as the vacant plot was redeveloped with new housing. (Courtesy of John Iden)*

38. *The east end of Franklin Place comes under the demolition men's hammers in 1967. The building in the foreground is No. 1 New Park Road and beyond it are Nos 44–50 Franklin Place, at one time known as Oaklands Cottages. Only the distant council houses in Spitalfield Lane give any clue to the location of this scene today; the old buildings have gone and the road realigned northwards. A large roundabout now occupies the site. (Courtesy of Ken Green)*

by keeping the road as single carriageway but widened to 24ft and realigned was approved in February 1966. Only two houses were lost: No. 8 at the Westgate end and No. 111 the school caretakers' house on the north-west side.[38] The Ministry of Transport (MoT) issued a grant for this in March 1967 and work commenced under a six-week closure the following August.[39]

Franklin Place was also largely reprieved by cutting a new dual carriageway (Oaklands Way) across the bottom of Northgate car park to join up with the north end of New Park Road. However, nine houses at the eastern end had been acquired by the Corporation from 1964, falling empty and finally being demolished in 1967; their site was later used for the large roundabout at the junction with New Park Road. Oaklands Way, along with the associated Northgate and Eastgate circulatory systems, finally completed the ring road in 1974. The 1966 Town Plan also envisaged a pedestrian precinct in parts of the four main streets which finally came about in 1975.

BILLETING THE MOTOR CAR

Not only did the motor car make its invasive presence felt by clogging up city centre streets and demanding the creation of ring roads, space was also needed to park the things. Thomas Sharp advocated the creation of several new car stands (as he quaintly called them), the largest of which – with 189 spaces – was be on the Sloe Fair Field at Northgate.

Sloe Fair Field was an area of rough grassland used to hold the eponymous annual fair on 20 October, and, as it was unused for the rest of the year, it should not come as any great surprise that it was seen to be ripe for conversion to a car park, as Sharp had recommended.

The Corporation Highways Committee resolved to appropriate the Sloe Fair Field to build a car park in December 1959, but with a capacity of 600 rather than the 189 envisaged by Sharp, and work was due to commence in June 1960. It was intended that Sloe Fair would continue to be held on the site, in accordance with its ancient charter, thus requiring car parking to be suspended for the three days around 20 October. A contract was let to D.H. Coll in April 1960, but mobilisation took so long that the start clashed with Sloe Fair, which seemed to have crept up on them unannounced. As such the contract had to be varied to stop work to accommodate Sloe Fair and then start up again afterwards. Construction was very slow for, a year later on 10 October 1961, it was announced that work would have to stop again for Sloe Fair and the work of final surfacing deferred until afterwards.[40] Once completed the new car park also served the new Festival Theatre.

39. *The Northgate car park under construction. It does not appear to be a hive of activity, which may account for the lengthy construction period. The buildings in the background, marking the northern boundary of the site, are the hospital laundry. They have since been demolished and housing now occupies the site. (Courtesy of Ken Green)*

40. *The demolition of Halsted's iron foundry in 1960 in readiness for its conversion into the Baffins Lane car park. The building in the centre is all that remains of the furnace house. In the background are the backs of properties on the south side of East Street. (WSRO)*

Another new car park recommended by Sharp was constructed in 1960 on the site of the former iron foundry of Halsted & Sons, situated between North and East Pallants.[41] The foundry had closed in 1932 but the buildings remained, having been put to a variety of other uses. All was razed to the ground in 1960 when the car park, to be known as Baffin's Lane, was created, but in the entrance from East Pallant the gate piers, complete with their hinge pins, are still to be seen, souvenirs of Chichester's industrial past.[42]

Mercifully a proposal made at a meeting of the Highways Committee on 15 October 1963 to fill in the canal basin to create another car park was not pursued.

TOWARDS A CONSERVATION AREA

It was doubtless the public displays of opprobrium heaped upon the city council's collective heads over the planned destruction of Somerstown (see Chapter Four) that brought about that hardening attitude of the Planning Committee to demolition that we have already encountered. It also seemed to usher in a reconsideration of the delicate matter of conserving that which gave Chichester its essential character – namely its predominantly Georgian buildings.

In July 1963 a joint meeting had been held between the city and county council planning committees to discuss the thorny issue of controlling development in the City of Chichester. Amongst the many problems over which cud was chewed were indeed those of trying to preserve the character of the city, the fact that too much recent development was 'architecturally undistinguished', owners who deliberately neglected their properties with the idea of forcing the planning authority to acquiesce to ultimate demolition and the difficulty caused by refusals of inappropriate new buildings being overturned at appeal. It was resolved that the Minister for Housing and Local Government would be approached with a view to declaring the centre of the city an area where special architectural control would be exercised.

An audience with the Ministry was duly granted and a report thereon was made to the October 1963 meeting of the Planning Committee. The Ministry agreed there to be a *prima facie* case for issuing building protection orders in respect of Grade III-listed buildings,* especially where they occurred in groups, and felt that more Chichester buildings should be added to the statutory list. As a result West Sussex County Council proposed to declare, in their next revision of the Town Map, the central part of Chichester to be an area over which strict control would be exercised for new buildings, and that it would be planning policy to

---

* At the time the three grades of listing were I, II and III. This was later changed to I, II★ and II.

preserve existing buildings of merit. In parallel with this, the Corporation would publicise the fact that, under Section 69 of the Town and Country Planning Act 1962, they were willing to acquire those buildings on which Building Preservation Orders had been served. This was a step in the right direction – and the first towards creating what we now understand as a conservation area.

The City of Lincoln had produced a survey and report dealing with their identical problems and, on receiving a copy, Chichester City Council Planning Committee resolved to ask the county planning officer to undertake a similar study – which he readily agreed to do. Work on this started in January 1964 and the study would look at exercising strict control over advertising in the main streets – a move which was not to prove popular with traders.[43]

The next step came in June 1965 when the town clerk, Eric Banks, presented a memo to the Planning Committee entitled 'Preservation of Georgian Buildings in Chichester'. In it he refers to a meeting he had held with Chichester MP Walter Loveys on 3 May, arising from which a deputation had been arranged to meet the Joint Parliamentary Secretary for the Ministry of Housing and Local Government. Banks opined that:

> If the present destruction of buildings of architectural or historic interest in the main streets of the city continues it would not be too much to say that in ten years time all the character and interest of the City will be destroyed leaving only a few ecclesiastical buildings of the cathedral, The Close and the Cross to remind the citizens and visitors alike of the city's historic past.

How true, how very true; another brake application had been made. The high-level meeting took place on 28 October 1965 and the town clerk was able to report back that the deputation had received a sympathetic hearing and that the Joint Parliamentary Secretary had promised to consider the various suggestions put to him. The upshot of that meeting, announced in May 1966, was that Chichester had been chosen to take part in a pilot study into the preservation of character and amenity of historic towns. The city council readily resolved to take part.[44]

Later that year the Minister of Housing and Local Government commissioned, in conjunction with associated city and county councils, studies of the four cities of Chichester, Bath, York and Chester. Their stated purpose was '... to discover how to reconcile our old towns with the twentieth century without actually knocking them down. They are a great cultural asset, and, with the growth of tourism, they are increasingly an economic asset as well.' As the studies progressed the findings were fed into the Civic Amenities Bill, sponsored by Duncan Sandys, MP, which was making its way through Parliament at the time.[45]

41. The cover of the 'Chichester: A Study in Conservation', whose publication in 1968 was a pivotal moment in Chichester's planning history. (HMSO)

In Chichester the study was led by G.S. Burrows, the county planning officer, and carried out by a joint team of staff from the county planning, architects, surveyors and valuers departments and also of the city engineer and surveyor.

Their work was completed in September 1967 and the report, entitled 'Chichester: A Study in Conservation', was published in 1968, nearly twenty years after that of Thomas Sharp. Running to 203 A4-sized pages and twelve appendices, the report was a much more substantial work than Sharp's and addressed head-on the problems of traffic congestion, blending necessary new development with old and – most importantly – putting existing buildings to new uses without spoiling their character, thus avoiding knocking them down.

The Civic Amenities Act reached the Statute Book in 1967 and required local planning authorities to designate 'conservation areas', paying special attention to enhancing their character and appearance. A national conference dealing with the implications of the new Act was run in London on 27 October 1967 and the town clerk and the chairman of the City Planning Committee attended.

Chichester was honoured with a visit by the Minister of Housing and Local Government, the Rt Hon. Anthony Greenwood, MP himself, in July 1968, who came to discuss the implications of the study. The city surveyor submitted plans for three possible areas for designation as 'conservation areas' in April 1969, namely:

1. Central area of the city covered by the Town Map
2. The west side of Somerstown (Parchment, Cavendish and Washington streets) and
3. The area of Fishbourne surrounding the Roman Palace

These were forwarded to the county planning officer for his consideration. The decision to include the west side of Somerstown was doubtless political in order to recover some credibility after the wanton destruction of the east side. This was still something of an open wound in the city, especially as the cleared site was still lying empty five years on.

At their meeting of 15 October 1969, the Planning Committee resolved that they were generally in agreement with the recommendations set out in the Conservation Study and that a programme for implementation would be prepared, so far as was consistent with the review of the Town Map, availability of funding and availability of the necessary powers. In January 1970 a draft report into the implementation of the study was prepared and approved and the recommended Conservation Area (now deemed worthy of capital letters in the minute book) would comprise the area within the walls plus Westgate, St Paul's Road, Northgate, St Pancras and Southgate. In March 1970 Lionel French was appointed area planning officer for the county – a man who was to be very influential in the establishment of the Conservation Area.[46]

Coda – the Conservation Area and its Advisory Committee

Although the establishment of the Conservation Area was to occur beyond the era of this work, it is appropriate to take a brief look at what happened next. The Conservation Area was formally designated by West Sussex County Council in March 1970, Lionel French ensuring that the area covered went well outside the city walls as had been suggested by the city council.

Chichester District Council became the local planning authority in 1974 under local government reorganisation, and in May 1976 they floated the idea of setting up a Conservation Area Advisory Committee, something recommended, but not mandated, by the Civic Amenities Act.

The proposal was set out in a report supported by Lionel French, which canvassed views on establishing an independent committee made up of people who would represent professional bodies, amenity societies and local interest groups to advise the district council on planning applications and assist with the development of enhancement schemes. The committee members would give their time for free but the council would make available a small grant to cover the expenses of a secretariat. After a year's successful trial the Chichester Conservation Area Advisory Committee became a permanent fixture in 1978.[47] It exists to this day.*

---

* Your author became a member of CCAAC in 2005 and was elected chairman in 2010.

Notes

1   Thomas Sharp, *Georgian City – A Plan for the preservation and improvement of Chichester* (Southern Publishing Co. Ltd for Chichester Corporation, 1949).

2   WSRO CV/3, Chichester City Council, minutes of Town Planning and Buildings Committee, 1955–63.

3   *Ibid.*

4   The *Chichester Observer*, 18 January 1963.

5   WSRO CV/3, op. cit.

6   *Ibid.*

7   WSRO CD/3, Chichester City Council, minutes of the Finance and General Purposes Committee, 1959–66.

8   WSRO CD/4, Chichester City Council, minutes of the Finance and General Purposes Committee, 1966–74.

9   WSRO CG/2, Chichester City Council, minutes of the Highway Committee, 1950–68.

10 Green, Alan H.J., 'Fork 'andles – Chichester's lost Ironmongers and Decorators' Merchants', Chapter 7 in Paul Foster and Sheila Hale (eds), *A Baker's Dozen – Chichester's Lost Retailers* (Otter Memorial Paper No. 29 University of Chichester, 2011).

11 WSRO CV/3, op. cit.

12 *Chichester Observer*, 3 August 1962.

13 WSRO CV/4, Chichester City Council, minutes of Town Planning and Buildings Committee, 1963–68.

14 *Ibid.*

15 WSRO CD/4, op. cit.

16 WSRO Add.MS 31399, Chichester Civic Society File.

17 Abstract of Title to East Broyle Farm – East Broyle Residents' Association.

18 WSRO CV/3, op. cit.

19 *Ibid.*

20 WSRO CV/4, op. cit.

21 WSRO CV/4, op. cit.

22 WSRO CG/2, op. cit.

23 I am grateful to Mr Ian Crewick for sight of the deeds to his house.

24 WSRO CD/3, op. cit.

25 WSRO CV/4, op. cit.

26 Told to the author by Gerry Adams who was the city council's director of housing in the 1960s.

27 WSRO CJ/4 Chichester City Council, minutes of Public Health and Hosing Committee, 1966–74.

28 *Ibid.*

29 *Ibid.*

30 Green, Alan H.J., *St John's Chapel and the New Town, Chichester* (Phillimore, 2005).

31 Down, A., *Chichester Excavations*, Vol. 2 (Phillimore, 1974).

32 WSRO CV/4, op. cit.

33 WSRO Add.MS 31397, Chichester Civic Society file relating to development in Chichester carries a letter from the town clerk advising of the 1972 Traffic Order for the new road.

34   Sharp, T., op. cit.

35   The *Chichester Observer*, 26 October 1962.

36   WSRO CJ/3, Chichester City Council, minutes of the Public Health and Housing Committee, 1959–66.

37   WSRO Add.MS 31397, op. cit., carries a copy of the 1970 public notice for the CPO of properties in Southgate and also the 1972 Traffic Order bringing the new road into use.

38   WSRO WOC/CM5/1/25, West Sussex County Council, minutes of Roads and Bridges Committee, 1965–66.

39   WSRO WOC/CM5/1/26, West Sussex County Council, minutes of Roads and Bridges Committee, 1966–67.

40   WSRO CG/2, op. cit.

41   *Ibid.*

42   Green, Alan H.J., 'Halsted & Sons of Chichester' in *Sussex Industrial History No. 35* (Sussex Industrial Archaeology Society, 2005).

43   WSRO CV/4, op. cit.

44   *Ibid.*

45   Burrows, G.S., *Chichester, A Study in Conservation* (London: HMSO, 1968).

46   WSRO CV/5, Chichester City Council, minutes of Town Planning and Buildings Committee, 1968–74.

47   The *Chichester Observer*, 30 April 1976, and 23 March 1978 and Templeton, J., 'The 40th Anniversary of Chichester's Conservation Area' (Chichester Society Newsletter No. 165, June 2010).

FOUR

WIELDING THE BESOM OF DESTRUCTION*

We have seen in Chapter Three how a number of historic buildings in the city centre were lost in the 1960s, but there were some highly destructive modernisation schemes in the first half of the decade that warrant this chapter of their own on account of both the scale of the damage they caused to the character of its city and its setting, and for the way they galvanised public opinion against destruction, opinion that succeeded in applying the brakes.

It may have been coincidence, but some of these schemes, which had been boiling away for some time, just happened to come to fruition in 1964 and coincided with certain unplanned happenings. As if that were not enough, in 1964 the city council became embroiled in an embarrassing scandal that made the national press. The year 1964 was to be Chichester's *annus horribilis*.

THE SACK OF SOMERSTOWN

There is no subject more guaranteed to raise the hackles of Cicestrians than the wholesale destruction of the east side of Somerstown in 1964. Somerstown was a late Georgian development of artisan housing outside the north gate of the city begun in 1810 and largely completed by 1835. It was built either side of what is now St Paul's Road, with three streets on the west side (Parchment, Cavendish and Washington) and three on the east (George, High and Cross), the east side being the larger of the two. The east side also included a terrace of houses on the east side of St Paul's Road and another on the west side of Broyle Road.

---

* '… and I will sweep it with the besom of destruction, saith the Lord of Hosts' (Isaiah xiv v 23).

Somerstown was a community in its own right with shops and pubs to support its inhabitants who scarcely needed to venture into the city centre for their day-to-day needs. In 1836 a new chapel of ease – St Paul's – was built in the parish of St Peter the Great to serve the northern part of Chichester including Somerstown, which in 1845 became a parish church in its own right.[1] By the census of 1851 the east side had a population of 625, spread amongst 148 households, who were largely working class.[2]

As the twentieth century wore on, Somerstown became somewhat run-down with several houses being occupied by large families who filled them to bursting point whilst uncaring landlords paid scant regard to the upkeep of their properties. As houses fell into disrepair they came into the council's sights as being ripe for 'slum clearance', a subject that was becoming fashionable in post-war town halls.

In this the council had been influenced by the Sharp Report that we first met in Chapter Three; here is Sharp on the subject of slums:

> There may, perhaps, be some reason why the city should grow so as to provide a better life for those living in it. It is important to examine this. What, for example, is the condition of the houses in which people live? If a large part of these are unsuitable because of their congestion then clearly rebuilding to house even the present population must increase the city's physical size. Fortunately the situation here, far from satisfactory as it is, is nothing like as bad as it is in many towns. There are some 250 houses that are slums. There are some 450 that are so blighted and outworn that they must be replaced at an early date. So what it amounts to is that some 700 new houses are required to replace present slums or near-slums.

That figure of 700 included the whole of Somerstown, which is shown on his master plan as being redeveloped with terraced housing. For an account of what happened in Somerstown during the uncertain years of the 1950s I would refer the reader to Joyce McKenzie's excellent book *Memories of Somerstown*, written by someone who was there, having been brought up on its east side and re-housed therefrom under the city council's infamous clearance scheme.[3]

The first of many death blows leading up to the destruction was dealt in February 1957 when the meeting of the full council resolved:

> (i) That the recommendations of the Public Health and Housing Committee be approved and (ii) That after the West Sussex (Southern Section) Development Plan has become operative, the County Council be requested to make application to the Minister for Housing and Local Government in accordance with Section 6(2) of the Town and Country Planning Act 1947 for the addition of the area shewn

on the plan now submitted as an area subject to compulsory acquisition for the purposes of comprehensive redevelopment.[4]

In 1958 Sir Hugh Casson was asked to draft an outline plan for the redevelopment of the east side of Somerstown. Whilst this was in progress the council's Housing Committee was preparing to instigate the compulsory purchase of all the properties in High, George and Cross streets, together with those adjoining in St Paul's and Broyle roads, under – not surprisingly – the aegis of 'slum clearance'.[5] Casson's scheme would have its principal access through St Paul's churchyard, a feature which did not endear it to the Parochial Church Council (PCC) who, in March 1959, rejected the idea by six votes to four. Undeterred, the town clerk invoked the Bishop of Chichester, resulting in a site meeting between the PCC and the city engineer. This time the PCC rejected the scheme unanimously, refusing to permit access through their land.[6]

The proposals for Somerstown, once publicly known, caused bitter resentment in the city, and local architect Stanley Roth suggested renovating and modernising the condemned houses instead. In a report in the *Chichester Observer* of 11 March 1960 he was quoted as saying, 'They [the city council] should not step in ruthlessly like this, demolishing and replacing the whole area.' In the same article the chairman of the Housing Committee, Cllr Maurice Evans, who emerges as the villain of the piece, admitted that not all the 171 houses were slums, preferring instead to call them 'worn out' (echoing the words of Thomas Sharp some eleven years earlier) and saying 'we use the term substandard houses. We just don't think they are good enough to be made satisfactory to last for 50–60 years.' Stanley Roth estimated that the cost to ratepayers of the council carrying out the redevelopment would be three quarters of a million pounds, and in so doing they would be 'pulling down perfectly good places and tearing up roads that were quite satisfactory'. He then hits the nail right on the head: 'There are many people who would have bought these cottages in the ordinary way and done them up to every satisfaction.' How right he was.

A week later the *Chichester Observer* carried a front-page article about Casson's plans for the site which the paper dubbed 'Chichester's Mayfair', implying that the mixed development of up to 160 houses, flats and shops would be beyond the reach of many Cicestrians, especially as Casson was saying that there was a need to attract back into the city people who would provide a 'nucleus of leaders' – people who had moved to live outside it.

The objections fell on deaf ears since the council was determined to proceed with their intentions and, as families were moved out, the empty houses began to be the target of vandals and presented an increasingly sorry sight. I remember regularly walking through Somerstown with my father en route to Oaklands Park

42. *Nos 48–57 George Street pictured on 19 May 1963 when their fate had been sealed by Chichester City Council. The empty houses have been partly boarded up and they are falling prey to vandals. (Courtesy of John Iden)*

43. *Somerstown also included this terrace on the east side of Broyle Road that also was doomed when this photograph was taken on 19 May 1963. The shop half in the picture to the left is No. 7 Broyle Road, the grocer's shop of Ernest Hay, whilst by the lamppost, at No. 11, is the barber's shop of Jimmy Ewen. Your author received his regular severe boyhood 'short back and sides' here. After demolition in 1964 Jimmy Ewen moved his business to Oving Road – fortunately deemed too far for me to walk from Orchard Street! (Courtesy of John Iden)*

44. Another view of the Broyle Road terrace. The antique shop on the corner of George Street, formerly a pub called The Beehive, was empty in May 1963 when this photograph was taken, and the windows have been smashed. (Courtesy of John Iden)

to exercise the dog. The sorry plight of the condemned houses provided a sharp contrast to the new Festival Theatre being built on the other side of Broyle Road.

In 1962 the protest went national when Sir Laurence Olivier, then the Artistic Director of Chichester Festival Theatre, wrote a highly critical letter to a variety of national and provincial newspapers. The letter, co-signed by Sir Michael Redgrave and Dame Sybil Thorndike, began:

> There has been great prominence given recently to the redevelopment of sites containing buildings of historical interest.
>
> We have just completed a season at Chichester, surely one of our most uniformly beautiful cities. It has come to our notice that a row of early *[sic]* Georgian terraced houses abutting the theatre [i.e. in Broyle Road] and extending over a small area have been condemned for demolition in spite of the fact that a certain section of the City have put forward a plan for renovation and preservation of these unique buildings … [7]

In response, the city's chief public health inspector, Thomas Ward, in an interview that was reported in the *Chichester Observer* of 12 October 1962, described Sir Laurence's protest as 'absolutely ridiculous' and went on to declare that the council's decision to demolish the houses was the only method possible 'because of their size, layout and structural conditions the properties were incapable of being repaired and improved to modern standards without destroying the whole character of the area'.

What an ignorant indictment of Georgian building! The work that was later carried out to similar properties on the west side proved just how wrong the council could be and how right were the protestors and Stanley Roth. The following month the vicar of St Paul's, the Revd John Jackson, also jumped on the bandwagon, writing in the parish newsletter:

> Should the scheme of complete destruction be carried out the planners and architects of the scheme will undoubtedly be condemned as we now condemn those who in the past destroyed the gems of the Tudor era.[8]

Another national attack came from an unexpected source, namely the architectural historian Ian Nairn who was compiling part of the Sussex volume of *Pevsner* at the time. In it he described some 'comfortable early C19 terraces, part of a suburb called Somerstown' and went on to say:

> Much of it (e.g. High Street and George Street) is about to be pulled down. If this is supposed to be 'slum clearance' in a city as completely unslummy as Chichester, it seems ridiculous. This area needed piecemeal reconditioning, not demolition. Its unpretentious virtues are worth a look while they stand.[9]

Unfortunately his advice to view Somerstown came too late, for the book was not published until 1965 by when the east side had all but gone.

Demolition began in January 1964, the contract having been awarded to H. Geall Ltd of Bognor, a firm who did rather well out of the destruction of Chichester in those days.[10]

However, the works were not without their problems since the owner of No. 17 Broyle Road had referred his case to the Lands Tribunal as the compensation offered was inadequate, and this was not heard until 24 June, delaying the demolition.[11] Further difficulties were created in March 1964 by 71-year-old widow Alice Gilbert, a feisty lady who refused to move out of her house at No. 10 Broyle Road as the £250 offered in compensation was only half what she expected. As such, demolition had to stop at the properties either side and she was still fighting two months later.[12] Indeed the demolition spread into 1965 owing to the difficulties in gaining entry.

Public attacks on the city council continued whilst this destructive act was in progress, firstly by Lady Sayer speaking for the Chichester Civic Society and then the architect Stanley Roth, and these were met with a robust public riposte by the town clerk who claimed that the houses had been thoroughly inspected

45. The demolition of the last corner of the Waggon & Horses on the corner of High Street and St Paul's Road in 1964. This pub was similar to The Bell in Broyle Road which, mercifully, has survived. (Author's collection)

46. Looking across the remains of Somerstown in March 1964 with the Waggon & Horses completely gone, along with all the houses on the south side of High Street. The houses on the north side of High Street are still there and to the right can be seen the houses on the south side of George Street which were awaiting the demolition men's sledgehammers. (Courtesy of John Templeton)

before the decision was taken and that only twelve were found to be capable of being restored. In this he was supported by the Archdeacon of Chichester, the Ven. Lancelot Mason, who stated '… I do not take it to be tolerable to condemn people to live in slum conditions for the sake of olde-wordliness'.[13]

Fortunately the west side of Somerstown was not covered by the 1958 compulsory scheme, probably because, although also still a poor area, the buildings were in a better state of repair. However, these buildings could well have perished later, along with all the other areas of older houses that the council had in its sights. Part of the reason for the survival may have been the aforementioned Festival Theatre which opened in 1962, causing Chichester to add many famous visitors to its list of seasonal residents. These included Bill Frazer and Doris Hare, both of whom bought cottages on the west side of Somerstown. Gradually these three remaining streets moved up the social scale and, once taken on by owner-occupiers, they were refurbished and could no longer be classed as potential slums. Today they are highly sought after and, at the time of writing, even the smallest of them is selling in excess of £250,000.

After demolition the site of the east side of Somerstown lay waste for nearly ten years, ten years of shameful indecision until, in the early 1970s, a redevelopment was began by Downland Fourth Housing Society. This uninspiring development (one resident describes it as 'architecturally challenged') in no way compensates for what has been lost and, to add insult to injury, the old streets were abolished, and the new development known by the generic appellation 'Somerstown', ignoring the fact that this title applied on the other side of St Paul's Road as well. This has resulted in many newer Chichester residents not being aware that Parchment, Cavendish and Washington streets are actually – and rightfully – part of Somerstown.

Two original buildings of the east side, both public houses, did manage to survive however, one at each end of what had once been George Street. At the west end is The Rainbow while at the east end is The Bell. Both sit on corners of truncated sections of George Street and represent the only tangible reminders of the past delights of this area.

SHARP GARLAND'S SHOP, NO. 1 EASTGATE SQUARE

Eastgate Square was a square that, by the start of the 1960s, was in just the wrong position, sited as it was at the confluence of four major roads, one of which, Market Road, had been earmarked to form a sector of the ring road. The cenotaph had long since been removed to the Litten Ground as it was in the way of traffic but, strangely, Eastgate Square had been left unscathed on

47. Eastgate Square around 1960. The tall white-painted building on the right-hand (north) side of the square is Sharp Garland's famous grocer's shop, whilst nearest the camera on the same side is Vera Humphy's (née Brazier) wool shop. Between them is Bennett's the florist. In the centre of the square is a floral roundabout that marked the spot where the cenotaph stood before it was moved to the Litten Ground. The buildings on the south side of the square have all survived but the north side has been completely redeveloped. (Author's collection)

Thomas Sharp's master plan as he proposed taking the ring road straight across the Cattle Market to join up with the end of New Park Road.

However, when Sharp Garland's grocer's shop on the corner of East Walls began to show signs of structural distress in January 1964, a gift must have seemed to have landed right in the highway engineer's lap – a road widening was probably to be had on the back of a 'dangerous building' notice.

Sharp Garland's shop was a legend and widely believed to have been the oldest grocer's business in the country. It opened in 1665 and in 1860 was bought by Sharp Garland, remaining under the family name for 104 years until that fateful year of 1964.[14] The Garland family had played a major role in the civic life of the city, both Sharp Garland and his son, Sir Sharp Archibald Garland, holding the office of mayor.

The shop was decidedly old-fashioned by the standards of the Swinging Sixties with groceries kept in fitted cabinets around the walls and tea and coffee stored loose in large tin canisters. There was always the heady aroma of freshly roasted coffee wafting into the square from the shop, and inside the coffee aroma became mixed with smoked ham and cheese. It was the sort of shop where customers still awaited their turn to be served from behind the long counter; self-service was inconceivable. If required, orders would be delivered using the firm's red Ford van driven by my uncle, Tom Green.

The building was timber framed and had been clad in Georgian times with brick, as had many similar shops in Chichester, and in January 1964 cracks began to appear in the façade. The city council was swift to act and the district valuer submitted a report to the Finance and General Purposes Committee on 27 January with a recommendation to purchase it and No. 2 next door occupied by Bennett's the florists. Consideration of the report was deferred by the committee in order to:

> … enable the City Surveyor (i) to report on the condition of the property; and (ii) to submit to the County Planning Committee an outline planning application to redevelop the area.

On 24 February the city surveyor duly reported on the poor condition of Sharp Garland's shop on the back of which the district valuer continued negotiations for its purchase and the city surveyor produced a redevelopment scheme for the site.[15] By the beginning of March the city surveyor became so concerned about the state of the building that he told Alf Peat, who ran the business, that the shop could collapse at any moment and that he must move out immediately. Eastgate Square was cordoned off and Chichester Magistrates granted an order for the owners to make the building safe. The Civic Society called for the building to be shored up whilst an investigation was carried out into saving the building, but to no avail. Demolition began on 5 March 1964, once again under the hammers of Mr Geall of Bognor.

48. Eastgate Square in March 1964 with Sharp Garland's, shrouded in scaffolding, being demolished in the background. The florist and woolshop were spared this time – but perished in the next decade. (Courtesy of John Templeton)

49. Doomed – the once-proud frontage of Sharp Garland's shop peers through the scaffolding. Within a few hours it would be joining the rubble already raining down on to the pavement from the roofline. (Courtesy of John Templeton)

Under a headline 'Sharp Garland could not be saved' the *Chichester Observer* of 13 March carried a lengthy report of a crowded public meeting at which the mayor, Cllr Brookes, the town clerk and the county surveyor had vigorously denied allegations that the Corporation had exploited the shaky state of England's oldest grocer's shop as a means to have it demolished for road widening purposes, whilst the magistrate who granted the order – the architect Stanley Roth who had so vigorously opposed the demolition of Somerstown – tried to extricate himself from an embarrassing imbroglio by saying that the Bench had hoped the owners would limit the amount of work needed to making the building safe. 'We would not want it to be said that the building was pulled down at the order of the magistrates,' he said.[16]

It is clear that little or no serious consideration was given to conserving the fabric of this historic shop, demolition was seen as the easy option – something that would be unthinkable today.

By July the district valuer was able to report to the Finance and General Purposes Committee that he had negotiated a purchase price for both Nos 1 and 2 Eastgate Square for £14,750 with a further £430 4s to cover surveyor's fees and legal costs. A resolution was taken to purchase both properties, redeveloping the site of demolished No. 1, but retaining No. 2 and leasing it to the existing tenant.

The purchase of the two properties was completed on 30 November 1964. The city surveyor's plans for the site were called in by the ministry in November 1965 but were permitted following a public inquiry held on 18 May 1966. Nothing happened, however, and No. 2 continued to be leased out until November 1968 when it was condemned. No. 3* was compulsorily purchased at this time but both buildings were left derelict until the early 1970s when redevelopment finally took place. The building on the corner was named Sharp Garland House, commemorating its past, but most Cicestrians would have preferred retention of what was there before.

WESTGATE FIELDS

The settings of the cathedral cities of Salisbury and Winchester are considerably enhanced by their being bordered on their southern sides by attractive water meadows. Today's visitors to Chichester may be surprised to learn that this city was once so blessed; those long-lost water meadows were colloquially known as Westgate Fields.

The meadows were bounded on the east by South Street and Southgate, to the north by the city wall and Westgate, and to the south by the railway. South of the railway the fields between it and the bypass were rapidly being swallowed by the expanding Terminus Road Industrial Estate, but beyond the bypass further unbroken fields swept away south and west to the shores of Chichester Harbour, intersected only by the by-pass and Apuldram Lane.

Westgate Fields was criss-crossed by footpaths and meandering branches of the River Lavant and were used for grazing cattle, particularly those being held over until market day. For schoolboys such as me, Westgate Fields was a lotus land where we could keep ourselves amused all day: water, mud, tadpoles, dogs and a busy railway – what more could a boy possibly ask for?

As we played there in the 1950s we were blissfully unaware that plans were being argued over that were going to destroy our lotus land in the next decade.

Thomas Sharp, in his aforementioned 1949 report, had praised Westgate Fields and the contribution it made to the setting of the cathedral, saying:

---

* In December 1966, during the school holidays, I assisted my father in installing a new floor in No. 3, Vera Humphry's wool shop, as the existing one was collapsing under the effects of dry rot. Neither Mrs Humphry nor we had any idea how short a life that new floor was to have.

50. A view to Chichester Cathedral from Westgate Fields taken in 1960. Until 1964 cattle famously still grazed right up to the city wall. (Author's collection)

In spite of its unusual impingement on the very centre of the city on one side, the Cathedral has kept an unusual freedom on the other. To the south, over a few large houses in the Close and beyond the city walls, it faces straight on to the meadows of open country – not merely on to an 'open space' of river banks or trim gardens such as some other cathedrals have, but just on to the ordinary green fields of the everyday countryside where cattle and sheep graze as it might be in the shadow of a village church. Though the railway runs beyond these few fields, it serves well to keep back the scattered building that has taken place to the south of it: and the effect here remains very like what it must have been in most cathedral cities until about a hundred and fifty years ago.[17]

Praise indeed, but if from those sentiments you would assume he was proposing to retain this idyllic feature you would be wrong – very wrong indeed. His master plan showed that he intended to push a dual-carriageway ring road, along with a link through to the west end of the bypass, right across Westgate Fields and turn the rest of the 'countryside' he had so praised into the sort of 'open space' he had so derided.

Sharp's ideas were taken up by West Sussex County Council and incorporated into their development plan, which was addressed by two public inquiries in 1952 and 1957. By 1957 the ring-road proposal had been joined by a further education college and a secondary modern school, which would effectively cover 62 per cent of Westgate Fields. At the two-day 1957 inquiry there was much public opposition from, *inter alia*, the Cathedral Chapter, the *Chichester Observer* and Sussex Archaeological Society as well as rank and file Cicestrians. After the inspector filed his report, the Minister of Housing and Local Government pronounced that the college was approved – but not the school or the ring road; some sort of victory seemed to have been won but it was to be short lived.[18] The 1960s were to see to that.

When Ian Nairn visited Chichester in researching the Sussex *Pevsner*, as well as viewing the still standing Somerstown as we have seen, he too visited Westgate Fields and was impressed, writing:

> Closer to, the famous view of the cathedral seen across fields from the by-pass to the SW cannot be matched in England. And this can still just be carried through on foot over the railway to the walls of the Close, still in rough pasture (or in reverse a walk of two hundred yards out of the busy South Street leads to fields from which, turning round suddenly, the image of the cathedral almost knocks the viewer over). But in 1960, after a long struggle, the Westgate Fields were designated for a ring road and two schools. However well designed and landscaped, the old essence will have gone. It is up to the twentieth century to construct something just as exciting, and will have its work cut out.[19]

This last was to prove a masterly understatement. Nairn had become aware of the result of a third public inquiry that had taken place in 1960 when West Sussex County Council, as the education authority, applied for a compulsory purchase order to buy the land needed to build a new college of further education and to reinstate the concept of a ring road, but without the school. In this they were successful as the order was duly granted.[20]

In 1962 work commenced on building the college, which was situated well to the west of the proposed alignment of the new road. This site had met with much local opposition, the view of the citizenry being that it should be built next to the railway station, on the site now occupied by the Waitrose supermarket. This was rejected by planners who felt that there it would be subjected to too much background noise against which it would be difficult to insulate.

51. Chichester College of Further Education seen on 28 August 1964 when it had risen out of the grass of Westgate Fields, but was still very much a building site and seemingly some way off being ready to receive its first students in two weeks' time – which it was! (Courtesy of John Iden)

The college opened its doors on 28 September 1964, two weeks after the official start of term owing to construction overruns.[21] The college grew rapidly and expanded westwards, northwards and southwards so as to occupy all the land between the river and the railway.

Although the college had got off to a prompt start, the construction of the new road to link the South and West Gates did not. In December 1960 the county Roads and Bridges Committee considered the report of a joint meeting that had taken place between officers of the city and county councils to discuss the alternative schemes they had each produced. Although the schemes were broadly similar, the Corporation wanted to have a large roundabout at Westgate in the middle of which would be erected a building to provide an architectural stop* to West Street, in place of Nos 1 and 2 North Walls which currently provided this service but were doomed to be swept away. In this ideal they were supported by the Chichester Civic Society who wished to see provided 'an exceptional architectural stop to preserve a sense of enclosure'. The county's scheme did

---

* An architectural stop is an important tenet of classical town planning – a feature which draws the viewer's eye to the end of an important street, closing off the vista. A good example is Great Pulteney Street in Bath were the 'stop' was provided by the Sydney Gardens Hotel, now the Holburne Museum.

52. Westgate seen in July 1962, looking west. The buildings in the foreground are Nos 1 and 2 North Walls (No. 2 had been the home of the artist Eric Gill from 1897–1900) which provided an architectural stop to West Street. Beyond are Nos 2 to 10 (evens) Westgate. All these buildings constituted an inconvenient narrowing of the western entry into the city (known as 'the bottleneck') and were thus doomed anyway. The need for a roundabout in conjunction with the proposed ring road sealed their fate. (Courtesy of John Iden)

not include this feature, the county surveyor opining that a roundabout without buildings 'would be more desirable from a highway point of view', so the county decided that their own scheme was preferable and should be discussed again with the Corporation.

In January 1961, having considered the report of a further meeting with the Corporation, the county Roads and Bridges Committee resolved to approve the county surveyor's scheme 'slightly amended to meet certain points raised by the City Engineer' at an estimated cost of £120,000 subject to government funding.[22]

The Corporation were clearly not prepared to roll over in front of the senior planning authority and so sent a resolution to the county council in February agreeing to the county surveyor's scheme for the new road on condition that sufficient land was purchased to facilitate an architectural stop 'if it is considered desirable at a later date and the county council agree to construct a building when requested by the City Council'. Needless to say the county council were not prepared to be so bound and resolved to submit a formal planning application to the city council and at the same time inform them that they could not undertake unconditionally to build an architectural stop but that 'very careful consideration will be given to a request for such a stop once the scheme has been completed'.

53. *A last look at Westgate Fields with the cathedral looming large over the city wall. The rough fence in the middle ground marks the line of the River Lavant which was straightened out in 1964 by the Sussex River Authority. The ring road and the Prebendal School playing field now occupy this pasture land. (Courtesy of John Iden)*

The city council then pressed for any dispute arising on this issue to be referred to arbitration, a condition which – not surprisingly – the county refused to entertain.

In June 1961 the MoT unhelpfully advised the county council that any grant towards the £120,000 needed for the road scheme 'might not be forthcoming for several years', so, as the new road (or at least part of it) would be required to provide access to the new college, the county surveyor reviewed his scheme, looking to reduce its cost to around £70,000. Things were not looking too rosy.[23]

In February 1962 the county surveyor was again pressing the MoT to indicate when it might make a grant available. The answer that came back, namely 1965/66, did not please the county council's Roads and Bridges Committee, who resolved to press the MoT again so as to achieve completion in 1964 when the college was expected to open.

It was decided to issue a compulsory purchase order for the land under Section 214 of the Highways Act of 1959 which included terms that prevented 'the erection of buildings detrimental to the view from such [new] highway'. At least a nod had been made in the direction of retaining an open aspect.[24]

However, when the county council applied for the necessary compulsory purchase order they felt it necessary to advise the minister that there was a 'difference of opinion' over the architectural stop (i.e. they did not want it!) but that this would not affect the order. When the city council heard of this they resolved to inform the minister that an end stop *was* definitely required. The minister's view on this was one of disinterest – he told the town clerk that it was simply a planning matter and had nothing at all to do with the compulsory purchase order.[25]

The compulsory purchase order for the fields attracted two objections which necessitated yet another public inquiry. This was held on 3 December 1963 and the inspector allowed the order to proceed in February 1964 but removed from it the land needed at Westgate to build a roundabout as he was not convinced

54. The Southgate end of the new Westgate Fields road under construction in 1965. Although by this time the carriageway was complete, work on the junction with Southgate had not commenced. Site access through to Southgate had been made by the demolition of the property of C.A. Colborne, the electrical contractor, but the range of buildings to the right, which included Rugby House, were also needed to complete the job. (Courtesy of John Iden)

55. The buildings on the west side of Southgate that were to be demolished to make way for the new ring road. Seen here in September 1963 they included Messrs Wadham's car showroom and Rugby House, which was occupied by Bottrill the coal merchant. Colbourne's premises to the right were demolished in 1964 to give construction access on to the new road, the remainder, as far as Wadhams, succumbed to demolition hammers the following year. (Courtesy of John Iden)

that enough land had been identified. Notices were at once served on owners and occupiers and the contract for constructing the road was awarded to Everymans of Maudlin in the sum of £54,521 10s 3d.

The new road was built as dual carriageway and work proceeded very quickly, for by December 1964 it was largely complete leaving only the junctions at Southgate and Westgate to be built.[26]

Despite the perceived urgency the road did not open until 7 September 1965[27] but, regardless of the measure of incompletion, it did afford me a convenient, shorter cycle route to the Boys' High School from my home in Orchard Street throughout that year.

WESTGATE

The junction of the new ring road with Orchard Street at Westgate called for some wholesale clearance work. The city's West Gate proper had been removed in 1772 but the houses on both sides of the approaching street were left standing, constituting a 'bottleneck' on one of the four principal accesses to the city, in this case what had been the A27 up to 1939. The construction of the ring road finally presented the opportunity to remove this bottleneck.

56. Westgate in July 1962, looking east with No. 2 Westgate in the foreground. The excavations are in connection with the building of a new sewer along Orchard Street that commenced earlier that year. To the left of No. 2 Westgate can be seen No. 4 Orchard Street. All these buildings were to be demolished in late 1963. (Courtesy of John Iden)

57. This terrace of humble late-Georgian cottages at the Westgate end of Orchard Street (Nos 16–40) was demolished in 1961 to make way for highway improvements. The south end of their site is now under the Westgate roundabout and the north end was made into a car park. The only clue to the location is the house in the background, No. 63, which still stands next to the entrance to the twitten to Parchment Street. (WSRO)

As we have seen the design for the new road across Westgate Fields provided for a large roundabout at Westgate to smooth traffic flows around the ring road whilst linking to West Street and West Gate. Unfortunately wholesale demolition was inevitable. In October 1961 the county council made a compulsory purchase of a terrace of late Georgian cottages on the east side of Orchard Street (Nos 16–40 evens) for £2,680. They were demolished and the portion of the site not reserved for the highway improvements was sold to the city council who converted it into a car park, the car park opposite which the West Sussex Record Office was to be built in 1989.

The houses on the north side of Westgate (Nos 2, 4, 6, 8 and 10) and those on the corners of North Walls (Nos 1 and 2) and Orchard Street (Nos 4 and 6) were already in the ownership of the county council who, in September 1963, decided to invite tenders for their demolition. These buildings, having been blighted for several years previously, were rapidly falling into disrepair. They were demolished in November 1963 and the Corporation pressed for steps to be taken to prevent the cleared site from becoming an eyesore until construction of the new road commenced.[28]

58. A view west along West Street with demolition of Nos 1 and 2 North Walls in progress. From this view the narrowness of the Westgate can be appreciated as can the effect of an architectural stop provided by the North Walls building. (Courtesy of John Templeton)

59. Another view of the Westgate demolition. On the right most of the buildings on the north side have gone but the northern pier of the old West Gate has still to be razed. On the south side – amazingly – only the building with the gable end, the former White Horse, perished. (Courtesy of John Templeton)

Although the city council had not opposed the demolition of Westgate (as they were pressing for the new road they presumably had no option but to support it), they insisted that the building known (erroneously) as the Old Toll House be preserved. In this they were successful and the building stands today used as an Indian restaurant.

When the new road first opened it made a temporary junction with Westgate and Orchard Street whilst the design of the Orchard Street section of the ring road was being thrashed out. In March 1967 the MoT issued a grant for the Orchard Street ring-road works which included the construction of the roundabout at Westgate, for which, in June 1968, two more properties were acquired. These were Nos 34 and 35 West Street, situated on the north side, which were demolished by Mr Geall of Bognor in July 1969. After this the long-awaited roundabout was finally constructed.[29]

The architectural stop never materialised, so this was a battle lost by the city council to its mightier planning overlord. However, a fine horse chestnut tree formerly in the garden of No. 4 Orchard Street just happened to end up in the middle of said roundabout and provided an alternative feature until its untimely demise from disease in 2009.

SCANDAL!

In January 1964 there broke out a scandal involving Chichester City Council that was to occupy the front pages of the *Chichester Observer* for several months, as well as making the nationals. The scandal, which precipitated some councillor resignations, stemmed from the previous year when, as a result of what was reported as 'complaints', a police inquiry lasting several months had been launched into the conduct of both the city and county councils, with corruption and fraud being alleged. It was intended that the papers resulting from the police inquiry would be sent to the Director of Public Prosecutions for action.

As part of the investigation detectives sat in on council meetings and Cllr George Foote stormed out of the January 1964 meeting of the full council saying that there was 'a poisonous atmosphere' in the council chamber and that no one had gleaned thousands of pounds from the public purse, all that had occurred was a few breaches of the Local Government Act. At the same meeting the town clerk, Eric Banks, denied the detectives' allegations that he had withheld documents from the police. Foote then resigned from the council.[30] This also made the pages of the *Daily Telegraph* and the *Daily Mail*.

In the meantime Cllr Anthony Halliwell had not appeared for three consecutive council meetings and Alderman Alan Mason, chairman of the Finance and General Purposes Committee, was considering his position. The public interest in what was going on became so great that they crowded out the council meetings. The front page of the *Chichester Observer* of 21 January carried the banner headline 'Summons against former Chichester Councillors' and reported a lengthy statement from Chichester Police to the effect that summonses had been applied for against George Foote under the Larceny Act and against Anthony Halliwell and his wife for attempted fraud. The five-month police investigation was said to be complete and the papers were being sent to the Director of Public Prosecutions. Halliwell resigned his place on the council in March and all three were summonsed to appear before Chichester Magistrates on 9 and 15 April.[31]

Chichester Magistrates heard that George Foote appeared before them on charges relating to theft over the purchase of, and works to, houses in St Pancras, but was cleared of all charges and awarded costs of 75 guineas. Foote announced that as his good name had been damaged he would not be standing for election again.

The charges against the Halliwells related to allegedly fraudulent attempts to obtain a mortgage from the Corporation on their house in Summersdale. On the strength of the charges they were committed for trial at the county assizes in Lewes. This they duly did in May and were acquitted but the judge ordered that the papers be sent to the Ministry of Housing and Local Government who would be asked to investigate the city council's affairs. He considered that the blame 'lay fairly and squarely on the shoulders of the Council's permanent officials'. Chichester City Council had agreed to cooperate with the inquiry.[32]

In November Hugh Griffiths, QC was appointed by the Bar Council to conduct the inquiry which began in April 1965 and his thirty-seven page report, published the following month, absolved Corporation officials from any blame over the Halliwell incident, concluding that 'The facts, when investigated, do not bear the sinister interpretation that misunderstanding and rumour had placed upon them.'[33] A copy of the report was duly sent to the minister and another was made available for public consultation at Greyfriars, but there it ended with all three accused being acquitted and no case being found against any council officers either.[34] A great deal of public time and money, to say nothing of private angst, had been expended on inquiries and court appearances, all – apparently – for nothing.

The name of the complainant and the nature of his/her 'complaints' that sparked off the original inquiry is not revealed in either the city council minute books or the newspaper reports. All very strange.

A BRIGHTER LIGHT

Fortunately the gloom of 1964 was pierced – literally – by an anonymous donor who had provided the dean and chapter with £3,000 to fund the installation of fifty-three floodlights around the cathedral. These were switched on in August, bathing the cathedral in a dramatic silvery light.[35] This was seen to best effect from the top of the Trundle, but those approaching Chichester at night from the west, along the Old Broyle, were rewarded by its suddenly springing into view when they crossed the bridge over the Midhurst railway line. I remember cycling up there to view it in that first week, and the novelty has never worn off, even fifty years on.

Notes

1   Green, Alan H.J., *St Paul's Chichester: The Church, its Parish and People, St Paul's* (PCC, 2010).
2   Eccleston, C., 'A Thesis – A study of demographic and Social Structures in Somerstown (East)', a copy of which is held at WSRO as MP 3947.
3   McKenzie, J., *Memories of Somerstown – A Tribute to a Community* (Purbeck Books, 2008).
4   WSRO CV/3 Chichester City Council, minutes of Town Planning and Buildings Committee, 1955–63.
5   WSRO Chichester City DE/1, a 1:500 scale plan of the east side of Somerstown showing the properties to be acquired by CPO for demolition.
6   WSRO Par 43/14/3, St Paul's PCC minute book, 1953–62.
7   The *Chichester Observer* of 12 October 1962 carried the full text of the letter.
8   WSRO Par43/7/9, St Paul's parish newsletters, 1960–79.
9   Nairn, I., and Pevsner, N., *The Buildings of England: Sussex* (Penguin, 1965).
10   WSRO CJ/3, Chichester City Council Public Health and Housing Committee minute book, 1959–66.
11   WSRO C/32 Chichester City Council minute book, 1954–65.
12   The *Chichester Observer*, 13 March and 8 May 1964.
13   The *Chichester Observer*, 13 March, 26 June and 3 July 1964.
14   Green, K., and Hale, S., 'Provisioning the Kitchen Cabinet', a paper in *A Baker's Dozen – Chichester's Lost Retailers* Otter Memorial Paper No. 29, Edit Paul Foster (University of Chichester, 2011).
15   WSRO CD/3, Chichester City Council, minutes of the Finance and General Purposes Committee, 1959–66.
16   The *Chichester Observer*, 6 and 13 March 1964.
17   Sharp, T., op. cit.
18   Childs, R., *Civil War over Westgate Fields Fifty Years Ago* (Chichester Society Newsletter, December 2011).
19   Nairn, I., and Pevsner, N., op. cit.

20 Childs, R., op. cit.

21 Walker, R., *The History of Chichester College 1964–2004* (Chichester College, 2004).

22 WSRO WOC/CM5/1/21, West Sussex County Council minutes of Roads and Bridges Committee, 1960–61.

23 *Ibid.*

24 WSRO WOC/CM5/1/22, West Sussex County Council minutes of Roads and Bridges Committee, 1961–63.

25 WSRO CG/2, Chichester City Council, minutes of Highway Committee, 1950–68.

26 WSRO WOC/CM5/1/23, West Sussex County Council minutes of Roads and Bridges Committee, 1963–64.

27 The *Chichester Observer*, 10 September 1965.

28 WSRO WOC/CM5/1/22 op. cit. and CG/2 op. cit.

29 WSRO WOC/CM5/1/26 and /29, West Sussex County Council minutes of Roads and Bridges Committee, 1966–67 and 1969 respectively.

30 The *Chichester Observer*, 22 November 1963 and 3 January 1964.

31 The *Chichester Observer*, 14, 10 and 21 January, and 23 February 1964 and the *Evening Argus*, 21 January 1964.

32 The *Chichester Observer*, 17 April and 22 May 1964.

33 The *Chichester Observer*, 6 November 1964, 23 April and 28 May 1965.

34 WRSO C/33, Chichester City Council minute book, 1965–74.

35 The *Chichester Observer*, 28 August 1964.

FIVE

CITY OF CULTURE

Whilst the city's attitude to its architectural heritage might appear to have been somewhat philistine in the 1960s, its attitude to its cultural heritage was anything but.

Cathedral cities have long been crucibles of artistic invention and Chichester was no exception. Central to this is the cathedral which, the Puritan period apart, had traditionally patronised the arts of painting, music and sculpture.

Chichester had reached new cultural heights in the eighteenth century when a large new Assembly Room was provided in North Street* (1783) and a theatre in South Street (1764). At the former, culture was available in the form of recitals, concerts and lectures, whilst at the latter the latest plays were to be seen. Following its enlargement by rebuilding in 1791, the theatre attracted repertory companies to Chichester, and even the great Edmund Kean trod the boards here.[1]

In the 1960s the arts in Chichester were alive and well and the tradition was built on with initiatives that were to see Chichester's cultural life reach greater heights in subsequent decades when it became the vibrant city of culture that it is today. The 1960s renaissance included the building of a theatre of national importance, the creation of a museum and the building of a large new branch library, all of which took place alongside an expansion in amateur creativity. The 1960s were to be a creative and uplifting time on the arts front.

---

* There had been an earlier, much smaller, Assembly Room in North Pallant (the site now occupied by the modern house No. 20) which was largely made redundant in 1783 and had been demolished by 1820.

LACKING – A THEATRE

The theatre in South Street closed in 1850, after which theatrical performances transferred to the Assembly Room and the Corn Exchange. The Corn Exchange had been converted into a combined theatre and cinema, known as the **Exchange Theatre**, with raked seating and a full proscenium-arch stage and was used for both staged works and the showing of films.[2]

In 1948, under the tenancy of Granada Ltd, the Exchange Theatre was again remodelled, this time exclusively as a cinema, known as the **Granada Exchange**, leaving the Assembly Room as the only performance space – and unfortunately one still without a stage.

In 1946 the ailing Chichester Corn Exchange Company was wound up and the following year its buildings were purchased by George Booth, the philanthropic owner of the Booth Shipping Line and onetime director of the Bank of England, who had retired with his family to nearby Funtington Lodge. Booth was a remarkable man with a deep love of the arts and a kindly disposition. He loved to foster artistic appreciation and allowed 9-year-old Eve Denyer, who lived in the cottage next door, the run of his garden and library and encouraged her to listen in to the musical recitals in his music room.[3]

60. In the 1960s the long-closed 'old' theatre in South Street was Messrs Lewis & Co.'s furniture and pram shop. The road alongside is still called Theatre Lane. The building is currently an Italian restaurant. (WSRO)

Booth proposed to continue to lease the cinema to Granada but demolish the other buildings in Baffins Lane and St John's Street in order to build **The Chichester Arts Centre**, a centre which would include a much-needed 500-seat theatre.[4]

Booth engaged the architect Harry Sherwood to produce a set of outline drawings for the centre. Unfortunately by the summer of 1949 Booth realised – having sought advice from the Arts Council and others– that his plans were perhaps a bit too ambitious, being on too-large a scale for a town the size of Chichester. He felt that 'it would be unrealistic to attempt to provide a centre mainly designed for professional musical and dramatic performers', so he intended to scale down the auditorium to 300 seats.[5]

To add to Booth's problems, in January 1951 the Corporation announced that, having consulted with local performing societies, it intended to refurbish the Assembly Room, inserting a proscenium-arch stage and new dressing rooms. This proved the final nail in the Chichester Arts Centre coffin, and in July 1951 Booth gave up, saying that the facilities proposed for the Assembly Room would be better than his project would have offered. Local artist David Goodman tried to keep the project going by appealing for shareholders but to no avail; in December 1951 the Chichester Arts Centre idea was abandoned and so remained just an interesting might have been.[6]

The need for a proper theatre had not gone away though. The refurbished Assembly Room, which finally reopened in 1953, did now have a stage but it was too small to attract professional companies to perform. Not only that, the room still (of necessity) had a flat floor which was far from ideal from an audience point of view.[*]

However, Booth's vision of a new theatre for Chichester was not lost. In 1962 Chichester was to gain a 1,350-seat theatre of national repute; George Booth *was* a visionary but, sadly, one a little too much ahead of his time.

CHICHESTER FESTIVAL THEATRE – FULFILLING THE NEED

If I find myself at a gathering in London (or even beyond) and announce to strangers that I live in Chichester, I can guarantee that I will be faced with two questions, namely: 'Do you sail?' and 'Do you go to the Festival Theatre?' The answer to the first is definitely 'no' and to the second a most definite 'yes'.

---

[*]   The new stage, welcome as it was, unfortunately spoiled the double-cube proportion of the Assembly Room since it occupied the full width and height of its east end. It was removed in 2002.

The fact that the latter question is invariably asked reflects the fact that one-horse-town Chichester had been put firmly on the map in 1962 with the opening of Chichester Festival Theatre. In 2012, Chichester Festival Theatre marked its fiftieth anniversary in fine style and published a celebratory book entitled *Chichester Festival Theatre at Fifty*, written by Kate Mosse. As the theatre's creator also detailed the founding history in his 1971 book *The Impossible Theatre*[7] only a brief account of its 1960s life is required here.

Chichester Festival Theatre had been the brainchild of Leslie Evershed-Martin, a Chichester optician, keen theatre-goer and founder of the Chichester Players. He was also the city councillor whom we met in Chapter Three express-ing his enthusiastic support for the Sharp Report; this was in 1949, just at the time that George Booth's grand scheme was beginning to run into problems.

Evershed-Martin had been inspired by a January 1959 television programme on the construction of a new amphitheatre-like theatre in Stratford, Ontario. The aforesaid Stratford, Ontario, had a population that matched that of Chichester and Evershed-Martin asked himself the question *why not such a theatre in Chichester?* Having secured the support of Tyrone Guthrie, the great theatrical producer, Evershed-Martin single-mindedly set about planning a new 1,400-seat open-stage theatre to be built in Oaklands Park. Whilst George Booth had lost confidence in the ability of Chichester to support a 500-seat theatre, Evershed-Martin pressed doggedly ahead, ultimately proving the pundits wrong, and created in the city an auditorium of nearly three times that size – and one of national standing.[8]

This is not to denigrate the efforts of George Booth: it was just unfortunate that his vision came too early, at a time when, in the immediate post-war years, enthusiasm tended to be dampened by caution. The passing of eight years had changed all that. Naturally Booth became a subscriber to, and supporter of, the new project, and put his experience of making national appeals to good use. In addition, Harry Sherwood, who had designed Booth's aborted Arts Centre, was consulted over the design of the new theatre.

Evershed-Martin surrendered his seat of eighteen years on the city council in May 1959 in order to devote his time fully to his project. Very quickly he established a large committee of like-minded individuals including the Duke of Richmond; the Very Revd Walter Hussey, Dean of Chichester; Eric Banks, the town clerk; Geoffrey Marwood, the chairman of the Planning Committee and my chemistry master at Chichester High School for Boys, the artist David Goodman who had been involved with Booth's project; and Dr C.W.W. Read, the director of education for West Sussex County Council. The Duke of Norfolk agreed to be patron. The committee immediately got to grips with the thorny problem of fundraising.

Unfortunately it was over fundraising appeals that Booth and Evershed-Martin were to have a major disagreement. Being well connected in London financial circles, Booth advocated the production of a glossy brochure setting out what we would now term a 'business plan' in order to persuade big banks and insurance companies to back the idea. As such a brochure would be expensive to produce, George Booth volunteered to put up the necessary £500. Evershed-Martin disagreed with this approach, feeling that the big institutions were only interested in their shareholders and the benefits that subscribing to a theatrical project might bring them – which would be minimal. Instead he wanted to appeal to the potential users of the theatre – i.e. the future audiences.

Booth and Evershed-Martin clashed again over the architect for the new theatre. Sherwood's outline design was abandoned and he was replaced as architect by the modernist practice of Philip Powell and Hidalgo Moya. Powell & Moya had worked in Chichester in 1948 designing a pair of avant-garde bungalows in Mount Lane, one of which was for Philip Powell's father, who was a canon of Chichester Cathedral. The other bungalow was also occupied by the Powell family*. Shortly after this Powell & Moya designed the **Skylon**, the famous symbol of the 1951 Festival of Britain. It was through his Chichester connection that Leslie Evershed-Martin, who had been impressed by Skylon, met Philip Powell. Powell was approached about executing the design for the Festival Theatre and Powell & Moya accepted the commission in August 1959, proffering their initial design the following November. The consulting structural engineer was Charles Weiss.

Booth attacked Powell & Moya's design as being too ambitious – doubtless as a result of experience with his own project – and was supported in this view by Sherwood and several others. Although he then retreated and desired that his name would not be associated with the new plan, George Booth still gave the promised £500, so his name appears on a board in the foyer as one of the founders of Chichester Festival Theatre. Booth was a true philanthropist.[9]

In 1960, as part of the fundraising initiative, a Festival Theatre Society was set up and Evershed-Martin's main committee became the Festival Theatre Trust. As we saw in Chapter Three, Barratt's former bookshop on the corner of South and West streets had been acquired by the city council in 1959, and in March 1960 the Festival Theatre Trust was granted a free lease of the ground floor for

---

* Sadly the two Mount Lane bungalows are no more. They were not listed despite being considered to be of sufficient importance to feature predominantly in a monograph about Powell & Moya published by the RIBA. One was quietly demolished in 1996 and Chichester District Council, in the face of strong public criticism, gave planning permission for the remaining one to be demolished in March 2010 to enable the site to be redeveloped.

INTERIOR OF THE CHICHESTER FESTIVAL THEATRE MODEL

61. A postcard showing the model of Powell & Moya's final design for Chichester Festival Theatre that was made in 1960 and travelled extensively as part of the fundraising process. This clearly shows the novel design for an open, thrust stage auditorium rather than the traditional proscenium arch arrangement. (Author's collection)

use as a fundraising and display centre for the project, a prime city-centre location which could not fail to attract the attention of the public.[10]

Powell & Moya's design was a bold one being of hexagonal plan and executed in reinforced concrete. We will look at the design in detail in Chapter Nine. Once it was finalised a model was made which was taken to be shown to prospective benefactors and also to local schoolchildren. I remember it coming to the Central Junior Boys' School in New Park Road where we were entranced by it. Doubtless wishing to be seen to be clever, I contributed to the eager questioning by asking how many bricks would be used. I was somewhat abashed to be told, quite simply, 'none'!

A contract was let to Sir Robert McAlpine when full funding was still far from secure, and work started on 1 May 1961. The foundation stone was laid on 12 May following by Princess Alexandra, a ceremony attended by many thousands of Cicestrians and local schoolchildren with the Band of the Royal Marines and the Martlet Swordsmen and Folk Dancers contributing to a scene which Evershed-Martin described as being 'typically Merrie England'.

Work proceeded apace and I kept a watchful 11-year-old eye on it from Oaklands Park whilst exercising the family dog. In March 1961 Evershed-Martin achieved another coup when he secured the services of Sir Laurence Olivier as the theatre's first artistic director. Topping out was achieved on 23 November 1961, attended by Sir Laurence, and soon the building was roofed in.

62. The Festival Theatre under construction in December 1961 with the main structure already substantially complete. (Author's collection)

On 10 January 1962 Sir Laurence Olivier took the bold step of announcing that Chichester Festival Theatre would open on 5 July that year. His faith in the contractor was well placed and the work was completed well in time for this to happen. The theatre duly opened on 5 July with the 1,350 first-night tickets being allocated by ballot and the full £110,000 needed for the venture finally secured. The queen and the Duke of Edinburgh attended a performance on 31 July, following Goodwood week.[11]

The first season ran for just nine weeks from 5 July until 18 September 1962 and featured three plays: two seventeenth-century works, *The Chances* by John Fletcher and *The Broken Heart* by John Ford, followed by *Uncle Vanya* by Anton Chekhov. Surprisingly for many, there was no Shakespeare. The glittering casts included Keith Michell, Joan Plowright, Joan Greenwood, Fay Compton, Sybil Thorndike and Michael Redgrave. All three plays were directed by Laurence Olivier, who also starred in *The Broken Heart* and *Uncle Vanya*.

The following season, 1963, obviously had something to live up to, and the three plays chosen were *St Joan* by Bernard Shaw, a reprise of *Uncle Vanya* and the first performance of *The Workhouse Donkey* by John Arden. 'Big names' in the casts were very much as for 1962, but joined by Frank Finlay, Rosemary Harris and Derek Jacobi. This time Sir Laurence only directed and starred in *Uncle Vanya*, the Shaw being directed by John Dexter and the Arden by Stuart Burge.

Shakespeare finally arrived on that open stage in the 1964 season with *Othello* starring Frank Finlay, Derek Jacobi, Laurence Olivier and Maggie Smith, the

112

63. *Chichester Festival Theatre seen from the north in 1967 with theatre-goers sitting on the grass. Behind can be seen the timber administration building. (Author's collection)*

64. *The interior of the Festival Theatre as built showing the thrust stage with its balcony level. It was intended at first that the stage sets would be somewhat minimalist hence no scenery dock was provided. This was a decision that was soon reversed. (Author's collection)*

65. *The cover of the first season's programme in 1962. (Author's collection)*

1962

CHICHESTER

FESTIVAL THEATRE

first season

66. A postcard bearing a commemorative postmark for the first season of Chichester Festival Theatre in 1962. Note that the postmark puts Chichester in 'Sussex', not 'West Sussex'; although the county had been split for administrative purposes for over seventy years it did not then have a split identity as far as its native inhabitants were concerned. This remained the case until the local government reorganisation of 1974. (Author's collection)

67. Smartly dressed theatre-goers arriving on the penultimate night of the 1962 season to see Uncle Vanya. The young people seated on the ground were intending to camp out all night in order to be first in the queue for the cheap tickets for the final night. Sir Laurence Olivier was so impressed by their enthusiasm he ordered the foyer be left open so that they could sleep indoors until the box office opened in the morning! The three young ladies are, left to right, Penelope Smith, Carolyn Smith and Marian Pilbeam. (Courtesy of Marian Pilbeam)

other plays being *The Royal Hunt of the Sun* by Peter Shaffer and *The Dutch Courtesan* by John Marston. Ticket prices in the 1964 season ranged from 5*s* (25p) to 30*s* (£1.50). The cheapest seats were in the back row of the balconies along the sides of the stage and could only be had by queuing on the day of the performance. Tickets priced 10*s* (50p) and above could be booked in advance.[12]

The theatre had no heating system as it was only intended to be used for a short summer season, so throughout the 1960s there were no winter programmes. That was to come later, but no matter: professional theatre had well and truly arrived in Chichester and played to full houses. The ritual of theatre-going had been added to the pleasures of Chichester summers.

AMATEUR DRAMATICS

Although, as we have seen, George Booth's arts centre project crashed, the former Corn Exchange building in St John's Street was kept by him and converted into a dancing school, eponymously named **The Booth Rooms**. The school opened in 1951 and was run by Marian Lombard and thousands of Chichester girls – and a handful of boys – passed through her hands. Characteristically Booth also introduced his young neighbour Eve Denyer to Marion Lombard and signed her up for Saturday morning dance lessons to which she cycled from Funtington.

Every New Year Marion Lombard put on a public production, which usually sold out and got glowing reviews in the local press. The Lombard School of Dancing, and its annual productions, continued until 1980 when Miss Lombard retired, after which The Booth Rooms became part of Wiley's expanding publishing empire. Sadly The Booth Rooms appellation was then lost and this remarkable man's association with Chichester is rapidly becoming forgotten; the plaque in the foyer of the Festival Theatre listing the founders is the only place in the city where his name is to be found displayed.

Alongside the professional theatre there was still room for an amateur dramatic society – or AmDrams as they were generally known – and the long-established Chichester Players continued to hold sway. Chichester Players was founded in 1953 by Leslie Evershed-Martin and a leading light in it was – yes – Geoffrey Marwood, my chemistry master at Chichester High School for Boys whom we have already met in other capacities. He had many strings to his bow!

Their usual theatre was the Assembly Room, but they had a short spell at The Booth Rooms in 1951/2 when the Assembly Room closed for a major refurbishment. In November 1960 they presented *The Gioconda Smile* by Aldous Huxley, which ran for four nights with tickets priced at 2*s*, 3*s* 6*d* and 5*s*. The Chichester Players are still going strong and now have a home at the New Park Centre.

NEEDED – 'A PROPER CITY MUSEUM'

A city with an ancient foundation and an educated population naturally stimulated an interest in its past, as well as in wider history. In the nineteenth century municipal and private museums and art galleries were established in larger towns and cities to provide enlightenment for their citizens.

Around 1848 the combined Chichester Literary and Philosophical Society and Mechanics' Institute had established, at their premises at No. 45 South Street, 'a valuable and curious collection' of objects mainly obtained through generous donations. The collection included many important local archaeological finds and was held in high regard. Unfortunately the society fell on hard financial times in the late nineteenth century, and in 1891 objects from the collection began to be sold off, a process which continued until, by 1924, everything had gone. The sales in that final year included the 'municipal moon'* and the city stocks, both to Worthing Museum. The ethos of the society then changed from cultural to social, and it was accordingly renamed The Regnum Club. Chichester Museum was now a thing of the past.[13]

Items of archaeological interest continued to be unearthed in Chichester, and when the Chichester Civic Society was formed in 1945 it established an Excavations Committee who investigated and recorded the many redevelopment sites that were underway around the city. They too unearthed many Roman items and these were stored in the Guildhall in Priory Park in the hope that one day they might be displayed for the benefit of the public.

Doubtless as a result of pressure by the city's archaeologists, the Corporation had formed a Museum Subcommittee of the Finance and General Purposes Committee, whose first meeting was held on 19 April 1949. They brought about the establishment of a museum in the Guildhall under an honorary curator, Dr Wilson, which opened to the public only during the summer months. It was resolved that the additions to the collections would be limited to objects of 'local interest'. The seasonal openings included special exhibitions, with which the Civic Society assisted, and they proved so popular with the public that the need for bigger and better premises soon became obvious.[14]

In 1954 an approach was made to Worthing Museum for the return of the municipal moon, the city stocks and some Roman artefacts, and in November 1955 a full-time curator was finally appointed in the person of Miss Gilchrist.

The catalyst precipitating action on creating a new museum was the co-option on to the Museum Subcommittee of Francis Steer, the county archivist,

---

* The municipal moon is a large seventeenth-century processional lantern used by much earlier mayors at night. Its spherical shape gave rise to its name.

on 9 December 1959. As well as being the brilliant antiquarian who produced the Chichester Papers*, Steer was a campaigner – and just the influence the Corporation needed.[15]

To mark the twenty-fifth anniversary of Eric Banks becoming town clerk, an exhibition was staged in the Assembly Room during summer of 1961 entitled 'Changing Chichester'. Under a headline 'Exhibition Stresses the Need for A Proper City Museum', the *Chichester Observer* of 18 August 1961 reviewed the exhibition and interviewed Banks on the subject of a new museum – 'I am more and more convinced that an ancient city like Chichester should have one,' he said. With the combined impetus of the town clerk and the county archivist things were bound to happen.

Need Fulfilled – Chichester City Museum

In 1961 Fred Sadler, head of the long-established Chichester firm of corn and seed merchants, died aged 94, and his house, No. 30 Little London and the grain stores next door, came on to the market and were bought by the architect Stanley Roth. No. 30 was converted into flats, and Mr Roth intended to convert the grain stores into offices. However, he soon spotted the fact that the redundant grain stores would make a marvellous museum, so he prepared an outline scheme for such a conversion.

It was at their meeting of 20 September 1961 that the Museum Subcommittee took the momentous decision to create what was to be known as **Chichester City Museum**. Stanley Roth had been invited to attend and he tabled his scheme to the committee and explained that he was prepared to grant 'a very long lease' of the building to the Corporation after conversion into a museum on 'reasonable terms'. Following this a lengthy memorandum from Francis Steer was read out which began by citing the success of the summer exhibitions in the Guildhall and pointed out that much material was available on loan or as gifts which would be lost unless the opportunity to create a new museum was not seized quickly. The Guildhall, he pointed out, was unsuitable. He then got into his stride with typically powerful locution:

> Chichester cannot afford to lag behind other towns in Sussex and elsewhere which have permanent and flourishing museums … the disaster of the previous museum in Chichester must not be repeated: the only way to avoid such an event is for a museum to be under the control of the City Council and served by a full-time curator.

---

* See Chapter Two.

68. The house of Fred Sadler at No. 30 Little London and the former Sadler grain store at No. 29. The grain store was to be converted into the new Chichester City Museum. (Courtesy of Geoffrey Claridge)

He recommended retaining the Guildhall for pre-history and Roman studies and acquiring 'suitable premises of character' for medieval and later items. He also felt that the collecting policy should only relate to Chichester and its locality with 'no ethnological, foreign natural history or general collections of coins, porcelain etc.' being included. He further recommended that a friends' group should be formed to generate income for the purchase of new objects and was very bullish about charging admission:

> There is no need for free admission to the museum; people are willing to pay up
> to one shilling for admission provided the display, whilst being instructive, is not
> 'above their heads'.

In this opinion he was (fortunately) to be overruled. Whilst we cannot disprove that the making of Roth's offer and the presentation of Steer's memo at the same meeting was purely coincidental, the combination of the scheme and the latter's fighting talk, referring as it did to the shameful dispersal of Chichester's erstwhile private museum, brought about the necessary decision. The subcommittee resolved to agree in principle to Roth's proposal and to instruct the town clerk to enquire of the Carnegie Trust and the Museum Association about grants. News of Roth's offer was reported in the *Chichester Observer* on 6 October leaving little scope for the Corporation to turn it down.

Stanley Roth and his partner Geoffrey Claridge designed and carried out the conversion work as an act of pure philanthropy. The museum building had a basement for storage of artefacts not on display and on the ground floor a reception area, office and display room. On the first floor were the main display rooms, an exhibition room and another office. A flat for the curator was provided on the second floor.[16]

Representatives from the Museums Association and the Carnegie UK Trust visited Chichester to inspect the Little London and Guildhall sites in December 1961 and advised on the layout of both buildings. They opined that an assistant curator would also be needed as the proposed custodian would not be able to carry out the duties of this post. Their advice was heeded.[17]

A new curator, Miss J.M. Cook, was appointed in July 1962, having been chosen from eleven applicants, and prior to their meeting of 18 September following, the Museum Subcommittee were conducted around No. 29 Little London by Stanley Roth to view the works in what was now referred to as 'The New Museum, 29 Little London'. Miss Cook presented her first curatorial report to the effect that she had begun accessioning the collections in the Guildhall and revealed the remarkable fact that at the summer 1962 Guildhall exhibition 4,887 visitors had paid a total of £97 19s to come in – a record since that of 1954. At that same meeting Stanley Roth was co-opted on to the committee.

The next meeting, on 11 December 1962, was held in the new museum where Dr Wilson resigned as a member of the committee but expressed his willingness to help run the new venture in an unofficial capacity. It was resolved that, despite Francis Steer's opinion on the matter of admission charges, none would be levied in the opening year.

An appeal to set up a group to be called **The Friends of Chichester Museum** attracted eighty-seven annual and thirty-one life subscriptions, and its first meeting was held on 11 December 1962. Membership cost half a guinea annually but those subscribing more than 5 guineas were granted life membership.[18] Work on the new museum proceeded apace during 1963 and a nameplate by the sculptor John Skelton was commissioned, with the Museum Society contributing half the £60 cost – the very first time they were to assist financially in the project.[19]

69. The nameplate for Chichester City Museum, designed and made by the sculptor John Skelton in 1963. (Photographed by the author)

Before the handover and opening of the new museum, Stanley Roth organised some exhibitions on the premises in 1963. Most momentous of these was one devoted to the works of the Sussex sculptor John Skelton who had a Chichester connection, being the nephew, and onetime apprentice, of Eric Gill. The exhibition of drawings and sculptures was opened on 13 July by Sir Charles Wheeler, president of the Royal Academy. The highlight of the opening was Sir Charles' unveiling of a large piece of Skelton's sculpture, entitled *Symbol of Discovery*, sited on a cobbled area outside the museum's front door. This impressive work had been commissioned by Stanley Roth and was in the form of a pair of hands carved from Westmorland slate, holding a Perspex 'jewel' in which were embedded small pieces of gold leaf. A slate plaque, lettered by Skelton and set into the cobbles at its base, reads 'Museums present to the world the precious offerings of the earth.'[20] *Symbol of Discovery* is perfectly suited to the setting for which it was conceived and is much admired and photographed by visitors to the city.

By December 1963, under the chairmanship of Lancelot Mason, Archdeacon of Chichester, membership of the Museum Society had reached 217 and they had held six meetings. One member, the antiquarian Lyndsey Fleming, had purchased some components of an historic staircase from the Grange in Tower Street, which was being demolished, and he donated the elaborately carved string thereof to the new museum.* This was the first of many objects to be donated to the City Museum by the society.[21] Indeed, the bulk of the museum's collection was donated by local people.

The official opening of Chichester City Museum took place on Wednesday, 22 April 1964 (probably the best thing to happen in that dread year) by the Rt Hon., the Countess of Albermarle, DBE, DCL, LLD, a Carnegie (UK) Trustee. Stanley Roth, in his role as president of the Museum Society, provided hospitality at the museum whilst the Corporation entertained her to lunch. In her speech the countess said, 'A museum must not be dead. It should be humming and vital. It should be a meeting place not only for societies but for all the arts, a place where things are always happening and people are developing new interests.'[22]

By 9 July 1964, 8,929 visitors had passed through the new museum, contributing over £20 to the collecting box in lieu of paying an admission charge. That month Miss C.A. Fisher replaced Miss Cook as curator. Regular temporary exhibitions were staged in the exhibition room which served to keep visitors coming back again and again as there was always something new to see.

---

* The Grange was a Victorian Gothic fantasy house built in 1840 on the site of a perfectly good Georgian house of the same name that was demolished to make way for it. The new house incorporated much fabric salvaged from the derelict Halnaker House, including this elaborately carved seventeenth-century oak staircase.

70. *John Skelton working on* Symbol of Discovery *on a hot day at his studio in Streat, beneath Ditchling Beacon in Sussex. (Courtesy of Ditchling Museum)*

71. Symbol of Discovery *in situ outside Chichester City Museum. (Courtesy of Geoffrey Claridge)*

72. *The opening of Chichester City Museum on 22 April 1964 by the Countess of Albermarle. She is standing with the Mayor of Chichester, Cllr William Brookes, and the curator, Miss J.M. Cook, next to a display of cooking utensils. The municipal moon is in the background. (WSRO, Chichester Photographic Archive, CPS2241–2)*

News of the new museum obviously reached the British Travel and Holidays Association whose September 1964 newsletter contained the following glowing report:

> The new museum in Chichester, Sussex, is no dusty storehouse – but a lively building where one's sense of wonder is aroused. Since it opened in early summer, many thousands of visitors – four thousand in the first month – have seen the treasures it contains …

The following month the Museum Subcommittee once again examined the issue of admission charges but resolved to defer any such introduction for another twelve months as £69 had been placed in the collecting box by grateful and generous visitors. In fact admission charges were never made, and the City Museum remained free for its entire existence at Little London, ensuring that visitor numbers stayed up[*].

Councillor Gilbert took on the chairmanship of the Museum Subcommittee in July 1967, the summer in which the Guildhall reopened after a year of closure when repairs were carried out to the roof. No fewer than 2,000 visitors came in to see it between June and September. The Little London museum had, since its opening in April 1964, been open to the public for six days a week during the summer months but in April 1968 it was decided to extend the winter Monday closing to the rest of the year, a practice that was set to continue.[23]

In those free and easy days there was no security beyond the display cases, and no means of monitoring the more-unwelcome antics of visitors, so, inevitably, thefts did occur. In June 1968 two boys from the Lancastrian School were caught breaking into the upstairs collecting boxes and were taken to the police station where the full majesty of the law descended upon them. After this it was decided to move the collecting boxes downstairs and to provide an enquiry window in the office so that comings and goings might better be observed.

That same year attendances at the Tuesdays-only openings of the Guildhall attracted 2,648 visitors who donated more than those to Little London. However, the fact that it had to close during the lunch hour was not popular with the public, so from April 1969 the Guildhall was opened on Tuesdays and Fridays from 10 a.m. to 4.30 p.m. – including the lunch hour. Museum visiting had become a very popular Chichester pastime.[24]

---

[*] When the Conservative Thatcher government introduced museum entry charges in the 1980s, visitor numbers at the Victoria and Albert Museum in London dropped by two thirds and overall less income was derived as fewer people were buying in the shop and café. Lunchtime visitors were not prepared to pay £8 when they could only stay for half an hour. Mercifully this decision was reversed by a subsequent government and the visitors and revenue returned.

Under the local government reorganisation of 1974 control of the City Museum passed to the new Chichester District Council. They changed the collecting policy to include the whole of the Chichester District area and renamed it Chichester District Museum to suit, though fortunately the Skelton nameplate proclaiming 'Chichester City Museum' was allowed to remain.

From the very start the Little London museum was only able to display a small portion of its collection and as time wore on this situation got worse, and by the twentieth century the lack of public toilets and disabled access to the first floor became unacceptable. As such a new museum was planned for the Roman Baths site in Tower Street and the Little London premises closed in 2010 to allow the collection to be packed up ready for the move. After lengthy delays the new museum finally opened in July 2012 and the Little London premises were sold.

Sadly, after forty-eight years of free museum entry, Cicestrians and visitors alike now had to pay to see the city's heritage and for many Cicestrians this meant paying to see items that they themselves had donated to the museum in good faith in times past. *Sic transit.* Fortunately, on 17 November 2014, the entrance fee was dropped following low visitor numbers.

CHICHESTER LIBRARY 'IS QUITE INADEQUATE ...'

Under the Libraries Act of 1919 West Sussex County Council had been established as the public library authority for Chichester, and the city council collaborated with them to establish a branch library in the city which opened in 1927 in the Old Theatre in South Street.[25] It moved above the Market House in 1932 but in May 1947 the branch library came to land in premises at No. 22 West Street, where they were to remain until 1967. The county Library Headquarters were in Ede's House (then known as 'Wren House') just down the road.[26]

No. 22 West Street was a fine Regency house of 1812 that had been modified to provide two entrances – that on the left being the way in, that on the right being the exit. At the time this building represented to me the archetypal library: squeaky brown lino on the floors, 'SILENCE' notices everywhere and sensibly shoed lady staff with their hair in buns ever waiting to pounce and utter '*Shhh!*' to noisy boys.*

From 1948 to 1960 the Library Subcommittee was chaired by Miss Jessie Younghusband, a redoubtable lady whose name is permanently

---

* It is quite possible that I am doing the staff of the pre-1967 library a great disservice – I'm sure they were all very nice really. It's just strange how early impressions tend to stick in the mind.

associated with the new primary school opened to serve the East Broyle Estate (see Chapter Seven). She was born in Eastbourne in 1892 and in Chichester was much involved with voluntary work in the city, including the Red Cross.[27] On her death the Library Subcommittee stood in silent tribute to her at their meeting of 1 July 1960. The chair was then taken by another redoubtable lady, Cllr Alice Eastland, whom we met in Chapter Two.

In October 1961 the county librarian, Gordon Bearman, sent a report to the subcommittee about the future of Chichester's library as the premises at No. 22 West Street were now too small. He put forward two alternatives: adapt Fernleigh (No. 40 North Street) or build new premises as part of the next extension to County Hall. The subcommittee decided in favour of the second option. Meanwhile a temporary extension to No. 22 was authorised as a matter of urgency and opened to house the children's library in 1963.[28]

The county council's capital building programme now provided for the building of a new branch library and headquarters in Chichester, the desperate need for which was justified in the entry made on 7 May 1963:

> County Library Headquarters is quite inadequate to serve a library system which has undergone considerable expansion in recent years and which will continue to expand. Chichester Branch is in sub-standard (leased) premises which are inadequate to meet the needs of the population served.

It was seen that premises with a floor area of 6,000sq.ft were needed for this dual role and £131,000 was earmarked for the project.[29]

SOLUTION – THE TOWER STREET LIBRARY

Tower Street is another of Chichester's charming lost backwaters; its east side was steadily eroded away in the post-war years, generally under slum clearance, and in the 1960s the county council progressively acquired most of its west side to extend County Hall. In October 1964 the Ship Inn and the buildings either side of it were compulsorily purchased to make way for the new combined branch library and county library HQ.

At the March 1963 meeting the county architect, F.R. Steele, presented sketch plans for the new library building to the county's Sites and Buildings Subcommittee who were not too happy about the cost. After this the plans were refined and another estimate was produced:

73. A view south along Tower Street on 30 March 1964. In the foreground is the pub The Ship and beyond it cottages and storehouses. These buildings, as far south as the white-fronted house, were soon to be demolished to make way for the new library. (Courtesy of John Iden)

	£
Buildings	85,000
Fixed furniture	8,000
External works	5,300
QS Fees and drawings	2,420
Structural consultants	2,000
Clerk of Works	1,350
Total	104,070

The architect pointed out that the extra-over cost of double-glazing the building would be £3,000 but such measure would only save £39 12s per annum in heating costs. The director of education expressed dismay at the paucity of the energy savings, so it was resolved to proceed without the luxury of double-glazing.[30]

The design for the new building was, famously, circular. Now I had always fondly imagined that the choice of this shape was in answer to the new Festival Theatre – Chichester has a hexagonal theatre, so why not a circular library? This is far from the truth, as was explained to me by the architect for the scheme, Rod Funnell. Apparently, when a large-scale OS map was tabled showing the land to be acquired for the extensions to County Hall, a circle was drawn on it labelled 'site reserved for new library'. The committee took this as indicating the intended plan shape and jumped at the idea, so Rod, the in-house architect allocated the job, had to make it work.[31] Fact truly is stranger than fiction!

The attractive 92ft-diameter drum-like structure was formed of radial pre-cast concrete ribs with large, segmentally headed windows in each bay. The roof was flat but had an unusual circular roof light consisting of twenty-four small, copper-clad gabled roofs radiating from the centre and ending in triangular windows. The structural engineer appointed was Ove Arup, who led the field in pre-cast design at the time. In January 1965 the tender for constructing the new library of local builder J.G. Snelling was accepted in the sum of £104,474 and work soon started on site.[32]

By the summer of 1966 the building was substantially complete and promised for handover on 15 November to allow fitting out to commence. The official opening was provisionally set for 24 January 1967. Alice Eastland had stood down as chairman of the Library Committee in October 1966 but agreed to remain a member until May 1967 to see in the new venture.[33]

The new library was on two floors: the lending library on the ground and the reference library on the first. The reference library included a fine collection of books on Sussex and was well stocked with copies of the latest quality magazines and newspapers. One welcome innovation was the provision of study desks; these could be booked free of charge and were a great boon for those studying for 'O' and 'A' levels who could not find the requisite peace and quiet at home.

74. *Construction underway in 1965 showing the pre-cast concrete first-floor ribs supported on the inner brick wall. A further rib unit is lying on the ground ready to be hoisted into position. The cathedral spire keeps a watchful eye over the proceedings. (Courtesy of Rod Funnell)*

75. *Another construction view in 1965 looking across Tower Street. In the foreground can be seen the temporary car park that was created between Chapel and Tower streets with a bubble car in evidence. The road known as 'Woolstaplers' now occupies this site. (Courtesy of Rod Funnell)*

76. *Nearly there. The new library, seen in July 1966 when nearing completion. Opposite can be seen the former Lancastrian Boys' School of 1811 which closed in 1911 and was annexed by Priors' woolstapling business which occupied the lofty building next door. Priors ceased trading in 1967 and the buildings were demolished. After lying derelict for over thirty years the site was developed as the new district museum. (Courtesy of Rod Funnell)*

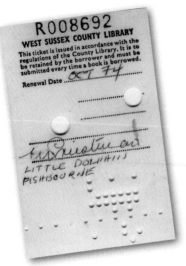

77. *One of the original computer library tickets issued for the new Chichester branch library. (Author's collection)*

78. *The system in use. Here a reader (who bears a striking resemblance to Dr Beeching) watches as his card is inserted in the reader by a librarian. The old-fashioned date stamp had not been obviated by the technology though. (West Sussex County Council Library Service)*

Another novel feature was a state-of-the-art computer issuing system, one of the first to be installed in the country, which replaced those much-loved paper tickets in cardboard pockets that had to be filed manually in racks. Each reader now had a ticket in the form of a plastic card punched with a series of holes through which the card was read. Each book had a similar ticket and, on issuing books, the reader's card was put in one slot and the books in the other, and the computer married the two together. The same process was used on return. Details of the issues were punched on to paper tape and read by the central computer at County Hall.

Although I did not at first take kindly to having my identity reduced to a series of holes, the system did work well. Indeed I once left my ticket in my shirt pocket and it inadvertently went through the wash. Although slightly buckled it was none the worse for its experience for it still worked perfectly!

The opening duly took place on 24 January 1967 by Professor Asa Briggs, Vice Chancellor of Sussex University. Professor Briggs described the new library as an 'exciting new building' which housed 80,000 books and the 4,000-book Sussex collection. He opined that 'books are a necessity of life'. After the cutting of the ribbon, Gordon Bearman presented the professor with two volumes of a catalogue of sixteenth- and seventeenth-century British drawings for the university library.[34]

At the meeting of the Library Committee on 1 February 1967 the new chairman, Mrs Baxendale, congratulated everyone on the smoothness of the

79. *Professor Asa Briggs performing the opening ceremony of the new Chichester branch library on 24 January 1967 watched by Gordon Bearman, county librarian (centre) and John Snelling the builder (rear). (WSRO)*

80. *The crowd of dignitaries assembled inside the library listen attentively to the speeches on the opening day. Against the wall on the left is Francis Steer, the county archivist, and next to him Dean Walter Hussey. (WSRO)*

changeover from the old premises to the new but reported that complaints had been received on behalf of disabled people who found access to the first floor difficult or impossible (there was no lift), a problem that had not existed at No. 22 West Street. In reply the county librarian explained that two-storey libraries were county policy for new builds but that the problem for the disabled 'was not insoluble and arrangements would be made for non-accessible material to be brought by staff to the ground floor on application'. On the face of it a not very helpful response but there was no law on disability discrimination in those far-off days.

Disabled access apart, the new library was an instant success. By April 1967 the number of readers had increased by 3,000 and 2,000 additions had been made to the stock of fiction. Between April and June 1967 there had been a 50 per cent increase in adult readers, so Cicestrians valued their new repository of learning, the new building obviously being seen as much more approachable than the old premises in West Street[*].

It is appropriate to have a brief look at the remarkable career of Gordon Bearman who was not only the county librarian who oversaw the provision of the new library but a pivotal figure in the life of Chichester through five decades. Gordon Bearman had been appointed county librarian way back in 1937 and, in addition to his paid job, he ran two youth fellowships at St Paul's church and acted as an ARP warden. He was called up in January 1943 and did not return to civvy street until October 1946. Gordon Bearman then took an increasing role in the life of the Church of England in Chichester. He remained a lay reader at St Paul's until 1951 and on 20 May that year he was ordained deacon and, whilst continuing as county librarian, he took up the duties of curate at Bosham churchs giving his services for free. He was priested in 1962 at Bosham and continued to serve as curate there on a non-stipendiary basis until he was appointed as Priest-in-Charge of the new St Wilfrid's church in Parklands on 31 May 1968.[35] When he left Bosham to take on St Wilfrid's, Gordon Bearman did not, as one might have expected, relinquish his county librarian duties but kept them on, not retiring from that post until 1970.[36]

WALTER HUSSEY – PATRON OF ART

A highly influential figure in Chichester's artistic renaissance in the 1960s – and beyond – was Walter Hussey, whose name has already cropped up in this text. Born in 1909 into a clerical family, he went to Oxford and then trained for ordination into the Anglican Church. He became vicar of his father's church, St Matthew's,

---

[*] No. 22 West Street still exists – it is now the offices of Edward Hayes the solicitor.

81. Walter Hussey when Dean of Chichester at the deanery. The sculpture on the bookcase behind him is a seated woman by Henry Moore. (WSRO, Hussey, MS65, courtesy of the Dean of Chichester)

Northampton, in 1937 and whilst there embarked upon a mission to re-ignite the role of patronage of the arts by the Church. Hussey was a very cultured man, deeply interested in music and modern art, and at St Matthew's he commissioned a number of musical and art works. In 1944 he engaged the relatively unknown sculptor Henry Moore to produce a large Madonna and Child statue for the church – an act which won him more opprobrium than approbation.[37] He also commissioned an up-and-coming composer, Benjamin Britten, to write a piece for his choir to mark the fiftieth anniversary of the consecration of the church in 1943. That work was *Rejoice in the Lamb*.[38]

When, in 1955, candidates were being sought for a new Dean of Chichester to replace Dean Duncan-Jones, Bishop George Bell added his recommendation to Walter Hussey's name. Bell himself was a lover of contemporary art and no stranger to the controversy it can raise – as he found when he allowed the Bloomsbury Group to decorate Berwick church after the war*.

Hussey was duly installed as Dean of Chichester on 30 June 1955 and took up his artistic mission again but did so slowly. He obviously realised that he was in Sussex and that – as the saying goes – 'Sussex won't be druv', especially here in deeply conservative Chichester. He needed time to get his feet under the table first, so the new works did not begin to arrive until the 1960s.

The first commission was in 1960 for a painting by Graham Sutherland in connection with the refurbishment of the Chapel of St Mary Magdalene. Entitled 'Noli me Tangere', the artist prepared two versions: one was paid for by the Friends of Chichester Cathedral and installed, whilst Hussey kept the other.

---

* The Bloomsbury Group was a set of artists who lived at Charleston Farm near Lewes and included Duncan Grant, Clive and Venessa Bell and Roger Fry. Their lifestyle was widely regarded as Bohemian and hence they were seen by many as highly unsuited for decorating a church. They covered the walls with paintings which included, at the chancel arch, Bishop Bell himself. It is well worth a visit.

It was unveiled in May 1961 and, as was to be expected, was met with some hostility. The refurbishment of the chapel also included a new stone altar by Robert Potter and a pair of candlesticks by Geoffrey Clark.

The next work arrived in the autumn of 1966 and this was to be the most striking modern addition to the cathedral. It was a huge tapestry by John Piper to hang on the dreary Victorian reredos behind the high altar. Depicting the Trinity and the four elements (earth, air, fire and water), the highly colourful tapestry was woven in seven strips at Frères in France and cost £3,269.[39] When, in 1961, the old Arundel Screen was re-erected at the crossing by Hussey as a memorial to Bishop Bell, it had the effect of cutting off the chancel when viewed from the west door. Piper's lively work provided a splash of colour which drew the eye through the screen to what lay beyond. Opinion was divided but (once again) was largely against this new addition. One man wrote to say that he believed the next generation would remove it as being 'in bad taste unsuitable to its surroundings ...' and ended by saying 'I entered to admire and left angry'.[40]

Suffice to say, forty-six years on it is still there and when it is traditionally taken down in Lent its absence is most noticeable.

Walter Hussey was a bachelor and hence was expected to opt to live in a small house rather than the vast deanery in Canon Lane. However, he chose the deanery as he could use the space to good advantage by amassing an impressive collection of artworks to adorn its walls.[41] In the 1970s Hussey went on influencing art in Chichester, including commissioning further works for the cathedral, right up until his retirement in 1977. In 1975 he was the driving force behind a three-week festival to mark the 900th anniversary of the moving of the cathedral from Selsey. Originally intended to be a one-off event, Cicestrians decided they rather liked the idea of an annual festival, so it continued, becoming the **Chichester Festivities**. This high-profile summer arts festival was to last for thirty-eight years until 2012 when, tragically, Chichester Festivities Ltd, the company that ran it, went into liquidation following heavy losses incurred that summer, leaving Chichester with something of a cultural vacuum.

Walter Hussey's final act was to bequeath his art collection to the city of Chichester on the condition that it would be displayed in a domestic setting in a restored Pallant House. This happened in 1982.

THE MUSIC MAKERS

Chichester may never have spawned a nationally famous orchestra, or built a monumental concert hall, but there was plenty of music making going on in

82. John Birch, organist and master of the choristers at Chichester Cathedral from 1958 to 1980, pictured in 2005 after he had returned to Chichester in retirement. (Courtesy of Cheryl Khoo)

the 1960s. Most of this music making was by enthusiastic – and very capable – amateurs, but there was one place where professional musicians performed six days a week, sadly unnoticed by most Cicestrians, namely the cathedral.

Chichester Cathedral sported a professional choir of twelve boys and six men who sang Choral Evensong every day except Wednesday, and on Sundays sang Choral Mattins and Choral Eucharist as well. It was one of the smallest cathedral choirs but perfectly suited to the size and acoustic of the cathedral, and they were accompanied on a fine organ, sections of which were by the seventeenth-century organ builder Renatus Harris.

Throughout the 1960s the organist and master of the choristers was John Birch who was appointed to the post in 1958 and remained in office until 1980*. Choral Evensong was sung to perfection to the Glory of God day in, day out, whether there was a full congregation or just one or two gathered to hear it. The tradition continues to this day.

Outside the cathedral there were several good church choirs in the early 1960s, the best of which was at St Peter the Great in West Street, under the direction of Ernest England.**

In the first half of the twentieth century you would expect to find two institutions in any self-respecting English town, a cricket team and a Gilbert and Sullivan society, two things so quintessentially English as to be *sine qua non*.

Chichester's Gilbert and Sullivan Society was founded in 1910 and gave its first performance – *The Pirates of Penzance* – at the Corn Exchange in January 1911. Known as **Chichester Amateur Operatic Society**, it traded on its amusing acronym 'CAOS' and its cast lists featured many well-known Chichester names. The treasurer was John Gilbert, a councillor and future Mayor of Chichester, who also acted as stage manager as he could not sing! The repertoire was purely G and S, apart from the odd excursion into *Merrie England*. In the 1960s CAOS

---

* Sadly John Birch died on 28 April 2012 during the writing of this chapter.

** St Peter the Great closed in August 1979 but maintained a traditional men-and-boys choir right to the end, the last parish church in Chichester to do so.

THE YEOMEN OF THE GUARD

OR

THE MERRYMAN AND HIS MAID

SIR RICHARD CHOLMONDELEY (Lieutenant of the Tower)	TIM BASTOW
COLONEL FAIRFAX (Under sentence of death)	STEWART WHITE
SERGEANT MERYLL (Of the Yeomen of the Guard) ...	JAMES WEST
LEONARD MERYLL (His Son)	JIM FIELDER
JACK POINT (A Strolling Jester)	JOHN MASON
WILFRED SHADBOLT (Head Jailer and Assistant Tormentor)	CHRISTOPHER DOMAN
FIRST YEOMAN	LEN MARCHANT
SECOND YEOMAN	BERNARD VICK
FIRST CITIZEN	GRAHAM SMART
SECOND CITIZEN	ROGER TADD
ELSIE MAYNARD (A Strolling Singer)	KAY POSTMA
PHOEBE MERYLL (Sgt. Meryll's Daughter)	NANCY PARKER
DAME CARRUTHERS (Housekeeper to the Tower) ...	MARGARET SMART
KATE (Her Niece)	EDNA HARMAN

* * * *

Chorus of Citizens and Yeomen:

Dick Blackman, Frederick French, Tom Hooker, Ted Josephs, Trevor Richards, Sydney Wellington.

Chorus of Townswomen:

Vanessa Bastow, Kathleen Blake, Doreen Boys, Edwina Brigden, Ann Cocks, Marjorie Davey, Joan Edwards, Elizabeth Foote, Sheila Hart, Ruth Lewis, Elsie Lipsham, Eileen Mathews, Susan Moir, Mollie de Pennington, Lesley Pearce, Marion Postma, Joyce Richards, Vanessa Smith, Anne Steer, Angela Stephens, Majella Taylor, Sarah Turner, Pauline Wall.

ACT I—TOWER GREEN—16th CENTURY.

ACT II—THE SAME, MOONLIGHT, TWO DAYS LATER.

There will be an interval of 15 minutes between Acts, during which soft drinks, etc. will be available from the attendants. Coffee, etc. is served in the Buffet downstairs.

12

83. The cast list in the programme for the 1964 production of Yeomen of the Guard *which includes many well-known Chichester names. (WSRO)*

was run by Margaret (Margot) Pink of the soft drinks family who acted as both producer and musical director, and the annual performance was held in the Assembly Rooms in October. The stage at the Assembly Rooms was far too small for the full company and the size of the auditorium necessitated a run of a full week in order to accommodate everyone who wished to attend. I was taken from an early age to these performances by my mother, who was an avid G and S fan, and I became hooked. The operettas were performed on a regular cycle and the 1960s productions were as follows:[42]

1960 *The Pirates of Penzance* (March) and *The Mikado* (October)
1961 *Ruddigore*
1962 *The Sorcerer* and *Trial by Jury*
1963 *Iolanthe*
1964 *Yeomen of the Guard*
1965 *HMS Pinafore*
1966 *Patience*
1967 *The Gondoliers*
1968 *The Mikado*
1969 *Princess Ida*
1970 *Ruddigore*

Reviewing the 1964 production of *Yeomen of the Guard*, the *Chichester Observer*'s arts critic commented upon the inadequacy of the Assembly Room stage: 'The company achieve the stage feat of "putting a quart into a pint pot" but the smallness of the Assembly Room stage does not hold them back for a minute'. He then went on to commend Christopher Doman who was making his first appearance in a leading role (as Wilfred Shadbolt) with CAOS: 'Doman does more than play the part adequately – he does it very well indeed.'

As the twentieth century wore on, interest in Gilbert and Sullivan began to wane, allegedly having little resonance with younger performers and audiences, and following the death of Margot Pink in 1975 CAOS began to move into other areas of production and put on two shows a year. Musicals gradually displaced the famous operettas – something of which Margot would not have approved – and G and S became the exception rather than the rule. This change in emphasis was reflected in a recent name change from *Chichester Amateur Operatic Society* to *CAOS Musical Productions Ltd*.

Today there are several secular choirs in the city but in the 1960s there was only one, The Chichester Singers, who had started life in 1953 as the Pamelia Singers under the direction of the then county music advisor, Doris Gould. They performed in the new main hall of Chichester College. As the numbers grew they became more by way of a choral society hence the change of name, and they still perform today.[43]

The Chichester Orchestral Society was reformed in 1967 taking its members from the Chichester Light Orchestra (CLO) which had provided the principal vehicle for orchestral music since the war. Conductors of the CLO in the 1960s included Ernest England, organist of St Peter the Great and Gordon Stables, another of my masters at Chichester High School for Boys, this time teaching me physics. Gordon Stables, who played the bassoon, continued as conductor under the orchestra's new guise alongside the Revd Humphrey Kempe who was principal conductor. In 1981 it was reformed again, becoming Chichester Symphony Orchestra which still performs today.[44]

SOUTHERN CATHEDRALS FESTIVAL

In 1960 the annual tradition of the three cathedral Choirs of Chichester, Winchester and Salisbury getting together for a weekend festival of music making within the Anglican liturgy was revived at Salisbury. The festival then alternated between the three cities, where it would be directed by the resident cathedral organist, and first came to Chichester in July 1962 under the direction of John Birch.

The festival was named **Southern Cathedrals Festival** (known to its followers as SCF) and in 1962 was held over just two days, 3 and 4 August, beginning on the Friday evening with Evensong and an organ recital.

By the time the festival came back to Chichester in 1965, SCF was getting into its stride and expanded into three days. The cover of the festival programme bore a dramatic full-page photograph of the floodlit cathedral; the floodlighting had only been introduced the year before and so was still something of a novelty. The festivals began to mark significant anniversaries of composers by featuring their works in the services and concerts, and in 1965 the organisers decided to feature Thomas Weelkes albeit so little was known about his dates that 1965 could not be claimed to mark a significant one!

Weelkes had been organist at Chichester in the early seventeenth century but, although a distinguished composer of both church music and madrigals, he was a constant source of irritation to the dean and chapter on account of his violent and drunken behaviour. His church music was sung at the festival's Friday Eucharist and Evensong and at the Saturday concert. The lecture on the Friday afternoon was given by Francis Steer, the county archivist (who happened also to be sub-librarian of the cathedral), on the subject 'Some historical aspects of

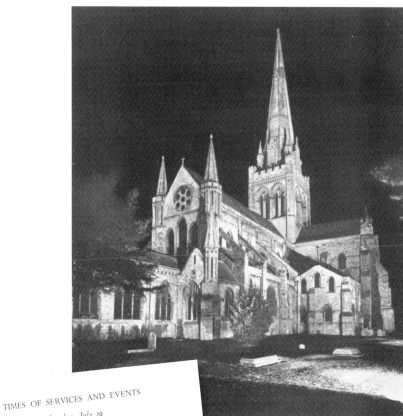

TIMES OF SERVICES AND EVENTS

Thursday, July 29

2.0 – 5.0　Garden of the Bishop's Palace open
5.15　EVENSONG
6.30　ORGAN RECITAL

Friday, July 30

11.15　SUNG EUCHARIST
1.0　The Festival Lunch
2.15　LECTURE
3.0 – 5.0　St. Mary's Hospital and The Theological College open
5.0 – 7.0　Gardens in the Close open, including
　　　　The Deanery (Canon Lane)
　　　　The Residentiary (Canon Lane)
　　　　The Prebendal School (entrance opposite the West
　　　　Door of the Cathedral)

5.15　EVENSONG
7.0　FIVE CENTURIES OF PRAISE IN MUSIC AND
　　　WORD

Saturday, July 31

11.0　Festival Coffee Party in the Residentiary Garden
　　　Cathedral Choirs in Open Rehearsal
12.30　Buffet Lunch
　　　Cathedral Choirs and Philomusica of London in Open
　　　Rehearsal
2.0 – 4.0　The Theological College open
4.15　EVENSONG
6.30　CONCERT

NOTICES

The Festival wishes to thank the Bishop of Chichester and Mrs. Wilson
for allowing the grounds of the Palace to be used, the Reverend Canon and
Mrs. D. R. Hutchinson for allowing the Garden of the Residentiary to be used,
and all those who have opened their gardens and buildings during the Festival.
The Festival also wishes to thank David Higham Associates Ltd. for permission
to reprint Randall Swingler's words in *A Canticle of Man*.
The Annual General Meeting, to which Patrons are invited, will be held at
Diocesan House, Winchester, on Saturday, October 9, at 2.30.
The Southern Cathedrals Festival, 1966, will be held at Winchester from
July 28 to July 30.

5

84. The cover of the programme for the 1965 Southern Cathedrals Festival held in Chichester from 29–31 July. It shows the floodlit cathedral but carries no wording to proclaim its contents! (Author's Collection)

85. An extract from the programme for the 1965 Southern Cathedrals Festival at Chichester showing the mixture of services, concerts and lectures spiced with the ability to visit private gardens in the close between events. (Author's collection)

Chichester Cathedral', in which he doubtless regaled his listeners with stories about Weelkes's exploits.[45]

The 1965 SCF was particularly remarkable for one of the commissioned works that received its first performance there. There were in fact two commissioned works that year, the first was a set of evening canticles in the key of C by Brian Kelly,[46] using syncopated Latin-American rhythms, which were sung by Chichester Cathedral Choir at the Thursday Evensong. These are less often heard now, but the second work was set to become famous the world over – *The Chichester Psalms* by the American composer Leonard Bernstein.

This work, a setting of five psalms in Hebrew, was commissioned by Dean Walter Hussey and John Birch but had actually received its first performance on 15 July 1965 in New York. However, the Chichester performance was to be the first by an all-male choir as the composer intended, a mixed choir having been used in America,[47] so it could claim to be the first *authentic* performance. Scored in three movements for treble (or countertenor) solo, strings, brass, mixed percussion and two harps, its explosive, percussive opening, marked *maestoso ma energico,* pinned the unsuspecting audience back into their seats. It took the musical world by storm and is the only Southern Cathedrals Festival commission to have become a 'standard' work in the choral society repertoire, although generally in the simplified version for choir, organ and harp rather than the demanding orchestration of the original.

Chichester City Museum staged an exhibition with an ecclesiastical theme (historic church plate) to coincide with the 1965 Festival and did so again when the festival came back to Chichester in 1968. Then the exhibition theme was 'make a joyful noise', being an exhibition of musical instruments used in country churches prior to the introduction of organs. In her report, the museum curator said that 'great interest was shown by the public'.[48]

The 1968 Southern Cathedrals Festival at Chichester marked the 50th anniversary of the death of C.H.H. Parry and featured a commissioned set of evening canticles by Herbert Howells. Howells had written a whole series of evening canticles for cathedral and collegiate choirs, each tailored to the sound of the choir and the acoustic of the building in which they sang. Although the majority of Howells' services remain in front line use, curiously the 'Chichester Service'[49] never really caught on – even in its home cathedral. Interestingly the Corporation agreed to make a grant against loss for the festival of not more than £100 – the grant was duly made indicating that then, as now, arts festivals find difficulty in covering costs.[50]

SCF is still a three-day event and still returns to Chichester every three years when church music lovers from all over the world descend upon the city and fill its little cathedral to bursting point.

PUBLIC ART

The 1960s saw the beginning of the provision of public art in Chichester; that is to say works of art – generally sculpture – which adorn public spaces for all to enjoy for free. We have already encountered John Skelton's 1963 *Symbol of Discovery*, commissioned for the new City Museum, but two years earlier, in 1961, he had made a mural in polished black marble to go outside Sainsbury's first Chichester store in North Street. The mural was in the form of a map of the area (helpfully giving directions to Sainsbury's other stores in Brighton, Bognor and Portsmouth) with vignettes of local features. Children were invited to interact with it by measuring themselves against a height-gauge labelled 'Children – are you

tall enough?' When Sainsbury moved out of Chichester to Westhampnett, the mural went with them and fortunately survived the fire that destroyed the premises in 1994. It can still be seen but regrettably has been condemned to hide behind squadrons of parked shopping trolleys.

Another mural, but sadly one rarely spotted by passers-by, arrived in 1966 when Sussex House was built on the corner of North and Crane streets on the site of Chitty's old shop*. It is by Yvonne Hudson and is a depiction of the goddess Minerva, surrounded by flying birds, executed in thirty-six large ceramic tiles. It is on the north face of the building and rather high up, hence the reason for its neglect, which is a pity because it adds a note of distinction to an otherwise very undistinguished building.

Many more public artworks were to follow in the decades to come.

86. Easily missed – Yvonne Hudson's mural of Minerva on the side of Sussex House. (Photographed by the author)

---

* See page 50.

ARTISTS IN CHICHESTER

Artists, both professional and amateur, flourished in 1960s Chichester, maintaining the centuries-long tradition, but there is space enough only to mention but a few.

Ronald Ossory Dunlop (always known as R.O. Dunlop) was born in Dublin in 1894 and moved to Barnham in the late 1940s where he lived in the old mill cottage until his death in 1973. He became a Royal Academician in 1950 (the only artist associated with Chichester during this time to be so honoured) and exhibited and sold his work at No. 7 St Pancras. A large, bearded figure of a man, R.O. Dunlop was often in need of a drink, this being something of an occupational hazard in his line of business. John Birch, then the cathedral organist, told me how he once called into Dunlop's shop to buy a picture. Dunlop pocketed the cash, and straightaway shut the shop to make his way to the pub to spend his takings.

Dunlop's work is in a highly distinctive impressionistic style and signed simply 'Dunlop' but unfortunately he generally spoiled the effect by using horrid cheap frames which did nothing to show his work to good advantage – quite the opposite in fact. His paintings now frequently command four-figure sums in London galleries.

87. R.O. Dunlop, 'Street Scene Duian, France' (1963). Oil on board signed 'Dunlop' lower right-hand corner. (Author's collection)

David Goodman was born in 1918, trained at St Martin's School of Art in London and moved to Chichester in 1944 when he married Cicestrian Pearl Turner. He began his Chichester career teaching at Chichester School of Art above the Market House, and was heavily involved with George Booth's arts centre project[*]. In 1952 he set up the David Paul Design Group with Paul Deggan, from whose Christian names the practice name was derived. They were responsible, with Rodney Symes, for designing all the literature for the Festival Theatre from 1960 to 1971 including the famous *Minerva* logo. David Goodman was a most prolific artist and produced masterly portraits and landscapes, using most media, all through the 1960s and was awarded a Gold Medal for painting at Ravenna in 1962 and again in 1968.[51]

His productivity and contribution to the arts scene in Chichester continued well beyond the 1960s, and between 1988 and 2000 he organised thirteen superb art exhibitions in the Tudor Room of the Bishop's Place in connection with the Chichester Festivities which were chosen and hung with great panache. He also founded the Chichester Society in 1974 of which he remained a member until his death in September 2013.

An artist whose Chichester career was launched in the 1960s was Peter Iden. Born in Bognor in 1945 he studied graphic design at the West Sussex College of Art and Design at Worthing and began his career as an architectural draughtsman, in which capacity he worked for Stanley Roth in the 1960s. He abandoned draughtsmanship in 1967 to devote himself full-time to painting, holding his first one-man show that year, before moving to Chichester in 1968. He then held some thirty one-man shows in the city, the previews for which were always very popular. I found that trying to buy a painting that had caught my eye was akin to trying to buy the last turkey on Christmas Eve as buyers queued up, hoping not to be beaten to the post.

His early work was in watercolour, a medium in which he excelled; the combination of his artistry and draughtsmanship produced street scenes of exquisite detail. Many of these are of Chichester.

As with many artists he changed his style over the years, changing exclusively to oils in the 1990s which better suited his downland and coastal scenes, then in the twenty-first century his work became abstract. Sadly he died in 2012 at the age of only 66 with a return of the lymphoma that had nearly killed him twenty years earlier. Although not a Royal Academician, he exhibited at the Summer Exhibition there in 1995 and had his first exhibition of abstract works at Messum's Gallery, Cork Street, London in 2003.[52]

---

[*] See page 108.

88.   *Peter Iden, St Martin's Square, Chichester, watercolour. Signed 'Peter Iden 71', this scene has not changed in over forty years. (Author's collection)*

NEEDED – AN ART GALLERY FOR CHICHESTER

What 1960s Chichester sadly lacked was a public art gallery – as opposed to dealers' galleries – and this fact was recognised by both the artistic populace and the city council. In the late 1960s an opportunity arose to create such a gallery in the ancient church of St Andrew, Oxmarket, hidden away behind the buildings on the north side of East Street.

St Andrew's had been badly damaged by the stick of bombs that fell across the city in February 1943 and the congregation moved to All Saints' church in the Pallant. The building was never repaired and was declared redundant in 1953. In the 1960s the archdeacon, the Ven. Lancelot Mason, was looking for new uses for redundant churches in his patch, and so the idea was conceived of converting St Andrew's into a gallery; local interest was kindled.

The city council had obviously also been considering an art gallery in some form or other, for a subcommittee of the Finance and General Purposes Committee was set up in 1968 for this purpose. It was agreed in June 1968 that discussions should take place with those promoting the St Andrew's idea, and the subcommittee reported back in November that such a meeting had taken place and they found that the St Andrew's project would produce 'no conflict with Corporation proposals for an art gallery at some future date'. Sadly we are not told the nature of the Corporation's proposals, but suffice it to say nothing was to happen on this front during the lifetime of the old city council.[53]

St Andrew's did eventually come to fruition and it opened in 1976 as The Chichester Centre of Arts (later The Oxmarket Centre of Arts) administered by a trust, and it provides a constant programme of interesting exhibitions of work by local artists.[54]

Cicestrians would have to wait until the 1980s for the next gallery – Pallant House – to materialise, a gallery that would display, *inter alia*, Walter Hussey's art collection.

TRADING IN CULTURE

A cultured community forms a ready market for artworks and books, and in the 1960s the city was fairly well served by dealers – for a city of its size.

In 1962 there were four art dealers in Chichester, The Little London Gallery (perversely situated in St Pancras) The David Paul Gallery in St John's Street, Leslie Hand in Lion House, St Pancras and O'Reilly's at No. 59 North Street. In addition Chichester Antiques, situated in the fine No. 43 North Street, included paintings in its stock in trade.

The best known of the galleries was the David Paul which was founded in 1960, taking its name from the David Paul General Design Group. David Goodman was one of the founders, jointly with Connie Fox and her daughter Shirley. It started in a small shop at the north end of St John's Street, adjoining Knight's the tobacconist on the corner of East Street, into which premises it soon spread.

Regarded as being one of the best provincial galleries at the time, the David Paul specialised in modern British art by acknowledged artists including local

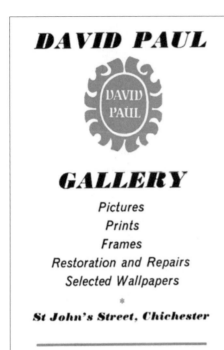

DAVID PAUL

GALLERY

Pictures
Prints
Frames
Restoration and Repairs
Selected Wallpapers

*

St John's Street, Chichester

89. An advert for the David Paul Gallery that appeared in the 1962 Festival Theatre programme. (Author's collection)

ones such as R.O. Dunlop and David Goodman himself. Exhibitions included the works by luminaries such as John Bratby and Elizabeth Frink. The gallery closed in 1980.[55]

Book lovers were also well catered for in the 1960s. Those seeking new tomes would make their way to the Wessex Bookshop at No. 24 South Street, next to Canon Gate. This was an independent bookshop (the only alternative for new books was WH Smith) and it was owned by Mr and Mrs Ball. Although small, the shop was well stocked but Mrs Ball could be a bit intimidating; she once pointedly reminded a school friend of mine that her shop was not a reference library when she judged (rightly, as it happened) that he had no intention of buying the book he had been studying for some considerable time. Later it became a branch of the book chain Dillon, surely their smallest shop!

Seekers after the second hand though would go to Messrs Offord & Meynell's shop at No. 50 East Street. Run in the 1960s by Vivien and Patsy Meynell (Mr Offord having long left the scene) this was more than a bookshop – it was an intellectual experience. Viv Meynell came from a distinguished literary line as his father was the author Everard Meynell* and his uncle, Sir Francis Meynell, founded the Nonesuch Press.[56] As well as being very well stocked with reasonably priced tomes, the shop contained a small coffee bar. This had been installed in the early 1950s and was probably the first in Chichester to serve *espresso* coffee from an Italian machine. With the coffee was served Patsy's homemade cake and biscuits, so the process of browsing and buying could – and frequently did – take a considerable time. This particular coffee bar experience was far more sophisticated than those on offer at the establishments we shall encounter in Chapter Eight!

---

* I was at school, at both the Central Junior Boys and the High School, with one of Viv's sons – named Everard after his grandfather. His other son, Richard, is a distinguished local architect.

90. *Offord & Meynell's bookshop at
No. 50 East Street. The window display
contains a selection of antiques as well
as books, and in the top right-hand corner
of the window a sign draws browsers'
attention to the added attraction of a
coffee bar. (Courtesy of the Meynell
family archive)*

91. *The coffee bar in Offord & Meynell's
bookshop. With its 1950s polka dot
wallpaper and Italian espresso machine to
the fore, it was probably the first of its kind
in Chichester. Note the shelf of books above
the counter, whose spines might attract the
attention of the coffee imbibers perched on
those lofty stools. (Courtesy of the Meynell
family archive)*

Conversation between book-minded customers and the proprietors was expected but was not intimidating for the young. As well as books Viv Meynell sold paintings and prints and a few small antiques, and so had plenty to offer the curious. He would potter around the shop with his glasses on the top of his head searching out volumes that might interest his customers.

In 1976, when the lease on No. 50 East Street expired, Viv Meynell moved to the Hornet, a former carriage works where artists Ken Child and Nigel Purchase ran the Eastgate Gallery. Meynell's Bookshop (now minus 'Offord') occupied the first floor. It closed in 1985.

A further second-hand bookshop opened in Chichester in 1967 at No. 39 Southgate. This was the Chichester Bookshop which occupied a late-Georgian house in what was once known as Richmond Terrace. The three-storey house was narrow and the shop occupied all floors, so one dreads to think what the weight of all those books did for the structure. It was run by John Dent, a man who was also involved with the scouting movement in Chichester. As well as books, Chichester Bookshop traded in sheet music, old magazines and theatre programmes and so had a larger and more eclectic stock than Offord & Meynell. It was also conveniently close to the Boys' High School and so was a favourite lunchtime haunt for sixth-formers. After several later changes of ownership the shop sadly closed in 2008.[57]

THE HERITAGE BENEATH OUR FEET

Evidence of Chichester's Roman past has been unearthed over the course of several centuries whenever excavations for new foundations have been undertaken, but interest in this rose to new levels in 1960. A workman digging a trench for a new water main at Fishbourne encountered some intriguing ancient rubble which precipitated an archaeological excavation by the Chichester Civic Society at Easter 1961; it revealed the remains of a once extensive Roman palace.[58]

I was only 10 when the excavations began and, having seen the report in the *Chichester Observer*, my friend and I set off on our scooters to see what was afoot and were amazed by what we saw. We had 'done' the Romans at school of course, but here Roman history was being revealed before our very eyes – it had suddenly come alive. In those carefree times small boys could wander freely around the unfenced excavations and ask the archaeologists what their trowels and brushes were revealing. The archaeologists, in their turn, were only too willing to answer our never-ending questions, thus firing youthful imaginations.

At the 1961 dig, odd fragments of pots and tiles (those deemed to be of little archaeological value) were sold off to visitors for a few pence. I readily parted with my pocket money for a few such shards and proudly showed them to my father who denounced them as being modern flowerpots, telling me that I had been 'had'. I did not believe him, of course, and the shards became the jewels in my eclectic schoolboy collection.

The excavations, which took place each year up to 1968, were carefully covered and backfilled before each winter until they were conserved and incorporated into the Fishbourne Roman Palace Museum which is known throughout the world.

In the 1960s the Civic Society raised the profile of archaeology in the city centre and every development site was excavated and recorded, largely under the watchful eye of Alec Down whose highly detailed recordings were later published in nine volumes of *Chichester Excavations*.[59]

Notes

1   Green, Alan H.J., *The Building of Georgian Chichester* (Phillimore, 2007).
2   WSRO Add.MS5296, Corn Exchange Co. Directors' minute book, 1919–33
3   As told to the author by Eve Willard who, amongst many, holds George Booth in high regard.
4   WSRO Raper Uncatalogued Acc 7820 Box 2, a bundle of printed notices of annual general meetings of the Chichester Corn Exchange Co.
5   *Chichester Quarterly*, Issues Michaelmas 1948 and summer 1949.
6   The *Chichester Observer*, 6 January and 8 December 1951.
7   Evershed-Martin, L., *The Impossible Theatre* (Phillimore, 1971).
8   *Ibid.*
9   *Ibid.*
10 WSRO CD/3, Chichester City Council, minutes of the Finance and General Purposes Committee, 1959–66.
11 Evershed-Martin, op. cit.
12 Chichester Festival Theatre programmes, 1962, 1963 and 1964.
13 Steer, F., The Chichester Literary and Philosophical Society and Mechanics' Institute 1831–1924, Chichester Paper No. 29 (CP 29) (Chichester City Council, 1962).
14 WSRO CAH/1, Chichester City Council Museum Subcommittee minute book, 1949–68.
15 WSRO CAH/1, op. cit.
16 *Ibid.*
17 The *Chichester Observer*, 6 December 1961.
18 WSRO Add.MS 26882, Francis Steer's file of museum papers contains a copy of the Friends' constitution.
19 WSRO CAH/1, op. cit.
20 Report of the Chichester Museum Society Committee for the (first) year ended December 1963.
21 *Ibid.*

22 The *Chichester Observer*, 24 April 1964.

23 WSRO CAH/1, op. cit.

24 WSRO CD/4, Chichester City Council, minutes of the Finance and General Purposes Committee 1966–74. Curiously the minutes of the Museum Subcommittee in CAH/1 (op. cit.) cease abruptly in April 1968 even though the minute book was not full. They are appended to the full F&GP minutes in CD/4 though.

25 WSRO WOC/CM/44/39/1, West Sussex County Council, minutes of Chichester Branch Library Committee, 1927–37.

26 WSRO WOC/CM/44/1/42, West Sussex County Council, minutes of Education Subcommittee 1945–48.

27 Jessie Younghusband School, Chichester. The website carries a short biography of their founder.

28 WSRO WOC/CM/44/39/2, West Sussex County Council, minutes of Chichester Branch Library Committee, 1937–71.

29 WSRO WDC/ED7/3/1, West Sussex County Council, Education Committee capital programme, 1962–69.

30 WSRO WOC/CM/44/9/13, West Sussex County Council, minutes of Sites and Buildings Subcommittee, 1963–64.

31 As told to the author by Rod Funnell.

32 WSRO WOC/CM/44/9/14, West Sussex County Council, minutes of Sites and Buildings Subcommittee, 1964–65.

33 WSRO WOC/CM/44/39/2, op. cit.

34 *Chichester Observer*, 27 January 1967.

35 WSRO Par 25/7/1, Bosham Parish Magazines and Crockford's Clerical Directory, 1968.

36 WSRO WOC/CM/44/39/2, op. cit.

37 Hussey, Walter, *Patron of Art – The revival of a great tradition among modern artists* (London, Weidenfeld & Nicholson, 1985).

38 Published by Boosey & Hawkes Cat. No. H 15567.

39 Hussey, W., op. cit.

40 *Ibid.*

41 Mason, L., *Walter Hussey* (a profile published in the 1977 Southern Cathedrals Festival programme, the year Hussey retired. Lancelot Mason was archdeacon at the time).

42 CAOS Musical Productions Ltd, programme for the centenary performance of *The Pirates of Penzance* (June 2011).

43 Osborne, N., 'The Chichester Singers and the St Richard's Singers', an essay in Chapter Six of *Chichester & The Arts 1944–2004 – A Celebration*, edited by Paul Foster (Otter Memorial Paper 18, University of Chichester, 2004).

44 Smith, J., 'The Chichester Symphony Orchestra', an essay in Chapter Six of *Chichester & The Arts 1944–2004 – A Celebration*, op. cit.

45 Festival Programme for 1965.

46 Published by Novello & Co., Cat. No. PCB 1419, 1965. It carries a dedication to John Birch and the Southern Cathedrals Festival.

47 Composer's note in the vocal score (G. Shirmer Inc., 1965).

48 WSRO CD/4, op. cit.

49 Published by Novello & Co., Cat. No. PCB 1439, 1968.

50 WSRO CD/4, op. cit.

51 Paul Foster and Gaynor Williams *David Goodman – Artist and Essayist* Chichester Modern Artists No. 2 (University of Chichester, 2006).

52 Iden, Peter, catalogue of exhibition held at the Oxmarket Centre of Arts, 2–9 October 1999 and David Messum, London, catalogue of Peter Iden exhibition 10–28 June 2003.

53 WSRO CD/4 Chichester City Council, minutes of Finance and General Purposes Committee, 1966–74.

54 Bluestone, L., 'Oxmarket Centre of Arts', Chapter Eight in *Chichester & The Arts 1944–2004* op. cit.

55 Cox, M. and Foster, P., *Feasting the Eye*, an essay in *A Baker's Dozen – Chichester's Lost Retailers* edited by Paul Foster (Otter Memorial Papers No. 29, University of Chichester, 2011).

56 Price, S., *Paper and Print*, an essay in *A Baker's Dozen – Chichester's Lost Retailers*, op. cit.

57 *Ibid.*

58 Cunliffe, Prof. B., *Fishbourne Roman Palace – A Guide to the Site* (Sussex Archaeological Society, 2002).

59 Published by Phillimore, the first appeared in 1971.

Six

Getting About:
Public Transport

In the early 1950s car ownership was a minority activity, along with holidays abroad, and this spawned what has become regarded as a post-war 'golden age' for public transport; leisure time had increased but not the means of affording a car. For the majority, going to work or school and getting out and about at the weekend meant using either the train or the bus. Holidays were taken in Britain,* typically at the seaside, again travelling by train or coach, and in the latter case coach companies vied with each other to provide the most modern and well-turned out vehicles to entice custom. Once at your seaside destination you would find serried ranks of coaches parked on the seafront offering evening excursions to local beauty spots or enticing mystery tours of whose destination only the driver was aware – or at least one hoped he was.

By 1960 car ownership was becoming more commonplace, the new 1959 Ford Anglia could be had for under £600 at Rowe's garage in the Hornet, and there were plenty of elderly second-hand cars available, vehicles that, having been laid-up for the war years, still had a bit more life left in them, but being decidedly old-fashioned were cheap to buy. More and more people were taking to the open road and forsaking the train and the bus.

For much of the 1960s Chichester was well served by public transport and most places within 30 miles could easily be reached by bus or train, but one did need to know how to read a timetable and possess the discipline of being able to turn up at the station or bus stop on time.

---

* As a result of the world financial crisis in 2010 many people began to holiday in Britain again, a phenomenon hideously known as a 'staycation'.

BY TRAIN …

Chichester was served by the West Coast line of the former London Brighton and South Coast Railway which was electrified by the Southern Railway in 1938 providing frequent electric services to Brighton, London (Victoria) and Portsmouth. The Second World War had stopped further expansion of the electrified system, thus westbound electric services from Chichester were constrained to going to Portsmouth. The Southern Railway became the Southern Region of British Railways in 1948.

There were, in the early 1960s, three through services each weekday morning to Southampton and beyond, but if you wanted to go west of Farlington Junction (to the north of Portsea Island) at any other time of day you had to go down into Fratton, change, and come back out again on a slow diesel service to Southampton Central; a journey from Chichester to Southampton this way took up to one hour thirty-one minutes to cover the 33 miles and so was not to be undertaken lightly.[*]

Chichester's Victorian station was in a rather run-down state following the war and, starting in 1958, had been rebuilt in a bold 'Festival of Britain' style. With its lofty ticket hall, mosaic-lined footbridge and steel and glass canopies it was the most modernistic building in the city in 1960, reflecting that 'golden age' of public transport. The level crossing at Stockbridge Road was then protected by heavy timber gates, operated by wheel by the signalman in the east box, but the nearby crossing in Basin Road, also gated, was operated by hand. The poor crossing keeper there had an impossible job in the afternoon when the schools in Kingsham were turning out. The throng of impatient pupils pressing against the gates often knocked the poor chap off his feet when he tried to open the crossing after the passage of a train.

A feature of Southern lines after electrification was regular-interval services, with the timetable repeating itself each off-peak hour. From the commencement of electric services on 3 July 1938 until 9 July 1967 the off-peak weekday timetable on the West Coast line remained – give or take a few minutes either way – essentially the same with hourly semi-fast and stopping services from Brighton to Portsmouth Harbour and an hourly service to Victoria.

There was an additional stopping train from Chichester to Portsmouth and Southsea (known as 'the motor' from steam days when it was a push-pull train)

---

[*]　The lines from Farlington Junction to Southampton and Eastleigh were finally electrified in 1990, changing travel patterns completely. Hourly services from Victoria to Southampton Central were introduced, reducing the journey time from Chichester to Southampton to fifty-one minutes.

which left from a bay at the country end of the down platform and provided connections for the halts out of the down semi-fast train. None of the journey times were too impressive, the fastest journey to Brighton was forty-five minutes and to Portsmouth Harbour twenty-eight minutes, whilst the Victoria trains covered the 69¾ miles in a plodding one hour and forty-seven minutes, with six stops including a longer one at Barnham for attaching a portion from Bognor.* The off-peak Victoria service travelled via the Mid Sussex line to Horsham and then headed north via Dorking North and Sutton. At this time there was no perceived need for a fast service to Gatwick Airport; to reach such an eccentric destination you needed to change at Barnham and join the stopping service to Victoria from Bognor, which first went down into Littlehampton before sallying forth up the Mid Sussex line calling at all stations. It was not until the early 1980s that all trains from Chichester were routed via Gatwick and East Croydon. One change that was made was in the stopping pattern of the Victoria trains, which in the 1966 timetable called additionally at Bosham and Southbourne in both directions giving these two stations three trains an hour, the best service they had had and, in the case of Bosham, was ever to have.

In addition to the regular electric services, there were the three daily through services, already alluded to, which were steam hauled via Southampton Central, leaving at 10.25 for Bournemouth West (summer months only) 11.49 for Cardiff General and 12.18 to Plymouth (via Salisbury and Okehampton). All three originated from Brighton and returned thence in the late afternoon.[1] The daily service to Bournemouth was withdrawn completely in September 1963, however the summer 1966 timetable shows a 'Saturdays only' service from Brighton to Brockenhurst which ran only from 23 July to 27 August; the reason for this strange destination, falling, as it did, short of Bournemouth, was probably the electrification works then in progress on the Bournemouth line. The Cardiff service was also withdrawn at the end of the 1963 summer timetable leaving just one through service to the west – that to Plymouth.

Another interesting steam working during early-1960s Augusts was in the other direction: a weekdays-only service from Totton (west of Southampton) to Littlehampton, which left Chichester for that resort at 10.33. This was a popular train with our family as the novelty of steam haulage was further enhanced by the vintage rolling stock that was garnered from the carriage sidings at Brockenhurst. It was not uncommon for purloined Western Region stock of GWR origin to appear if Brockenhurst could not come up with anything suitable. The return

---

* The fastest journey times are not much better fifty years on in 2011, namely forty minutes to Brighton, one hour thirty-seven minutes to Victoria and twenty-seven minutes to Portsmouth Harbour.

92. The return half of a day ticket from Chichester to Hayling Island. It is dated 1 August 1961 when the Hayling branch trains would have been packed with holiday makers and day trippers. (Author's collection)

service departed Littlehampton at 1837 giving a good long day on the beach. We fondly imagined the train crew sunning themselves on the same beach until it was time to go back home, but in practice they doubtless had to take the engine to Brighton to be turned and serviced in between times.

Although the Beeching Plan did not affect Chichester itself, it did kill off the nearby short branch from Havant to Hayling Island – a seaside destination popular with Cicestrians – in November 1963*. This line was steam worked right up to closure by the diminutive Brighton 'terriers', which added something to a day out in the way that the train ride to – say – Bognor, could not.

The local services along the West Coast line were in the hands of the ex Southern Railway '2BIL' and '2HAL' electric multiple units. These two-coach units would be joined together and the usual formation on the West Coast was of four or six coaches. All the passenger accommodation was in compartments which, in the 2BILs, were linked by a corridor to a lavatory in each coach, but the coaches were not gangwayed together. The lavatories were primitive but fascinating; at the bottom of the funnel-shaped pan, instead of the expected water trap, there was a brass flap operated by a lever on the wall. Pulling the lever lowered the flap, discharging the contents of the pan on to the track below and at the same time affording an interesting view of the passing sleepers. The 2HALs were decidedly inferior, only one coach had a corridor and lavatory, the other had full-width compartments which each seated twelve people. Their seats were very narrow and hard – in fact they were more by way of a perch than a seat – and the 2HALs were quite the most unpleasant trains ever to run on Southern metals. Having been built between 1935 and 1939, the BILs and HALs were reaching the end of their useful lives by the late 1960s and getting decidedly tatty. The last ones were withdrawn in 1971.

The London services were worked by the '4COR' express units characterised by their rough riding and terrifying gangways between the coaches. At Barnham the portion from Bognor was attached which always included a buffet car which

---

*   Although listed in the 'Good Doctor's' report, the decision to close the line had already been taken on account of the cost of replacing the rickety timber bridge across Langstone Harbour.

93. *'The motor' seen in the down bay at Chichester, with an unidentified 2 HAL leading. The 15 headcode denotes that it will call at all stations and halts to Portsmouth and Southsea. The picture was taken by schoolboy Bernard Ashley with his trusty Kodak Brownie 127 camera. After taking this picture he doubtless boarded the train to take him home to Southbourne. (Courtesy of Bernard Ashley)*

94. *SR Co-Co Electric locomotive No. 20001 stands in the down sidings in Chichester yard one evening in June 1962 awaiting its next turn of duty, whilst in the background Battle of Britain class No. 34055,* Fighter Pilot *hurries the up Plymouth train on the last leg of its journey to Brighton. (Photographed by the author)*

could be accessed from the whole train. The 4CORs were replaced in 1964 by new British Railways 4CEP units which made for smoother – if less exciting – journeys.

The through trains were generally in the hands of Bulleid pacifics of the West Country and Battle of Britain classes although Schools class 4–4–0s would often appear on the Bournemouth train until 1962 when the class was withdrawn. In the summer of 1963 the Bournemouth service became diesel hauled by the 'Crompton' type 3 locomotives. All three steam trains took on water at Chichester which allowed time for the small army of schoolboy trainspotters, strategically assembled by the water crane, to pester the drivers to let them ascend the hallowed footplate whilst the tender was replenished and the fireman hauled his coal forward.

Then, as now, hundreds of schoolchildren would travel to Chichester each day by train from Arundel, Littlehampton and Bognor in the east, and all stations from the Hampshire border in the west. In order to relieve the pressure on the station at the end of the school day, pupils at the Boys' High School bound for certain trains were held at school until ten minutes before their train was due. Wise members of the public avoided using the trains at this time of day unless they really had to.

In July 1967 the Southern Region timetable underwent its first major revision for nearly thirty years. The change was induced by the commissioning of the electrified service from Waterloo to Bournemouth which finally eliminated steam from the Southern, but the opportunity was taken to start again with a clean sheet of paper for the whole region. For Chichester the biggest casualty was 'the motor' which was withdrawn (save for one daily working at 09.37 to Portsmouth and Southsea) leaving Fishbourne, Nutbourne and Warblington halts with only an hourly service. This was a reflection of the fall-off in usage of the train owing to increased reliance on the horseless carriage for local journeys. The off-peak Monday to Friday service comprised hourly semi-fast and stopping services from Brighton to Portsmouth and an hourly service to London Victoria but confusingly at new times.

95. A 'Scholar Season Ticket' funded by West Sussex County Council to the tune of £6 10s 11d, which enabled Michael Brown to travel from Arundel to Chichester in 1968. Michael Brown was a pupil at Chichester High School for Boys. (Author's collection)

Journey times did not improve markedly as a result of the changes, it took one hour and forty minutes to Victoria (via Dorking North and Sutton), the fastest journey to Brighton was forty-five minutes and to Portsmouth Harbour, twenty-eight minutes. The semi-fast service to Brighton now called additionally at Lancing and Portslade in each direction.

As we have seen, the services to Bournemouth and Cardiff had been withdrawn in September 1963 leaving only the Plymouth train providing a through service to the west, but with the new timetable that commenced on 10 July 1967 this was cut back to terminate at Exeter St David's. This was in anticipation of the closure, between Okehampton and Bere Alston, of the Southern route across Dartmoor to Plymouth which *was* to fall victim of the Beeching Plan on 6 May the following year.[2] The summer Saturday service to Brockenhurst did not reappear in 1967.

In addition to its passenger services, Chichester was an important centre for freight traffic – it was what today would be termed a 'hub'. To the west

96. Rebuilt Battle of Britain class pacific No. 34087, 145 Squadron *makes a spirited departure from Chichester with a down early-morning freight in May 1965. The line in the foreground is the west side of the turning triangle. (Photographed by the author)*

of the station a large marshalling yard had developed over the years on both sides of the running lines, crossed by a lengthy footbridge which linked the severed portions of Westgate Fields. This footbridge was a haven for generations of grubby-kneed trainspotters (your author included) who would happily spend all day there in the school holidays watching the seemingly endless procession of mostly steam-hauled goods trains that came in from both directions to be re-marshalled for their onward journeys. Some trains from the east would arrive behind an electric locomotive – one of the three Southern Railway 'Hornbys' (Nos 20001–20003) or a British Railways E5000 class – but they did not work west of Chichester and spent much time languishing in the yard awaiting their next turn. No. 20001 is seen so languishing in Fig. 94 above.

In those days freight was carried in small four-wheeled wagons which often took several days to reach their destinations owing to the amount of re-marshalling of trains that had to go on. Much of this traffic was coal from South Wales and there was a large coal depot south of the station on the site of the former Selsey Tramway. As Chichester did not possess a turntable, locomotives were turned on a triangle whose sharp curves caused cacophonous flange squealing which could be heard all over the city. As a boy I had the good fortune to live a few doors away from one of the foremen shunters, Reg Brundish, who would allow myself and Phillip Laker, the boy who lived next door to me, to ride on the engines as they turned, for which we felt very privileged – and rightly so.

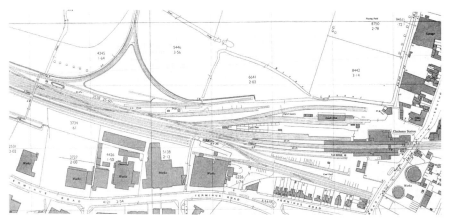

97. An extract from the 1964 Ordnance Survey at 1:2500-scale showing Chichester station and its vast goods yard. The long footbridge across the yard linked the portions of Westgate Fields severed by the railway, and the triangle on the north side was used for turning locomotives. The sidings to the south of the station next to Stockbridge Road served a large coal depot on the site of the former Selsey Tramway station. To the south of the railway the Terminus Road Industrial Estate has sprung up and has begun to expand on to the site of the extra sidings laid on the downside of the line during the war but which had recently been lifted. This accounts for the excessive length of the footbridge. (© Crown Copyright, 1964)

98. *A special train at Lavant on 12 March 1967. This was the occasion of a steam excursion hauled as far as Chichester by the preserved LNER K4 class 2–6–0 No. 3442* The Great Marquis. *At Chichester the K4 came off and the train was diesel hauled to Lavant and back. Here the train is seen at Lavant where 'Crompton' Type 3, D6544, has run round and is waiting to return to Chichester. In the foreground it can be seen that the platform has been raised in concrete to ease the loading of sugar beet which, unfortunately, prevented passenger trains from stopping alongside it. (Photographed by the author)*

The line from Chichester to Midhurst had lost its passenger services back in 1935, but a stump of it remained open for freight as far as Lavant. In the 1950s farmers around Chichester had turned their attentions to growing sugar beet and, in due season, Lavant was used as a 'rail-head' for loading the crop on to trains for onward conveyance to sugar manufactories. Lavant became a popular destination for enthusiasts' special trains in the 1960s as it provided the novelty of travelling over a line that had been closed to passengers for over thirty years.

In between the infrequent freight workings the line was deemed a right of way by many Cicestrians, especially in the blackberry season when the brambles on the cutting slopes yielded tons of the said fruit. Easy access on to the track was available at the Broyle Road bridge. The sugar beet traffic ceased in 1968 and later the line was used to transport gravel from the excavations at Hunter's Race to Drayton.

After the line closed completely in 1991 it was bought by West Sussex County Council who converted it into a cycle path known as **Centurion Way**, a singularly inappropriate appellation for a former railway line as the Romans never got round to inventing this particular means of transport. The fact that it was now an official right of way rather spoilt the sense of adventure when blackberrying.

... AND BY BUS

Southdown Motor Services

The principal provider of bus and coach services was Southdown Motor Services. Based in Brighton, Southdown covered the whole of the county of Sussex and made incursions over the border into Hampshire. The distinctive livery of Southdown's buses was apple green and cream (the cream was officially described as 'primrose yellow') and the vehicles were always immaculately turned out. Similarly the crews were always smartly attired; the basic uniform was black with green piping but in summer the black jacket gave way to a pale grey one and the peaked caps were given white tops.

Whilst some bus operators crammed as many seats into the vehicle as possible, thus ensuring that seated passengers were uncomfortable, Southdown's vehicles were of low seating capacity ensuring adequate leg room. This low capacity meant, of course, that at busy times the vehicles were soon full, but salvation was at hand with spare vehicles waiting at key locations, such as Chichester, to be pressed into use as reliefs, and standby crews were there to man them. Imagine that happening today.

Where to board your bus ...

Prior to September 1956 all services in Chichester served West Street; those terminating in the city ended their journeys outside the cathedral and then performed a three-point turn in the junction with Tower Street, next to St Peter's church. This manoeuvre contributed much to traffic congestion in West Street and, it was often alleged, damage to the fabric of the church of St Peter the Great.[3]

In September 1956 a smart new bus station had opened at Southgate, just across the road from the railway station.[4] This then became the centre of operations with all services, whether terminating or not, calling here. The inconvenient reversals in West Street at last ceased. The bus station was built by Southdown Motor Services on the site of the former police station, which had been bought in 1950, along with some garden ground in Basin Road, by Chichester City Council who leased the land to the company.[5] Its facilities included a spacious booking hall, enquiry office, waiting room, toilets, kiosks and also a licensed buffet, all reflecting the aspirations of this 'golden age'. The booking office was for those wishing to book seats on the long-distance coaches.

99. *The way things were. On 4 February 1956 Southdown 238 (FUF 238), an East Lancs-bodied Leyland TD5, has just reversed out of Tower Street having completed its three-point turn prior to returning to Selsey on service 52. Meanwhile No. 746 (MCD 746), an all-Leyland PD2/12, is starting the same manoeuvre in order to continue its journey from Midhurst to Bognor on service 60 as a schoolboy hurries past. Note the badly decaying stonework to the bell tower on the left of the picture. (Courtesy of John Iden)*

100. *An aerial view looking north over Chichester Bus Station in 1964. The railway line runs diagonally across the picture, and to the north of it the multi-arch-roofed building in the middle ground is the bus garage which has a pre-stressed concrete roof – an early example of thin-shell construction. To the west, on the other side of Basin Road (with its notorious level crossing) is the bus station proper. Surprisingly, there are only two buses on the stand but many are parked outside the garage, suggesting this may have been taken on a Sunday. The upper storey of the bus station building housed Southdown's offices and staff social club. At the top of the picture the new ring road (Avenue de Chartres) is under construction but the destruction of the buildings in Southgate to accommodate it has not yet begun. (Author's collection)*

101. An advert contained within the pages of the summer 1961 Southdown timetable extolling the virtues of the fully licensed buffet at Chichester Bus Station. At that time the bus station was only five years old. (Author's collection)

To the east of the bus station a large garage with an innovative clear-span, pre-stressed concrete roof was built in Basin Road.

The bus station and garage are still in use but the current tenants, Stagecoach (South) who acquired Southdown, have closed all the passenger facilities and sub-let the space for commercial purposes. Today when a long-distance coach arrives, the cross-legged passengers find to their dismay there are no toilets available for their use.

THE BUS AND THE CROSS

The ancient Market Cross has always proved an impediment to the progress of buses since it was difficult for large vehicles to circumnavigate it on the correct side, except in the east to west and north to south directions. With the opening of the bus station in 1956, the south to north services (19a, 58, 60, 62) had to pass the Cross on its east side and the west to south services on the south, both involving the navigation of a roundabout on its right-hand side in contravention of the Highway Code. For this the policeman, who was always on point duty, had to stop all traffic to allow the moves to take place.

The creation of the pedestrian precinct in 1975 removed all traffic from North and East streets, so all north and westbound bus services are now routed up South Street to the cathedral and thence via the ring road. Indeed traffic, which is mostly buses anyway, can now only pass the Cross at its south-west corner.

Services

The services at the start of the 1960s were fairly extensive with no fewer than fifteen Southdown routes operating, albeit on some of them the frequency left something to be desired. In the summer 1961 timetable the services were as follows:

Service	Destination/Route	Frequency	Notes
31	Brighton (Pool Valley) to Southsea (South Parade Pier)	fifteen minutes	
52/52A	Chichester (Summersdale) to Selsey. 52 via Hunston, 52A via Donnington	thirty minutes	alternate journeys via Donnington
53	Chichester (Sherbourne Rd) to E and W Wittering	thirty minutes	
54	Chichester Bus Stn to Petersfield via Compton	two hourly	
54A	Chichester Bus Stn to Hambrook	six per day, Weds, Sat and Sun only	
56	Chichester Bus Stn to Old Bosham	hourly	
57	Chichester (Whyke Church) to Bognor via Westergate	hourly	
58	Chichester Bus Stn to East Dean via Singleton	eight per day	
60	Bognor to Midhurst via Ructon and Singleton	hourly	after Midhurst the bus continued to Petworth and Brighton as Service 22
62/62A	Chichester Bus Stn to Petersfield via Chilgrove 62A also via Westhampnett and Goodwood	six per day, Weds, Sat and Sun only	only two travel via Goodwood
63/63A	Chichester Bus Stn to Horsham via Halnaker and Petworth. 63A also via Eartham	nine per day, one extra on Weds and Sun	
64	Chichester Bus Stn to Yapton via Tangmere, Westergate and Barnham	nine per day	
66	Chichester (Florence Rd) to Rustington via Slindon, Arundel and Littlehampton	thirty minutes	
164	Chichester Bus Stn to Oving via Shopwhyke	five per day, Sats only	

The Wednesdays-only services were, of course, run for the benefit of those attending Chichester Market. In 1960 one service was withdrawn, the 158 from Chichester to East Dean via Westerton and Goodwood, surely the most scenic of all routes serving the city. As we had relatives who were employees of the Goodwood Estate and lived in one of the Pilley Green lodges, our family regularly used this service as it passed by their front door. It was much missed. The 56 to Old Bosham was unusual in that if it reached the end of its run at high tide it had to turn in the sea, surely the only bus service in Britain that did this!

102. In 1946 Southdown began a programme of rebodying its stock of pre-war Leyland Titans in order to modernise the fleet. A number of these vehicles survived into the 1960s at Chichester garage, relegated to relief duties and school services. One such was 117 (BUF 217), a 1935 TD4 with a Saunders body that is seen here in West Street on standby for relief duties. All-Leyland PD2 335 (JCD 35), has pulled in behind it on the eastbound service 31 to Brighton. This photograph was taken on 7 July 1956 just before the new bus station opened, after which the Southdown office, which is seen in the background, closed. It was annexed by Morants, Chichester's only department store (now House of Fraser), and now houses their shoe department. (Courtesy of John Iden)

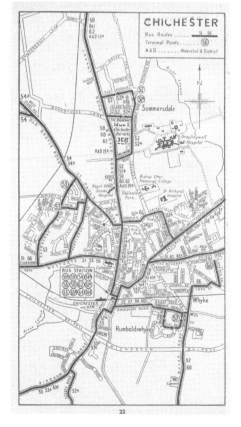

103. The map from the summer 1961 Southdown timetable showing the routes in Chichester. (Author's collection)

In addition to the Southdown services, Aldershot and District ran four buses a day from Midhurst to Bognor on their route 19A, as an extension of their half-hourly service from Aldershot to Midhurst. This brought Dennis vehicles into Chichester, making a change from the Leylands and Guys that formed the backbone of the Southdown fleet at the time.

The 31 from Brighton to Southsea was Southdown's flagship service and the newest double-decked vehicles were always put on to this route first. Indeed, as it took four hours to complete the 50-mile journey, intrepid travellers deserved some creature comforts. This route soon acquired the much-vaunted Northern Counties-bodied Leyland PD3s (known as Queen Marys owing to their unaccustomed large size), made distinctive by their full fronts and front entrances, which remained on the service for the whole of the 1960s. As the sixties wore on, and older rear-entrance vehicles were withdrawn, the Queen Marys' numbers increased in Chichester as they took over other routes, the last one to be conquered being the 60 in 1968.

104. An unidentified Southdown 'Queen Mary' of the batch new in 1961/62 calls at West Street. It is on the eastbound working of the 31 from Southsea to Brighton. When it leaves the stop it will pass the Market Cross on the wrong side into South Street and then call at the bus station before proceeding on its leisurely journey to Brighton. (Courtesy of John Templeton)

Southdown reduced the off-peak frequency of the 31 to half hourly on 24 January 1966, which caused John Heaver & Co., who were sand and gravel merchants in Quarry Lane, to object to the city council as the 31 was used by their staff between 12.30 and 14.30. Their complaint fell on unsympathetic ears as the council's Finance and General Purposes Committee felt that there was no demand for a more frequent service and thus resolved not to take the matter up with Southdown! The council were not usually averse to taking issue with Southdown whose regular applications for fares increases were routinely opposed.[6]

The first one-man-operated single-deckers had appeared in the late 1950s on the more lightly used routes such as the 54 and 58, but through the 1960s, as passenger numbers began to fall, other routes, such as the 63 and 66, were converted to this mode of operation in order to achieve economies.

COACHING DAYS

In addition to the stage services, Southdown operated an extensive number of long-distance coach services of which the most popular was to London. In the summer of 1961 there were seven services a day from Chichester to London's Victoria Coach Station taking three hours and five minutes for the 70-mile journey, travelling via Midhurst, Guildford and Kingston with a ten-minute 'comfort stop' at the Red Lion at Milford.*

Southdown also operated many touring coach holidays, both around Britain and the Continent, and it was scarcely possible to go on holiday anywhere in mainland Britain and not catch a glimpse of the familiar apple green on a touring coach at some time during the week. Strangely, coaching holidays are one of the few aspects of 1960s travel to survive and are just as popular today. Southdown coaches were available for private hire to any destination you could choose to think of. However, they were not the cheapest of coach hirers, and had to compete with the two local independent businesses, Bleaches and Everymans of whom more anon.

Better travel by *Southdown*

EXPRESS COACHES DAILY TO AND FROM LONDON

COACH EXCURSIONS	HIRE A COACH for any event!
Day, Half-day and Evening trips operating every day throughout the Summer season.	Our Private Hire Department will be pleased to give you a quotation. Ask now for full details of all our services.

SOUTHDOWN MOTOR SERVICES LTD
BUS STATION · CHICHESTER · Phone 3251

105. Southdown placed this advertisement in the 1963 Chichester City Guide extolling the virtues of their express services, excursions and private hire. (Author's collection)

---

* It was shown in the timetable as being 'for refreshments' but anyone who has tried to get served in a busy pub within ten minutes knows it is impossible – and even more so with a coach party of thirty.

106. A Southdown coach on private hire. A Duple-bodied Leyland Royal Tiger is seen at Heyshott in 1961 having brought members of the Chichester High School for Boys 'Bug Club' on a Saturday morning excursion to trawl nasty things out of Heyshott Pond. Notice that the driver, as expected, is smartly turned out wearing his white-topped peaked cap even though his passengers were just a load of unappreciative schoolboys. (Chichester High School for Boys/A.A.F. Bell)

Perhaps the most famous coach service to serve Chichester was the South Coast Express which ran between Margate and Bournemouth calling at all principal towns en route, including Portsmouth. It was jointly operated by Southdown, East Kent and Royal Blue, the latter's distinctively liveried Bristols having an air of opulence about them. On high-summer Saturdays there were many departures westwards from Chichester, some going beyond Bournemouth to serve destinations in Devon and Cornwall, but only three coaches per day operated right through from Margate taking twelve hours to reach Bournemouth, the others starting instead at Folkestone, Hastings or Eastbourne, but the journey times were equally leisurely. The main benefit of long-distance coach travel was economy as it offered considerable savings over travelling by rail for those who were not in any particular hurry to reach their destination. Express is, after all, only a relative term.

BLEACHES OF LAVANT

Back in 1921 Henry Edward Bleach bought a second-hand lorry and found work delivering milk to Portsmouth and bringing coal back to Chichester. He built a garage at Lavant, opposite the station, and in the 1930s added coaches to the lorries.

In 1949 the business was handed to his two sons Michael (Mick) and Anthony (Tony). Mick ran the transport side, adding three Duple-bodied Bedford OB coaches to the fleet. He had a contract for school runs to Downland villages and at weekends the coaches were available for private hire business, which continued well into the 1960s. The red-liveried Bedfords were a familiar sight around Chichester conveying darts clubs to matches, football supporters to often quite distant fixtures and the WI to gatherings. As the 1960s wore on and car usage increased there was a drop-off in demand for private hire, and as the Bedfords were now showing their age and needing replacement it was decided to end coaching and concentrate solely on haulage. Bleaches of Lavant are still in business, and in the same family, and their pale-green lorries can be seen all over the country.[7]

EVERYMANS OF MAUDLIN

Bleaches biggest rivals were not Southdown but Everymans Coaches of Maudlin. Everymans was founded by the Brockhurst family in 1946 as a garage on the site of Everymans's forge, by the A27 at Maudlin, to the west of the city. They built up a considerable coaching business which, by 1960, numbered eighteen vehicles. The fleet was very mixed and included half-cab Leyland tigers as well as more modern Bedfords – including the obligatory OBs.

They had a school contract for Chichester and a daily line up of their vehicles was to be seen outside the Lancastrian School in Orchard Street. In the early 1960s the livery was changed from cream, brown and orange to two-tone blue and, as well as the school work, they were operating an extensive private hire service. They could not, however, operate tours as the mighty Southdown always managed to block small operators' tour-licence applications. As with Bleaches, the onset of the motor car damaged the private hire business, and by 1969 the fleet had reduced to just six coaches. Curiously though, the business picked up again in the 1970s and new vehicles were acquired.[8] Today Everymans garage still exists at Maudlin, and in the same family, but it is now situated on a quiet backwater as the A27 has moved away from the village. The coaching is no more.

Notes

1   British Railways, Southern Region passenger timetable, 2 November 1959 to 12 June 1960.
2   Daniels, G. and Dench, L., *Passengers No More*, 3rd edition (London: Ian Allan Ltd, 1980).
3   Your author served on the Parochial Church Council of St Peter the Great in the 1970s

and it was much rumoured by older members thereof that the reason for the poor state of the fabric was the reversing buses. In fact that state owed more to the poor-quality materials used in its construction.

4   Southdown Motor Services, *The Southdown Story* (1965).
5   WSRO CD/2, Chichester City Council, minutes of Finance and General Purposes Committee, 1949–58.
6   WSRO CD/2, op. cit.
7   Told to the author by Mick Bleach, son of the founder.
8   Told to the author by Gerald Brockhurst, a current director of Everymans garage.

SEVEN

SCHOOLS: ANCIENT,
MODERN AND REVISED

U nlike Winchester, its Hampshire rival, Chichester could not boast a
famous public school, but its citizens were well served by many others,
both state and private. Indeed its growing population required the building of two completely new schools during the 1960s, the Jessie Younghusband
primary and the Bishop Luffa secondary.

The local education authority was West Sussex County Council, and under the
Education Act of 1944 the city's four secondary schools had been re-designated
as county grammar and county secondary modern schools. Entry to the grammar schools was now no longer conditional upon parents' ability to pay fees but
pupils' aptitude to learn and was thus dependent only upon passing the infamous
'eleven-plus' examination. Those who failed the eleven-plus were sent to one of
the secondary modern schools. This remained the case throughout the 1960s but
from 1963 the new Bishop Luffa School offered a mixed alternative to the existing four single-sex establishments.

My own education was in the state sector and began at the Lancastrian Infants
School, which was in sight of our house in Orchard Street. From there I progressed, in 1958, to the Central Junior Boys' School in New Park Road followed,
in 1962, by the Boys' High School where I remained until 1969.

In 1961 there were no fewer than seventeen educational establishments listed
in the local directories, some of which have long since vanished or metamor-
phosed into something else. They were as follows:

State Schools	
Chichester Nursery School	Woodlands Lane
Lancastrian Infants (County, mixed)	Orchard Gardens

Central Junior Boys (C of E)	New Park Road
Central Junior Girls (C of E)	Chapel Street
Kingsham Primary (County, mixed)	Hay Road
Rumboldswhyke Primary (C of E, mixed)	Whyke Road
St James' Primary (County, mixed)	St James' Road
St Richards' Primary (RC, mixed)	Market Avernue
Chichester High School for Boys (County Grammar)	Kingsham Road
Chichester High School for Girls (County Grammar)	Stockbridge Road
Lancastrian Boys (County Secondary Modern)	Kingsham Farm and Orchard Street
Lancastrian Girls (County Secondary Modern)	Kingsham Farm and Orchard Street
St Anthony's Special School	St Paul's Road
Private Schools	
Lindenau School (mixed ages 3–16)	No. 37 North Street
Prebendal School (boys prep)	Nos 53–54 West Street
Littlemead School (mixed prep)	No. 19 Stockbridge Road
Northgate House School (kindergarten and pre-prep)	North Street

Space does not permit a detailed examination of all these schools, so I will give brief details of a selected few.

THE PREBENDAL SCHOOL
(CATHEDRAL CHOIR SCHOOL)

By far the most ancient of Chichester's schools (indeed by 1960 it was the *only* truly ancient school) was the Prebendal in West Street which was founded in 1497 by Bishop Storey as a boys' grammar school. Bishop Storey it was who gave the Market Cross to the city in 1501. In 1931 the Prebendal became an independent preparatory school and through the 1960s the roll numbered around ninety-eight boys, twelve of whom were cathedral choristers and up to another six probationers. The school had spilled over into parts of the Bishop's Palace and other cathedral buildings as the West Street premises had become too small. The school, with its distinctive red blazers, went co-educational in 1972 and still educates the cathedral choristers today.[1]

Opposite: 107 (L): The Girls' Lancastrian badge, here seen on a beret, consisted of a monogram of the school's initials. (Courtesy of Linda Wilkinson); 108 (R): In November 1962 the Girls' Lancastrian School marked its bicentenary at a Jubilee Prize Giving. The programme showed that the Bishop of Chichester gave the address and the school orchestra performed several pieces. (Courtesy of Linda Wilkinson)

THE LANCASTRIAN SCHOOLS

The oldest-established of the Chichester schools that became part of the state system was the Lancastrian Boys'. This was founded in 1810 under the system of the Quaker educationalist Joseph Lancaster. It was a charity school run by a management committee and opened in temporary accommodation in North Pallant in February 1811 before moving into brand-new premises on the east side of Tower Street the following August.

A school for girls was opened on the same principle in 1812 in East Walls which later moved to Little London. In 1910 both Lancastrian schools moved to new, and adjacent, premises in Orchard Street. The old boys' building was then annexed by Priors the woolstaplers and survived into the late 1960s before being demolished[2] (it can be seen in Fig. 76), whilst the old girls' building still survives, hidden behind the Chichester Boys' Club.

Under the 1944 Act the two Lancastrian schools became secondary moderns, known as the Lancastrian County Secondary Schools, and were served by two boards of governors. One board ran the two boys' grammar and secondary modern schools, and the other did the same for the two girls' establishments.[3] As the Orchard Street premises had become too small, two new schools were constructed at Kingsham Farm with the boys moving in 1955 and the girls in 1958. The schools were always known locally as 'The Lancs'.

The head of the boys' school in the 1960s was Roy Lewis and that of the girls' Beatrice Tattersill – the latter known to pupils as 'Old Ma Tatt'.[4] The boys wore dark green blazers and their blazer badge was based upon the city crest but with only six droplets (goutes) instead of fourteen. The girls' uniform was navy blue and the badge is shown in Fig. 107 below.

There was a third Lancastrian School, one for infants, built next to the Orchard Street premises at the top of Orchard Gardens. In the 1960s the headmistress was Miss Olive Leach who had given long service to the school. Today this is the only school in Chichester that carries the title 'Lancastrian'.

LANCASTRIAN SCHOOL FOR GIRLS, CHICHESTER

Founded May 11th 1812

JUBILEE PRIZE GIVING

November 30th at 2.30 p.m.

THE CENTRAL JUNIOR BOYS' SCHOOL

Central Junior Boys' was a Church of England school that had been founded in New Park Road in 1812 as the Central Sussex Boys' School under the system of the Revd Dr Andrew Bell. The school had been rebuilt on the same site in 1888 but, electric lighting apart, by the 1960s the buildings had changed little since then. The windows were high up so that you could not see out, the lofty rooms were open to the rafters and heated by coal stoves whose warmth failed to radiate to the farthest corners but nonetheless roasted those boys who sat closest to them. There were seven classrooms, of which five were formed by sub-dividing the two largest rooms with folding timber and glass screens. The iron-framed desks were ancient, formed in pairs with a common hinged seat which necessitated both boys standing and sitting simultaneously. The wooden lids of the desks wore a rich fresco of marks, doodles and comments inscribed by hundreds of previous occupants, and set into the top ledges were ceramic inkwells. We were taught to write with dip-in pens whose cheap nibs became crossed and clicked like turnstiles, spattering the page with unwelcome spots. The ink was made up from powder and water and distributed to the ink wells each week by an ink

109. The Central Junior Boys' School building (dating from 1888) seen from the Litten Ground just after closure. (Courtesy of Ken Green)

110. A Central Junior Boys' School blazer badge. The CJB monogram is woven in gold on a light blue background, light and navy blue being the school colours. (Author's collection)

monitor; I know not the composition of this ink, but it must have been organic for in the summer months it developed an interesting culture of mould.

Running most of the length of the south side of the building was the lobby which had a row of cracked wash basins down one side and rows of coat pegs down the other and always smelled strongly of carbolic soap. The toilets, however, were outside and situated against the wall that separated us from the Shippam's Social Club to the west. They were open to the sky and hence always froze up in winter; the smell in summer is better imagined than described.

Another Victorian school building, on the corner of St Pancras and New Park Road (*olim* the Elizabeth Johnston Girls' School), formed an annexe to the school and this can be seen in the background of Fig. 2.

The dining hall was the most modern part of the school, dating as it did from 1950[5], and was a prefabricated building that also served as the assembly hall and gymnasium. At this time an outpost of the school had been established in the now-vacant former Lancastrian secondary buildings in Orchard Street, and every day the boys billeted there had to process, rain or shine, to New Park Road to partake of lunch in this building. I went home to lunch and hence never personally sampled the culinary delights of the CJB kitchen, but I heard the reports of those who did – and they were not too complimentary. The quality of the food may have been reflected in the fact that the bins, into which the scraps were placed for collection by a pig farmer in his battered Bradford van, always seemed to be filled to the brim.

The headmaster during the 1960s was Tom Greaves, a kindly man who hailed from the North East and took great pride in the number of his boys who passed the eleven-plus and went on to the high school.

In July 1964 the New Park Road school closed and the boys and staff moved to a new home in Orchard Street in the former Lancastrian Boys' School pending amalgamation with the Central Junior Girls' School of which more anon. Although the annexe in St Pancras has long since been demolished the main buildings have survived, being taken into community use and adapted into what is now the much-loved New Park Centre.

THE CENTRAL JUNIOR GIRLS' SCHOOL

The female counterpart to the Central Boy's School was also founded in 1812 under Bell's system in (as yet) unidentified temporary premises, but in 1884 it moved into a purpose-built facility on the west side of Chapel Street.

The new building was sub-divided internally by glass screens in the manner of the boys' school and in the 1960s still offered little in the way of creature comforts. Although there was a playground at the rear of the school there was no playing field and the girls had to go to Priory Park for their sports or use nearby Coronation Hall in Chapel Street if it were wet. Equally inconvenient was the fact that the canteen and kitchen were on the opposite side of Chapel Street, behind the clinic, ensuring a soaking on a wet day when going to lunch. The headmistress during the 1960s was Mrs Dora Taylor.[6]

The school closed in 1968 when it too became part of the new Central Junior School but its buildings lingered on until 1973 when, along with Coronation Hall and most of the other buildings nearby, it was demolished as part of the whole-sale Chapel Street redevelopment. Strangely, although the building survived so long after closure, it seems to have escaped the attentions of photographers (your author included) and all I can give you is a view of the back of the school taken during the demolition of Tower Street. A residential development known as Providence Place now occupies the site but there is nothing to record the former existence of a school here.

111. A view of the rear of the Central Junior Girls' School viewed from Tower Street during the wholesale demolition of the east side of the same. The school would itself suffer destruction in 1973. (Courtesy of the late Wally Dew)

THE CENTRAL CHURCH OF ENGLAND JUNIOR SCHOOL

The two Central Schools were run by a joint management committee on behalf of the Diocesan Education Committee, and the Dickensian nature of both the New Park Road and Chapel Street buildings was a major concern to them.[7] Back in 1946 the architect Stanley Roth had been asked to produce an outline scheme for rebuilding the boys' school[8] but it came to nought; instead the Management Committee expressed a preference for closing it, along with the girls' school in Chapel Street, and combining them on a new site in Orchard Street.[9] This 'new' site would be the two 1910 Lancastrian secondary modern schools that were due to be vacated.

Although, as we have seen, the two Lancastrian secondary schools duly moved out of Orchard Street in the 1950s, nothing much happened about the Central move. Finance had much to do with it and during my time at the Central Junior Boys' there was a Monday morning ritual of paying in contributions to 'The Building Fund'. Each boy was supposed to bring 3*d* for this and, although it was nominally a voluntary contribution, woe betide anyone who failed to pay up. Having accidentally spent it in Stephens' sweet shop en route to school was not accepted as a valid excuse. Over the years those threepenny bits must have amounted to a sizable sum, but we were not to see any benefit from it.

Work started at Orchard Street in 1962 but progressed slowly and only sufficient for the boys to transfer there at the start of the 1964 autumn term, where they continued their independent existence. Funding from the Department of Education and Science was halved in July 1965 causing further delays, and conversion work of the rest of the Orchard Street buildings did not resume until February 1967.

The two schools finally came together at the start of the autumn term in 1968 when, on 5 September, the Central Church of England School opened its doors as a mixed primary with Tom Greaves, the former head of the Central Boys' School, as headmaster. The school still flourishes and at the time of writing it is celebrating the 200th anniversary of the founding of the original Bell's schools in 1812.[10]

CHICHESTER HIGH SCHOOL FOR GIRLS

Chichester High School for Girls opened as a fee-paying grammar school in 1909 with twenty on the roll, in attractive new buildings in Stockbridge Road. Under the 1944 Education Act it became a county grammar school, with free admission, but retained its old name.

In 1959, to mark the fiftieth anniversary of the opening of the school, a £1,500 jubilee fund was launched to build a swimming pool which, when it opened in 1961, was the envy of Chichester as this was the only state school to have one at a time when the city at large lacked a public swimming bath.[11]

The headmistress during the 1960s was Miss Enid Dynes who set a high academic standard and the numbers going on to Oxbridge were impressive. The school expanded on its site and in the 1960s reached down as far as the bypass in hutted accommodation.

The girls wore blazers of an olive green hue, bearing on the breast pocket the blue and gold school badge. The badge carried six birds known as martlets, the footless swallows that featured on the Sussex crest. The school had an English, rather than a Latin, motto, namely 'Foster the inborn light'.

CHICHESTER HIGH SCHOOL FOR BOYS

Although the girls' grammar school had opened in 1909 it was not until 1928 that a similar facility was provided for boys when 'Chi High' was born in Kingsham Road.

Chichester High School for Boys also became a county grammar school under the 1944 Education Act and in the 1960s was the quintessential English grammar school providing a free first-class classical education and achieving excellent results at 'O' and 'A' Level with high numbers going on to university, particularly Oxbridge. The masters wore academic gowns for teaching which presented an unfamiliar, and rather awe-inspiring, sight for new boys such as me when, on 11 September 1962, I was one of eighty-seven who started the final phase of his school career at 'Chi High'.

The headmaster throughout this period was the redoubtable Kenneth Drummond Anderson, BSc (Cantab), MA (Oxon). Nicknamed 'KD', he was a military man of military bearing who ran a tight ship. To say that he expected excellence in all things would be an understatement, and he regularly fulminated against poor work, slackness in behaviour and poor standards of dress. Sometimes his outbursts bordered on the tyrannical and, although this was often with good cause, it did not make him very popular with his pupils or, one suspects, some of the staff.

The school roll during the 1960s averaged 689 in seven years (first to upper sixth) plus a small third-year sixth (VIS) for those staying on to try for Oxbridge scholarships. The catchment area was wide, from Littlehampton in the east to Emsworth in the west, Petworth in the north and Selsey in the south resulting in a great deal of commuting by train and bus.

112. The central portion of the (long) 1966 school photograph with the headmaster, K.D. Anderson, in the centre of the third row, flanked by thirteen of his staff. The boys range from short-trousered first-formers sitting cross-legged on the grass to sixth formers standing precariously on stacked benches at the rear. (CHSB Archive)

Two of the headmaster's obsessions were smartness and correct wearing of the school uniform. Long hair and the vagaries of fashion were particular *bêtes noire*, but, despite KD's lofty aspirations, the spirit of youthful rebellion for which the 1960s were famed ensured that sartorial transgressions continued, and the offence of long hair was often dealt with by the miscreant being made to go to the office to collect 5*s* and get his hair cut straightaway. One assumes the 5*s* only formed a loan, which had to be repaid by the offender's parents!

The core of the uniform was the famous – and highly conspicuous – emerald-green blazer bearing on its breast pocket a blue and gold martlet school badge, which was similar to that of the girls' school. A sixth-form privilege was the option of wearing grey suits instead of blazers but they had to be mid-grey; charcoal grey was banned.

Use of the matching school cap was gradually cut back throughout the 1960s. It was a much-hated garment and by 1965 it was only worn by the lower school – i.e. forms I to III. At the end of the third year there took place a ritual destruction; caps were hurled from train windows, cut into shreds or burnt, which is why so few have survived. The seeds of my interest in local history and conservation must have been sown at a very early age for I kept mine and still have it.

The school had a very active cultural life in the 1960s, the highlight of the year being the school play that was staged for a week in November. Full-length plays were tackled and pupils from the Girls' High School were borrowed for the

113. The cast and stage crew of the 1961 production of The Thieves' Kitchen. *Seated in the front row, numbering second from the left are the staff involved with the production namely J.A. Hyland (lighting); G. Marwood, in a very characteristic pose (producer); Messrs O'Brien, Thomas and Siviter (stage management); and N.F.H. Harries (décor). (CHSB Archive)*

female leads. The producer was Geoffrey Marwood (nicknamed 'Claude')* who taught chemistry and was a dedicated thespian; as we saw in Chapter Five he ran the Chichester Players and was a founder member of the Chichester Festival Theatre. The whole production was always to a very high standard and plays tackled included Bolt's *A Man for All Seasons* (1963), Shaw's *Devil's Disciple* (1966) and Shakespeare's *Hamlet* in 1968.

One now-famous name that recurs in the programmes of school plays is that of David Wood (student here in 1955–62). A gifted actor, he became school vice captain in 1962 and went on to enter the theatrical world being best known for his work for youth theatres. In 2007 he returned to Chichester for the Chichester Festival Youth Theatre's production of his adaptation of Roald Dahl's *James and the Giant Peach*. In a programme note he recalls his time at the high school, describing himself as having been 'theatre mad' and inspired by his English teacher Norman Siviter who had arranged for him to appear as an extra in *Saint Joan* and *The Workhouse Donkey* during the second season of the new Chichester Festival Theatre in 1963.[12]

The school boasted a large number of after-school societies catering for almost every conceivable interest and membership was actively encouraged by **KD** as not only did it widen interests but it gave opportunities for developing leadership skills and learning the essential art of public speaking. Indeed, a recurring admonition delivered in his Speech Day addresses was the failure to take part in these extramural activities, he suspected the fact that boys who refused to do so had after-school jobs to go to or were watching television.

---

* Claude was also the name of the school skeleton – the similarity between the two characters was often remarked upon.

At the end of each summer term the whole school processed to the cathedral for the end-of-year service. All the staff wore full academic dress for the occasion adding caps and hoods to their gowns, and with so many Oxbridge men there was plenty of fur around. I regret I cannot for the life of me remember whether KD headed up the procession in the manner of a general leading his troops into battle or brought up the rear like a bishop. He would, I feel, have aspired to either role, but either way the whole procession created quite a spectacle as it wound its way towards the mother church, stopping all the traffic en route.

My final term at Chi High took place in the gloriously hot summer of 1969, a term heralding the inevitable sitting of three 'A' Levels. The 'A' Level ordeal was made worse by the fact that some papers had to be sat in the gym which doubled as an examination hall; the acrid smell of stale body-sweat, exacerbated by the hot weather, doing little to help concentration.

THE JESSIE YOUNGHUSBAND PRIMARY SCHOOL

The non-Church (i.e. county) primary schools in Chichester were administered on behalf of the local education authority by a joint management committee under whose wing came the Lancastrian Infants, Kingsham Primary, St James' Primary and the Chichester Nursery schools. Since 1951 the committee had been chaired by Jessie Younghusband, whose name has already occurred several times in this narative, but she died suddenly in July 1960 and was replaced by Patricia Roth, wife of the architect Stanley Roth who has himself made several prior appearances in these pages.[13]

The population expansion required additional primary school places, and in the east of the city St James' Infants School was extended in 1962 to provide a primary department. Originally named the Evan Davies Primary School after a former director of education it was soon subsumed by the host school to become St James' Primary.

In the north of the city though, the expansion of Parklands and the prospect of the East Broyle Estate called for a completely new school, and at the managers' meeting of 12 July 1960 a Mr Parker came to present the county council's proposal for one such in the vicinity of St Paul's Road to fulfil this need. One of the managers expressed the view that there had been some 'lack of co-operation' between the managers and the authority over this, but nonetheless the proposal was approved. It was for an establishment of some 245 pupils aged 5 to 11 to be known by the rather ponderous and uninspiring title of Chichester (North) Primary and Infants School.

The construction started in 1961 of a prefabricated timber building on the Derwent system, the main contractor being the local firm of John G. Snelling Ltd. That same year the managers proposed that the name of the school be changed to the Jessie Younghusband School to commemorate their erstwhile chairman, to which the county council agreed. The school opened its doors in September 1961 under the headship of Miss Talbot, but in a hut at the Lancastrian Infants School as the new buildings were far from ready. The promised completion date of January 1962 was also missed, so the first week of the spring term that year, with fifty-one on the roll, was spent in huts at the adjacent St Anthony's Special School.[14]

The school's first register was begun on 9 January 1962 when fifty-one 8-year-old pupils were recorded, forty-seven of whom had come from the Lancastrian Infants School. All of these lived on the Parklands Estate bar one who came from the nearby Woodlands orphanage*. Indeed several children were enrolled from Woodlands until December 1964 after which it closed.[15]

A swimming pool, shared with St Anthony's, was provided in 1962 but pleas by the managers for a 'simple shelter' for changing were persistently dismissed by the county council as being too costly. One early pupil, Chris Butler who enrolled, aged 5, in September 1963, recalls that the pool was unheated and always seemed to be freezing regardless of the time of year and, in the absence of a shelter, pupils had to change into their swimwear in their classrooms before venturing forth. He also recalls that after swimming they ran around naked to dry off! (Well, this was the 'permissive '60s' after all.)

The school was keen on widening pupils' experience and one venture was a study of the life of Gladys Aylward, a missionary to China in the 1930s whose remarkable story was made into a film in 1957 starring Ingrid Bergman. The headmistress managed to get Gladys Aylward to visit the school and talk to the pupils, who gained a first-hand account without the Hollywood 'spin'.

The uniform at the start was traditional for the time. They all wore navy blue blazers with plain navy blue ties over white shirts with short trousers and long grey socks for boys and pleated skirts for girls. The shirts and ties were later dispensed with and replaced with dark blue roll-necks.[16]

By June 1964 the numbers on the roll had risen to 176 and from then on the roll began to embrace children from outside the Parklands area, including some from military families stationed at Chichester Barracks. The first seven East Broyle residents enrolled in September 1965 from addresses in Winchester Drive, Canterbury Close and Norwich Road.[17]

---

* The Woodlands Children's Home was off St Paul's Road. When it closed in 1964 it became a hall of residence for the College of Further Education. It was later demolished for a housing development that perpetuates the Woodlands name.

114 (L): Chris Butler, c.1965, sporting the original Jessie Younghusband blazer and tie. The blazer badge cannot be seen in this view. (Courtesy of Chris Butler); 115 (R): The Jessie Younghusband blazer badge which consisted of six blue martlets on a gold background surmounted the initials JYS. The badge was dropped when blazers ceased to be worn in the 1970s. (JYS Archive)

116. The Jessie Younghusband sports day, 9 June 1965, with the sack race in vigorous progress. The prefabricated school buildings can be seen in the background. (WSRO, Chichester Photographic Archive, CPS 2868-3)

117. The programme for the official opening of Jessie Younghusband School on 3 December 1965 (over four years after the school first started) by Brigadier L.L. Thwaytes, DL, the vice chairman of West Sussex County Council. (JYS Archive)

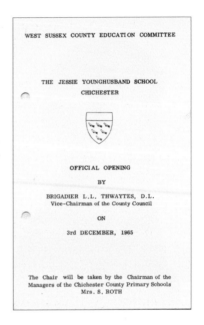

WEST SUSSEX COUNTY EDUCATION COMMITTEE

THE JESSIE YOUNGHUSBAND SCHOOL
CHICHESTER

OFFICIAL OPENING

BY

BRIGADIER L.L. THWAYTES, D.L.
Vice-Chairman of the County Council

ON

3rd DECEMBER, 1965

The Chair will be taken by the Chairman of the Managers of the Chichester County Primary Schools
Mrs. S. ROTH

Curiously, although the school had started trading back in 1961 it had never been officially opened and the managers first discussed this long overdue event at their meeting of October 1964. After months of failing to agree a convenient date, the opening, by Brigadier L.L. Thwaytes, DL, vice chairman of WSCC, finally took place on 3 December 1965 when there were 269 pupils on the roll.[18] The official programme shows that the Revd Gordon Bearman conducted the prayers of dedication, Mrs Roth introduced the brigadier and Miss Talbot, the headmistress, gave the vote of thanks. What the brigadier actually said is not recorded but he should have declared, of course, the school to be even more open than ever!

The building of the Little Breach Estate adjacent to the school (see Chapter Three) brought about the need for yet more school places and, as Jessie Younghusband was now full, it was decreed by the county council that Little Breach should come within the catchment area of the Lancastrian School as far as its infants were concerned.[19] However, primary-aged pupils from Little Breach began to arrive at Jessie Younghusband from September 1968.

The school roll peaked at 283 in 1966 and 1967, and of the forty-five leavers in July 1967 six went to the Boys' High, six to the Girls' High, six to the Lancastrian Boys' and sixteen to the Lancastrian Girls schools. Three went on to the new Bishop Luffa School.

Miss Talbot left the school at the end of the spring term 1968 and was replaced as head by Mr Highley, who maintained the high standards of his predecessor. Also long serving was Patricia Roth who remained chairman of the managers, with Mr S.W. (Bill) Bastow (who ran the famous chemist's shop in North Street) as vice chairman, throughout the 1960s.[20]

THE BISHOP LUFFA SCHOOL

West Sussex County Council had begun planning for an additional secondary modern school back in the 1950s in order to cater for the growing population and, as we saw in Chapter Four, this was to have been built in Westgate Fields. The new institution, to be known as the Regum School, would be four-form entry and co-educational and was programmed to be built in 1959/60. As a result of the public opposition to the loss of Westgate Fields that site was eventually dropped but, whilst the debate rumbled on, the idea was explored of opening it as a two-form entry school in the vacant Lancastrian buildings in Orchard Street pending construction of new buildings.

Breakthrough came in 1960 when the Diocesan Education Committee applied to the county council to take on the Regnum School as a grant-aided Church of England venture, pointing out that in a poll they had carried out 80 per cent of the 500 parents who responded were willing to let their children attend a Church secondary school. The county Secondary Education Subcommittee recommended 'no objection' to this idea, so a Church school it was to become.[21]

The diocese had taken on this project using the powers contained in the Education Act of 1959 which allowed the setting up of Church-aided secondary schools, and Chichester was one of four places chosen in Sussex as needing such a school. At their meeting of 26 January 1960 the Diocesan Education Committee voted to name the new school after Bishop Luffa, the Bishop of Chichester who completed the cathedral in 1108, and that the school would be opened as a two-form entry 'instalment' as soon as possible.

By November 1960 the necessary public notices were published over the signatures of 'six prominent citizens of Chichester who have consented to act as promoters of the scheme'.[22]

Following the rejection by public inquiry of the Westgate Fields site, a new site was found between Sherborne Road and the Midhurst railway line, which was purchased (albeit not without some difficulty) from the Corporation and John Daviel, of the Brighton practice of Clayton, Black and Daviel, was appointed architect.

Daviel's plans, for a building of unadventurous design, were approved in June 1961 and the planning application made the following November with the hope of the new buildings being ready for occupation in September 1963. The contract for constructing the new school was let to local builder John G. Snelling, who had just completed the Jessie Younghusband School for £138,833 in June 1962 and work started the following month. Unfortunately by the end of the year it was found that the new buildings were getting uncomfortably close to the site boundary, the reason being that the site was narrower than the Corporation's drawings indicated, and the diocesan legal advisor felt that they should receive a refund of £500 in respect of the shortfall in acreage![23]

A board of governors was up for the school which included five clerics, one of whom was the archdeacon and another the Revd Cecil Bennett, vicar of St Peter the Great.

The foundation stone was laid by the actress Dame Sybil Thordike on 26 June 1962, and in the December following Leslie Bartlett, DFC was appointed head-master with effect from 1 May 1963.[24]

Unfortunately the building work was seriously delayed by the hard winter of 1962/63 (see Chapter Ten), so the expected completion date to meet opening in September 1963 was missed. Instead the school opened in temporary accom-modation at the former Lancastrian School in Orchard Street with just sixty-two pupils on the roll and an establishment of four teachers.[25]

The uniform consisted of a maroon blazer with a badge carrying a bishop's mitre worn with white shirts or blouses. The boys wore short or long grey trou-sers and the girls grey skirts. Strangely, although the girls wore hats the boys do not seem to have been required to wear caps.

BISHOP LUFFA C.E. SECONDARY SCHOOL
CHICHESTER

OFFICIAL OPENING

BY

Her Majesty Queen Elizabeth
The Queen Mother

THURSDAY, 1st JULY, 1965
at 3.15 p.m.

118 (L): Her Majesty the Queen Mother at the official opening of Bishop Luffa School on 1 July 1965. The headmaster, Leslie Bartlett, is on the right of the picture and the Revd C.W.F. Bennett, vicar of St Peter the Great and chairman of the school governors, is to the left. (WSRO); 119 (R): The cover of the programme for the official opening of Bishop Luffa School on 1 July 1965. (WSRO)

The new school buildings were finally completed in September 1964 and the county Education Subcommittee authorised 160 extra cleaning hours to prepare the buildings on handover from the contractor.[26] The school began the autumn term 1964 on its new premises but the forms housed in Orchard Street had transferred to the new buildings on 7 January 1964.[27]

The official opening of the school was performed by the Queen Mother on 1 July 1965 as part of a busy state visit to Chichester. She was received at the cathedral by the Duke of Norfolk and a group of VIPs, following which she was taken to the school where she was greeted by the Bishop of Chichester, the Rt. Revd Roger Wilson, who introduced her to an assembled company that included the governors, members of the diocesan and county education committees, the architect and the contractor. After being presented with a bouquet by the youngest girl (Jillian Seward) the Queen Mother was taken on a tour of the school and unveiled a plaque recording the event. The assembled party then sat down to tea in the small hall, the two pupils chosen to be on the top table being John Enos and Pauline Parker.[28]

The county Education Subcommittee gave approval to expand Bishop Luffa into a sixth-form entry school of 1,080 pupils in June 1966, but by 1969 the roll had only risen to 313 pupils, the expansion occurred from the 1970s after it had become a comprehensive.[29]

THE COMPREHENSIVE CHALLENGE

In the 1950s, under a Conservative government, a new form of education – comprehensive – emerged alongside the grammar, secondary technical and secondary modern schools created under the 1944 Act. Comprehensive schools were non-selective, taking pupils of all abilities and thereby abolishing the stigma attached to failing the eleven-plus.

Comprehensive education featured large in the Labour Party manifesto that brought Harold Wilson to power in 1964, and it became the mantra of the Labour Government who resolved to sweep away all grammar schools as part of its plans to modernise Britain. With this in mind it may come as a surprise that the first recorded suggestion of Chichester schools going comprehensive came not from a government minister, nor an official from WSCC, but from Kenneth Drummond Anderson, headmaster of Chichester High School for Boys – a man of high Tory views whom one would not expect to have had any truck with what was now becoming seen as socialist dogma!

At the boys' joint school governors' meeting* of 24 February 1964, Mr Anderson – the minutes record – said that he had considered some form of comprehensive system which would embrace not only the Lancastrian School and his own, but others in the catchment area. This seems curious since KD was so obviously a grammar school champion who would not have been expected to propose changing a winning formula. Did it surprise the governors one wonders? Possibly Mr Anderson saw the writing on the wall since West Sussex County Council had opened its first comprehensive school, Thomas Bennett in Crawley, in 1958.[30]

The rumblings about the future of education in West Sussex reached the front page of the *Chichester Observer* on 28 January 1966 under the headline 'Go ahead with comprehensive education'. This was a report of a meeting of the West Sussex Association for the Advancement of State Education that had taken place at the Boys' High the previous Tuesday. The speaker was Mr P. Keyte who was the headmaster of Hazlewick Comprehensive School in Crawley. He urged politicians to 'take the brake off comprehensive education', which he believed to be much better, and cited his own school as being a good example of what could be achieved, dismissing as 'rubbish' suggestions that its large size (1,200 pupils) was a disadvantage.

On 14 February 1966 a special meeting of the joint High and Lancastrian Boys' schools governors was held to discuss the idea of reorganising as a comprehensive and, having agreed the case for the elimination of selection, they resolved:

> That the Governors are in favour of the reorganisation of the four county secondary schools as one mixed comprehensive school on the Kingsham campus when the necessary buildings are available.

Three days later a special joint meeting was held with the governors of the two girls' schools to consider the views that had been canvassed from the staffs of all four establishments.

A confidential interim report was presented to the county Secondary Education Subcommittee on 8 March 1966 recording the progress made so far with the scheme including a 'much greater acceptance', of the principle of comprehensive education. It recorded the results of a poll taken amongst the staffs of the High and Lancastrian schools which revealed that only the Boys' High staff had favoured one mixed comprehensive, the two girls' schools opted for single-sex status, whilst the Boys' Lancastrian proposed a mixed school with the two sexes

---

* The Boys' High and Lancastrian schools were served by a joint board of governors – the same applied to the two girls' schools.

taught separately from 11 to 16 before coming together in a mixed sixth-form college. The governors had resolved unanimously to eliminate selection at 11.[31]

A further meeting of the boys' governors was held on 28 February 1966 when ways of introducing closer working between the schools was discussed. The idea of a new common blazer was floated but it was agreed that nothing could be done until legal sanction was given to amalgamation. It was noted, however, that high school non-performers were already being transferred to the Lancastrian School where their educational needs might be better met.[*]

The boys' parents' association invited Dr Read, Director of Education for West Sussex, to address their open meeting in the summer term of 1966 but were 'disappointed that nothing was said about the future plans for the school'.[32] Parents' minds might have been eased at the AGM of their association on 22 September 1966 at which the headmaster spoke about the future of the school … 'which I think' – *The Martlet* correspondent recorded – 'alleviated many doubts parents might have had on this subject after having read the various reports in the press'.[33]

The press reports continued, and in the *Chichester Observer* of 14 October 1966, under a banner-headline 'PARENTS OF HIGH SCHOOL GIRLS ARE WORRIED', the date of 1971 was given as WSCC's target for reorganisation of secondary schools in Chichester. The report cited the general dissatisfaction of the two girls' schools, and their pupils' parents, about the proposals, one particular gripe being removal of the right of choice for a single-sex education. The matter had apparently been referred to Walter Loveys, the city's MP.

West Sussex County Council finally approved the comprehensive reorganisation in Chichester on 31 October 1966, but a decision on whether the new schools should also be coeducational was deferred.

Nothing more happens until 1970 when at the boys' governors' meeting of 23 March the matter resurfaces, and in following meetings the scene was set for two separate single-sex schools that might be amalgamated at some unspecified time in the future.

The reorganisations took place and the new comprehensives opened in September 1971, the boys' school having as its head, perhaps surprisingly, one Kenneth Drummond Anderson, BSc, MA (Oxon). Rather than herald a new beginning with a fresh identity, the name Chichester High School for Boys was perpetuated for the new establishment, as was the emerald green blazer to the understandable irritation of the former Lancastrian School pupils. The new girls' comprehensive was called Chichester High School for Girls but – wisely – a completely new uniform was devised. However, the girls suffered the inconvenience

---

[*]   This also worked in reverse. In my time one boy moved from the Lancastrian into the CHSB sixth form in order to take A levels.

of operating on a split site, involving much commuting between Stockbridge and Kingsham and the crossing of a major road en route.

Bishop Luffa also became a comprehensive in September 1971 but very smoothly; here no re-branding was necessary as it was the same school only with a changed ethos.[34]

Notes

1   Neville Ollerenshaw, *A History of the Prebendal School* (Phillimore, 1984).
2   Green, Alan H.J., *The Building of Georgian Chichester* (Phillimore, 2007).
3   WSRO E35N/1/2, Chichester High School for Boys and Lacastrian County Secondary School for Boys Governors' minute book, 1951–65.
4   Told to the author by Beryl Turner (*née* Green), his sister who attended this school.
5   WSRO E35A/1/7, minute book of the Central Schools Management Committee, 1946–52.
6   Told to the author by Beryl Turner (*née* Green), his sister who attended this school.
7   WSRO E35A/1/7, op. cit.
8   WSRO E35A/6/19, a plan of the proposed new school – it would have extended on to the park to the north.
9   WSRO E35A/1/7, op. cit.
10 Woollam, S., *A History of Central Schools, Chichester – The First 180 Years* (Governors of the Central School, 1992).
11 *The Greencoat, Jubilee Edition* (the magazine of Chichester High School for Girls, Summer Term, 1959).
12 Programme for *James and the Giant Peach* (Chichester Festival Theatre, 2007).
13 WSRO E35X/1/1, Minute Book of the Chichester County Primary Schools Managers, 1951–66.
14 *Ibid.*
15 Jessie Younghusband School Archive, School Register, 1962–69.
16 Told to the author by Chris Butler who started at Jessie Younghusband School in 1963.
17 JYS School Register, op. cit.
18 WSRO E35X/1/1, op. cit.
19 *Ibid.*
20 WSRO E35X/1/2, minute book of the Chichester County Primary Schools Managers, 1966–77.
21 WSRO WOC/CM44/4/18, minutes of WSCC Secondary Education Subcommittee, 1958–60.
22 WSRO Acc 9738, 14/1/3, Chichester Diocesan Education Committee minute book, 1950–63.
23 *Ibid.*
24 WSRO WOC/CM44/4/19, minutes of WSCC Secondary Education Subcommittee, 1960–63.

25 WSRO E35N/1/2 minutes of Chichester High and Lancastrian Boys' schools joint governors' meetings record the use of their premises by Bishop Luffa, and WOC/CM44/2/25, WSCC Education Committee Directory for 1962/63 records the establishment.

26 WSRO WOC/CM44/4/20, minutes of WSCC Secondary Education Subcommittee, 1963–66.

27 Bishop Luffa school governors' minute books – information extracted for the author by Bishop Luffa School staff.

28 WSRO PMP/1/2/2, a copy of the arrangements for the opening and PMP/1/2/3, op. cit.

29 WSRO WOC/CM44/4/21, minutes of WSCC Secondary Education Subcommittee, 1966–69 and WOC/CM44/2/32, WSCC Education Committee Directory for 1969/70.

30 Godrey, J., Leslie, K., and Zeuner, D., *A Very Special County – West Sussex County Council – the First 100 years* (WSCC, 1988).

31 WSRO WOC/CM44/4/21, op. cit.

32 *The Martlet*, Vol. 9, No. 3, carries a report of the meeting.

33 *The Martlet*, Vol. 9, No. 4, carries a report of the meeting.

34 Bishop Luffa School governors' minute books, op. cit.

EIGHT

CITY AT PLAY AND PRAYER

I have already intimated that for many of the city's youth 1960s Chichester was a 'dead and alive hole' with little to amuse them. Across the age ranges though there was plenty to do even if theatre and classical music was not your 'bag'. There were sports clubs for playing and watching cricket, rugby, football, tennis and bowls whilst sailing was available in the harbour for the better heeled. In 1960 the city boasted three cinemas but the number had dropped to only one by the end of the year.

The one thing that was missing was a public swimming pool but that was finally put right in 1967 with another addition to the city's assets.

Two major events of the year with all-age appeal were Gala Day and Sloe Fair, the former, sadly, no longer with us but the latter maintains its ancient foundation each 20 October.

Church going was already in sharp decline in the 1960s, despite the efforts of powerful evangelists such as Billy Graham, but there were still many more churches open then than now, and a new one, St Wilfrid's, was created to serve Parklands.

Finally, appealing to those over 18, there were myriad pubs of all descriptions dotted across the city, which is a good place to start …

LET'S GO DOWN THE PUB

The city's pub count in the 1960s was thirty-eight of which nineteen have since closed.[1] The earliest casualties were two in Somerstown, **The Waggon and Horses** and **The Star**, which perished in the destruction of 1964, but those apart the others kept going throughout the decade.

Pubs then were somewhat different from today's norm; serving food was an unusual attribute (you generally went to the pub after having eaten), they were places you went to have a pint and meet your friends ('the local') and chew the fat on the great issues of the day. Jukeboxes were making inroads in an attempt to attract a younger audience, but the now-universal live music was uncommon. One place where it was to be found though was **The Hole in the Wall** in St Martin's Street where the Chichester Folk Song Club was formed in 1961 and performed there every week throughout the decade.[2]

If you walked from the barracks to the railway station in 1962 you would pass eleven pubs*, so by partaking of half a pint of best bitter in each you would be well on the way to inebriation by the time you reached your destination. Those eleven pubs include four which have since ceased to be: **The Old House at Home**, **The Wellington**, **The Star** and the **White Horse**.

There was now no brewing going on in Chichester; its local brewery, Henty and Constable, having been taken over by Friary Meux of Guildford who used the buildings at Westgate simply as a local distribution depot. Beer at this time changed from being alive in a barrel to being pasteurised and served under pressure from a keg. Keg beer was not pleasant but it obviated the need for a landlord to have any cellaring skills – the real ale revival was, unfortunately, a long way off.

UNIFORMED YOUTH ORGANISATIONS

Chichester was well served by the uniformed youth organisations of the day and these had a great following. There were three Boy Scout troops, with attendant Cub packs, which catered mostly for the 8–15 age range. These were the 5th, the 8th and the 12th and of these the last was the one to undergo the most significant change in the 1960s. The troop had been revived in 1955 by local historian, writer, broadcaster and antiques expert Bernard Price, but he handed the helm to Len Eyles in 1962. Len Eyles campaigned for the troop to have a permanent HQ to improve upon the primitive hut they occupied at Woodlands. The city council finally granted them a lease of part of the Oliver Whitby playing field in Sherborne Road in 1968, and the spacious new building opened in April 1969, the ceremony being performed by Bernard Price.[3] The 12th Chichester Group and their HQ still flourishes today.

There were, by contrast, no fewer than five Girl Guide companies and seven Brownie packs, but their one and only Guide Hall was (and still is) in Whyke Lane. As the hall could not accommodate all the meetings, only the 2nd, 3rd, 6th and 9th companies met there, the 4th meeting at Woodlands, the 5th and the 9th

---

* This includes the **Ship Hotel** which had a popular bar open to non-residents.

120. The new 12th Chichester Scout HQ in Sherborne Road, nearing completion in 1969. (Courtesy of the 12th Chichester Scout Group)

121. Scouts and Cubs of the 12th Chichester Group watch Bernard Price, of Antiques Roadshow *fame, open their new HQ on 15 April 1969. The young cub in the foreground appears to be overawed by the great man's knotting skills. (Courtesy of the 12th Chichester Scout Group)*

Brownies at the Congregational Church Hall in South Street and the 7th Brownies at the Salvation Army Hall in Orchard Street.

The District Captain was the redoubtable Miss Fanny Silverlock, who also led the 3rd Company, and the treasurer of the local association was Mrs Banks, the wife of the town clerk. At Bishop Otter College was a Guide Club formed of student Guiders who helped with the running of the local companies.[4]

Another popular uniformed organisation was the Chichester Division of the St John Ambulance Brigade which had a large cadet force. This was the largest division in Sussex, and its president was John Selsby and superintendent of the ladies was Alice Eastland, both sometime mayors of the city. The divisional superintendent was Roy Clayton.[5] Fanny Silverlock was one of the nursing officers who, in addition to being an active ambulance woman, organised the jumble sales, cadet parties and the annual dinner-dance. What with her heavy involvement with the Girl Guides and being a Sunday school teacher at St Pancras, she must have had precious little time to herself. It is small wonder then that she was given an award at the 1960 AGM as the person who had 'contributed most in the year in every sphere of activity'.[6]

At the regular Monday drill meetings talks and demonstrations were given by local medics including Drs Collins, Lacy, Gough and Pailthorpe who also acted as examiners.

We will look at the key role the St John Ambulance Brigade played in the health-care of the city in Chapter Eleven.

122. District Captain Fanny Silverlock seen at a ceremony on 27 September 1963 when she was presented with a silver oak leaf in recognition of her services as a Guider. She is flanked by Julia Moore and Vivien Napper who received their Queen's Guide badges at the same time. (Courtesy of Pat Ware)

123. The Chichester St John Ambulance Brigade boy cadets seen in 1964 with some of their officers in the hall of the former Lancastrian Boys' School in Orchard Street, their usual meeting place for drill nights. (Courtesy of Allan and Pat Ware)

GALA DAY

Any self-respecting town would have a carnival day, a day when it would let its hair down and raise money for charity at the same time. Chichester joined the throng in 1955 when the ever-industrious Leslie Evershed-Martin, then mayor, founded Chichester Combined Charities who staged the first ever gala on the first Saturday in July.[7] It was an instant success and so thenceforward the first Saturday of July entered the Cicestrian calendar as **Gala Day.**

In the 1960s the gala reached its zenith when the week leading up to Gala Day itself was filled with events. One of these was a 'spot the cuckoo' competition when local shops would secrete in their window displays something that would not normally be there, which the eagle eyed were invited to spot. Other pre-events included a dance, six-a-side football competition and a flower show.

For many of us the highlight of Gala Week was the Soapbox Derby, in which teams of two raced their lovingly made boy-powered vehicles* around

---

* For the uninitiated, a soapbox cart consisted of a stout plank of wood carried on old pram wheels with a wooden soapbox serving as a body in which the driver sat. One boy pushed and the other steered. I have painful memories of my 'steam fire engine' coming to grief in an unfortunate prang.

124. The cover of the 1965 Gala Day programme, bearing the famous cornflower which was the emblem of the event. (Author's collection)

County Hall, often resulting in spectacular collisions and bloodied knees. There was also a *Concours d'Elegance* class for the more elaborate creations for which the Duke of Richmond provided a trophy. In 1960 this was won by two 13-year-old Scouts, Richard Hill and Roger Fox, from the 5th Chichester Group with their *Flying Dragon*.[8]

On the great day itself cornflowers, the gala emblem, would be on sale and were sported as buttonholes by one and all. These were supplied by Frampton's Nursery, and one year I was a volunteer picker sent by the Boys' High School but it came as something of a surprise to find that this morning off school was no sinecure; the tough stalks quickly cut the fingers to shreds.

A military band – often the Royal Marines – would parade around the city in the morning, then in the afternoon Priory Park would open its gates. There, in addition

125 (L): The 1965 Soapbox Derby with the leading teams rounding the fountain in front of County Hall. Behind the ranks of spectators can be seen a loudspeaker van, probably supplied by T.C. Daniels. (WSRO, Chichester Photographic Archive, CPS 2838–7); 126 (R): Another view of the 1965 Soapbox Derby. Here two teams compete in the obstacle race. The primitive nature of the vehicles can be appreciated. It seems incredible now that in those far-off days, before the invention of computer games and 'I-thingies', boys could amuse themselves for hours with a wooden box, plank of wood and some old pram wheels. (WSRO, Chichester Photographic Archive, CPS 2838–9)

127. *Pat Silver seen in West Street selling the gala emblem, the cornflower, from her blue and white barrow. (Courtesy of Pat Ware)*

128. *The 1962 gala procession in Market Road. This float, by Post Office Telephones, won third prize. Their Karrier lorry has been decked out with a display relating to* The Flintstones, *a popular TV cartoon programme about Stone Age characters who seem to have been saved by making a 999 call. (Courtesy of Ken Green)*

to a funfair and side shows, were arena events which, in 1965, included a search and rescue helicopter display and sheepdog demonstrations. One regular, but unscheduled, arena event was that staged by Ted Gobey, a one-armed cattle drover always the worse for drink, who would duck beneath the ropes and march up and down hurling abuse at the official performers. Sadly the strong arm of Sussex Police would all too quickly bring his highly entertaining performance to an end.

In the early evening the carnival procession would take place, consisting of floats prepared by local societies on vehicles loaned by local hauliers. The Corporation usually granted free use of a vehicle to convey the Gala Queen as well as staff to assist with the decorations.[9] The lengthy procession, headed by the guest military band, started from the Cattle Market and wove its way round the city streets thronged with onlookers. Following the band was the glamorous Gala Queen, and often in the 1960s the Dagenham Girl Pipers would take part, occupying the middle of the procession whilst the City Band brought up the rear. The St John Ambulance cadets would walk alongside the carnival procession carrying open blankets into which onlookers were exhorted to throw coins.

The funfair continued throughout the evening and then, when it got dark, there would be a torchlight procession involving bonfire societies from all over Sussex including, naturally, several from Lewes. The day ended with beating the retreat in Priory Park.

From the very start the city council made an annual grant to the gala, and in 1962 a deputation of Leslie Evershed-Martin and Jack Miller, chairman and secretary of the Combined Charities respectively, sought to have the £200 grant increased to £300, which was agreed to. Unfortunately this was to be short lived for the grant dropped to £100 in 1966 and was stopped altogether in 1967, when the Finance and General Purposes Committee opined that it had never been the council's intention to support the gala![10]

The success of the event from a fundraising point of view can be judged from the fact that in 1962 £2,000 was raised which was distributed amongst local charities.[11] Sadly in the 1980s Chichester seemed to run out of community spirit and the gala became reduced in scope and eventually petered out. Enterprisingly, in 2012 the city council staged a one-off revival of the gala to celebrate the Queen's Diamond Jubilee when once again Priory Park was thronged with fun-seeking Cicestrians.

SLOE FAIR

Sloe Fair was founded by Royal Charter of 1107 and named after a sloe tree that stood in the field outside the North Gate where the fair was held. By the early nineteenth century the date had settled on 20 October, but fairs then were general markets which came with other attractions and entertainments, not all of which were necessarily of a wholesome sort.[12] By the mid-twentieth century the Sloe Fair had lost its marketing aspect and was purely a noisy funfair, but for the young of Chichester and the surrounding villages it simply *had* to be attended, and it was something of a right of passage to be allowed to go to the fair for the first time without parental supervision.

For centuries the Sloe Fair field at Northgate really was a field, and as it always seemed to rain on 20 October, Sloe Fair was held in a sea of mud adding extra meaning to 'all the fun of the fair'. Indeed it was a source of great delight to many generations of schoolboys (including your author) to scour the field after the fair had retreated for balls lost from the coconut shies and any other interesting jetsam left behind by the showmen. As we saw in Chapter Three, this feature of Sloe Fair ended in 1961 when the Sloe Fair field was tarmacked over to form a car park. Much of the fair's intrinsic charm was thereby lost and the showmen now left nothing behind. True, it was still a *fairground* but hardly the 'fair ground' in which the lot fell unto the Psalmist and Rudyard Kipling*!

In 1963 the 20 October fell on a Sunday, so, under the terms of the charter, the fair was postponed to the following day. However, on the Sunday the Fairground Society held a religious service at which the Revd John Jackson, vicar of St Paul's, preached from the roundabout 'with white-robed choirboys by his side' and hymns were accompanied by the fairground organ. The roundabout was James Noyce's famous nineteenth-century 'Golden Gallopers', a magnificent ride usually powered by a steam showman's engine. The following day's fair was wet (as usual) and there were over 100 stalls and rides on offer.[13]

YOUTH

The widespread youthful disdain for their native city probably stemmed from the fact that it did not have a nightclub, but there were other gathering places, the best-known being the Chichester Boys' Club in Little London which offered mainly sporting opportunities, especially boxing, and the Youth Centre at Fernleigh in North Street which styled itself as a 'Young Adult Centre and Coffee Club'. There were also the coffee bars that so characterised 1950s and '60s popular culture. The three coffee bars colonised by the young were the **El Bolero** at No. 13 South Street, **Cary's Coffee Bar** in Cooper Street and the exotically named **Mehitabel** at No. 82 East Street, overtop John Temple, the tailors; all had their loyal followers.

The El Bolero, popularly known as 'The Elbo' occupied a corner site adjacent to the Vicar's Hall entrance to the cathedral (now occupied by Timothy Roe the jeweller) and so commanded views both down and across South Street enabling customers to see and be seen. My father sneered at its long-haired occupants and denounced them as 'beatnicks', no doubt suspecting that drugs were being dealt there. As with all coffee bars aimed at the younger generation it also had a jukebox which could be fed whilst trying to make a cup of coffee last as long as possible. Cary's Coffee Bar was not far away at the end of Cooper Street, now the Confucious Chinese Restaurant.

---

* Psalm 16, v 9 (BCP), 'The lot has fallen unto me in a fair ground: yea, I have a goodly heritage.' Rudyard Kipling used part of this in his famous poem 'Sussex' viz: 'The lot has fallen unto me in a fair ground – in a fair ground – yea Sussex by the Sea!'

129. The popular El Bolero coffee bar at No. 13 South Street, next to the Vicars' Hall entrance to the cathedral. (Courtesy of Ken Green)

The Mehitabel, run by French artist Michel Le Bourlier, occupied an upper floor, so had a rather different air looking down on to the street and was open late at night, but it closed in 1963 and its space was taken by the Dragon Spring Chinese Restaurant. A Wimpy Bar – Chichester's first burger outlet – had opened in 1966 on the corner of North and Crane streets proving very popular with the young, paving the way for the 'fast-food' obsession to come in subsequent decades.

Regular dances were held at the barracks and St George's Hall in Whyke, but many would repair to Bognor where Butlin's famous holiday camp opened its doors to day visitors, especially in the winter, and the Rex Ballroom hosted famous pop groups of the day.

On one memorable occasion very big names from the pop music world appeared in Chichester. On 12 February 1967 a drugs raid was made on the West Wittering home of Rolling Stone Keith Richards where a party, attended by, amongst others, Mick Jagger also of the Rolling Stones and the singer Marianne Faithful, was in full swing. Interesting substances were found on the scene and Miss Faithful was observed in a state of nature. Richards and Jagger were arrested and charged by Chichester Magistrates with being in possession of illegal drugs. They were brought to trial at the Quarter Sessions in Chichester on 22 June 1967, a much-publicised trial which really put Chichester on the map. Both men were imprisoned, Richards for a year and Jagger for three months. After a famous appeal, hinging on the small quantities of drugs involved and the fact that the judge concerned, Judge Block, admitted that he had gone out to crush the Rolling Stones, the sentences were quashed the following August.[14]

On the day of the trial most of the city's schoolgirls absented themselves from lessons to stand screaming outside the court when their idols appeared*.

---

* 1960s pop culture required girls to scream at the tops of their voices when in the presence of their pop idols, including at concerts, which ought to have made performing a trifle difficult but seemingly didn't.

THE SILVER SCREEN

In 1960 the population of Chichester was only some 19,000 souls but it had managed to support no fewer than three large cinemas in the decades before. These were the **Granada** in East Street, the **Odeon** in South Street and the **Gaumont** in Eastgate Square.

The Granada was housed in the former trading hall of the Corn Exchange and had been refitted in 1948 to seat 900. The Odeon had been rebuilt in 1936, when it was known as the **Plaza**, to give 1,036 seats, and in 1939 it was taken over by the Odeon circuit, being renamed the Odeon in 1945. The Gaumont had been purpose built in 1937 with a seating capacity of 1,278 and was the most luxurious of the three having a most sumptuous art deco interior.[15]

In the 1960s television became the harbinger of the death knell for many cinemas across the land; by 1960 the majority of households had a television, and with bigger screens, increasing channel choice and, from 1976, colour, going to 'the pictures' became less of a necessity. Regular cinema audiences fell away rapidly and would only be tempted to turn out now and again to see a 'blockbuster' film instead of going out twice a week.

All three cinemas held matinee performances for children, colloquially known as 'Saturday Morning Pictures', consisting of the standard – and unhealthily American-biased – mix of a western, a serial and a cartoon; by providing a serial, each episode of which ended with a cliff-hanger, the young audience was guaranteed to return next week, spending another sixpence to find out what happened.

Assembling anything up to 500, generally unaccompanied, children in one building to watch exciting films was a recipe for pandemonium, and, from experience of having attended the performances at the Granada in the 1950s and early 1960s, I can confirm that the recipe worked. Before the performances a long queue would form down Baffins Lane and this was presided over by a bristling commissionaire who would stamp out the first signs of any trouble with sharp words or, more likely, a clip around a recalcitrant boy's ear. We still went back for more. The introduction of children's daytime television hastened the demise of this market and Saturday Morning Pictures gradually fizzled out.

Sadly the year 1960 was to prove a watershed for cinema in Chichester. On 6 February the Odeon in South Street closed its doors for good and within eight months another closure was announced, this time the Gaumont. The Gaumont was owned by the Rank organisation who were also acquiring a major shareholding in Odeon at this time but had been refused permission by the government to amalgamate the two circuits on the grounds of monopoly.[16] As such it was perhaps surprising that two cinemas under the control of Rank had managed to survive in this small city for so long. The closure of both within a few months of each other caused much dismay, and under a banner headline 'GAUMONT CINEMA WILL CLOSE IN OCTOBER' the *Chichester Observer*, in its issue of 26 August 1960, reported:

> After October 15, Chichester with a 19,000 population, a large rural district with plenty of summer visitors, will be served by its one remaining cinema, the Granada in East Street.

The actual demise of the Gaumont went unrecorded by the local 'rag' and in its issue of 21 October, when the Granada first appeared alone on the entertainments page, it was advertising *Circus of Horrors* and *A Town Like Alice*, the latter starring Peter Finch.

One person who had lost her job when the Gaumont closed was Pam Jones who then joined the staff of the Granada as an usherette in 1961. Later she relieved in the kiosk and on the cash desk before being promoted to secretary and wages clerk. She recalls that the Rank organisation had 'done a deal' with the Bernsteins, who owned Granada, over which of the two remaining cinemas should continue to serve the dwindling band of Chichester cinema-goers.

130. The exterior of the Granada in 1966. It was now the only cinema in the city. Beyond can be seen the hoarding around the site that was to be developed to provide Stocklund House. (WSRO)

131. The Granada kiosk, c. 1965 with Pam Jones (left) and Mrs Aburrow attending to a youthful seeker after popcorn. (Courtesy of Pam Jones)

For Pam Jones, working at the Chichester Granada was like being part of a happy family; Cecil Bernstein, who lived nearby at Pagham, was a frequent visitor and took a genuine interest in the staff.

The manager at the Granada during the 1960s was Jack Harris, an ex-regimental sergeant major, whose walking stick was often used as a shepherd's crook to extract young troublemakers from the audience. He retired in March 1967 to be replaced by Frank Davis. Later Pam Jones became his assistant manager, but this was in the days when it was uncommon for women to hold such posts, so she had to be chaperoned by one of the operators in case of inappropriate attentions by the audience!

Another 1960s phenomenon was the fad (if that is the word) for bored teenagers mindlessly to slash cinema seats, and the Chichester Granada was not spared their attentions although the problem was less acute here than in many places. Other teenage practices were the sticking of chewing gum on to the seats and a scam whereby only one of a group would actually buy a ticket, and then let in the rest by opening the fire doors at the south end of the auditorium.[17]

The Odeon building still remains in South Street, having been occupied by a succession of supermarkets, but the Gaumont was converted into the city's first swimming pool, as we shall see. The Granada soldiered on until August 1980 when it too closed its doors leaving Chichester with no cinema. Fortunately the handsome Corn Exchange which housed it lived on and is now a branch of a fashion chain.

SHOPPING

On first unveiling his sight, a visitor parachuted blindfold into the centre of today's Chichester could imagine himself to be anywhere in the United Kingdom, for the vast majority of the shops are those to be seen everywhere, namely branches of the same chain stores all with identical shopfronts and stock. In the 1960s,

132. North Street in the 1960s. Two supermarkets, Victor Value and J. Sainsbury, vie for custom next door to each other. Notice the line-up bicycles on the kerb. Of these businesses only WH Smith is still trading here today. (Courtesy of Ken Green)

however, things were very different. Although there were the obligatory branches of Woolworths, Marks and Spencer, Currys, Boots, The International and the Home and Colonial, the majority of the shops were small and owned and run by local people, people who were generally also involved in the civic life of the city[*]. Housewives would shop several times a week and from several different shops.

The new-fangled supermarkets had arrived in Chichester in the early 1960s, the first, Victor Value in North Street, was a very small affair but introduced the city to the concept of self-service. Sainsbury opened a larger supermarket right next door in North Street in 1961, and Tesco – controversially as we have seen – did the same in East Street that same year, whilst the closed Odeon cinema became a branch of the Pricerite chain. The concept of 'one-stop shopping' was beginning to catch on, but these four supermarkets were positively diminutive by today's standards, so throughout the 1960s the small shops still managed to retain their loyal customers.

In the 1968 Kelly's Directory it can be seen that the city centre was still host to twelve butchers, ten greengrocers, thirty-four grocers, three fishmongers and

[*] For a fuller account of Chichester's lost shops I would refer the reader to *A Baker's Dozen*, Bishop Otter Memorial Paper No. 29, edited by Paul Foster and published by the University of Chichester in 2011.

six bakers for provisioning. Some of these were housed in the Market House (colloquially, but incorrectly, known as the *Butter Market*) such as Mrs Cripp's fish stall and Jock White's greengrocery – my mother would never dream of buying her vegetables from anyone else. It was still possible to buy fresh local fish and game from Byerley's in South Street, homemade sausages from Elphick's in East Street and wonderful fresh bread from Spurrier's shop in South Street.

In addition to provisioners, in 1968 there were still three ironmongers, seven cycle shops, three decorators' merchants, and six dispensing chemists, mostly independently owned. Pine's rambling ironmonger's shop in Eastgate Square was a legend and Geering's the drapers in North Street boasted a fascinating overhead cash carrier that spirited customers' money away from the counter to a central cash desk and promptly brought back the change and receipt.

There were myriad ladies' and gents' outfitters in the city but only two department stores. The best was Morants in West Street which had started as a draper's shop at Nos 13 and 14 just after the war, but in the 1950s spread progressively along West Street in both directions annexing, *inter alia*, the Oliver Whitby

133 (L): A bicycle bell bought from Chitty's cycle shop bearing the shop's proud name. (Author's collection)

134 (Below): An early 1960s view of West Street with part of Morants department store on the left. The brick-clad section, replacing Morants original shop, was then fairly new, but the white-fronted part – the shoe department – had been the Southdown bus office. Beyond Morants can be seen the post office and the Dolphin and Anchor Hotel whilst in the distance a car is negotiating the Cross. West Street is very quiet, suggesting this was either a Thursday afternoon (early closing) or a Sunday. (Author's collection)

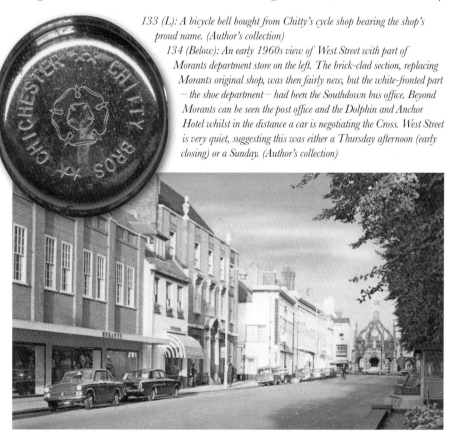

*135. A garment label for Morants.
To have 'own label' goods meant that
the shop had truly arrived. (Author's
collection)*

School and then backwards into Tower Street. It still exists, but although taken over firstly by Army and Navy and then House of Fraser, Cicestrians of a certain age still fondly refer to the shop by its old name.

The second department store was a creation of the 1960s, namely that of the Co-op who had a new store built on the site of the church of St Peter the Less in North Street. From its four floors it sold a range of household goods and clothing but was on a very much smaller scale than the famous Co-op store in Fratton Road, Portsmouth, to which many Cicestrians continued to repair. It was not to last long as a Co-op and is currently occupied by Lakeland Plastics. 'Morants' is still the only department store in the city centre.

136. The new Co-operative department store in North Street, seen in May 1966, two years after opening. Beyond it is the new road – St Peters – leading through to Priory Road. (Courtesy of Ken Green)

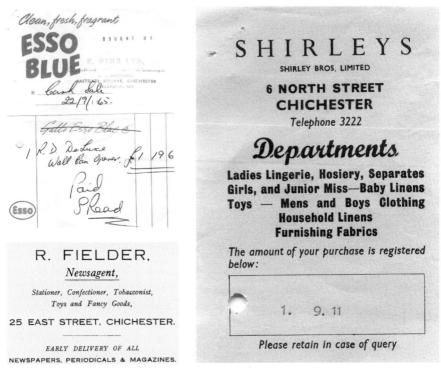

137. *Some souvenirs of lost Chichester businesses. Shirley Brothers at No. 6 North Street, whose receipt says it all, was gutted by fire in 1974. Pine's ironmonger's shop in Eastgate Square was a legend; this receipt for a deluxe wall can opener is written on an Esso Blue pro-forma. One is tempted to think that the claim for Esso Blue paraffin being 'fragrant' is a little far fetched. R. Fielder in East Street was Chichester's principal newsagent and employed a regiment of twenty-six paper boys in the 1960s. (Author's collection)*

Sadly the small independent shops were to disappear in subsequent decades and Chichester became the clone town that it is today as distant greedy landlords push up the rents to a level that anyone starting a business cannot afford. Also to come were the out-of-town shopping parks and vast supermarkets that sucked the very lifeblood out of the commercial heart of the city. To see what Chichester was once like shopping-wise, visit Lewes.

SERVING THE MOTORIST

The horseless carriage had made its presence felt in the city centre from the early 1900s when garages opened on all four main streets to fulfil motorists' needs. In the 1960s garages were still a feature of the city centre, the largest including Adcock's (which had opened in 1908) at the far end of East Street who sold cars

138. Southgate in 1959 with Mason's garage on the left sporting a wide canopy over its forecourt. The confectioner's shop in the foreground is The Bon Bon. The garage was demolished in the early 1980s to build a new Waitrose store, a building now occupied by Argos and The Vestry public house. (Courtesy of Mike Mason)

manufactured by the Rootes Group and Mason's in South Gate. Mason's garage was the city's Vauxhall dealership and their main premises and workshops were on the west side of Southgate at Nos 19 and 20 with a forecourt selling Cleveland petrol. To gain access to the forecourt motorists had to cross the pavement at the same time avoiding pedestrians.

In 1961 Mason's acquired the former Mechanic's Institute building, just down the road on the corner of Market Road and Southgate, which had been in the occupation of F.J. French the wholesalers. They converted it into a car showroom by the rather brutal insertion of huge plate glass windows at ground-floor level to display the Vauxhall cars within.

Other garages within the city centre were Wadham's in South Gate* who sold BMC cars, Page's (later Blue Star) at North Gate (Rootes Group) and Reed's on the south side of West Street. Buying petrol from Reed's involved trailing the pump hoses across the pavement via an overhead crane. Half way up South Street

---

* This garage appears in Fig. 55. It just managed to escape demolition for the ring road in 1965 but later succumbed to a 1970s office development.

139. Before: F.J. French's wholesale warehouse situated in the former Mechanics' Institute in Southgate, a building which had been little altered externally since it was built in 1835 to the design of local architect John Elliott. It is pictured here in 1961. (Courtesy of Mike Mason)

140. After: The same building after conversion into a car showroom for Masons Garage, later in 1961. The building still exists and is now a restaurant of the Café Rouge chain. (Courtesy of Mike Mason)

141. An advertisement in the 1962 Festival Theatre programme for D. Rowe & Co. from which it can be seen that car hire was another facet of the business. The car shown is a Ford Anglia, one of the best-selling family saloons of the time. (Author's collection)

was Field's garage, which later in the 1960s became Stringer's, who sold Austin cars. Outside the city walls there was the Northgate garage run by Alderman Pope but the largest garage was D Rowe & Co. in the Hornet, who were the city's main Ford dealers and also traded in farm machinery.

The approaching pedestianisation of the city centre sounded the death knell for the city centre garages and in the early 1970s they either closed down or moved to out-of-town locations on the industrial estates. Their sites were quickly redeveloped and little by way of signs remain, but the eagle-eyed may spot the fading wording 'Adcock's garage' painted on the side of what is now the Sussex Camera Centre in Eastgate Square

TO CHURCH ON SUNDAY

Sixties Chichester was quite well provided with churches of most denominations. Predominant, naturally, was the Church of England, with, at the centre, the cathedral which offered daily services in addition to three every Sunday. The little churches* had all closed by 1953 and their tiny parishes had been amalgamated into St Peter the Great, whose church, also known as **The Subdeanery**, was in West Street, opposite the cathedral. The vicar throughout the decade was Canon C.W.F. Bennett who had given long service to the city. The other parish churches were St Pancras in Eastgate Square, St Paul in Northgate and St George in Whyke. In addition, St John's, a proprietary chapel in St John's Street, which had been united with the benefice of St Pancras in 1955, continued a quasi-independent existence but was to close in 1973.[18] St Pancras and St John were evangelical, St Peter the Great and St Paul middle of the road, whilst St George was high in its churchmanship.

---

* These were St Peter the Less and St Olave in North Street, St Andrew in East Street, St Martin in St Martin's Street and All Saints in West Pallant.

One new Anglican church opened in the 1960s, namely St Wilfrid's built to serve Parklands. It began life as the church hall of St Bartholmew's church that had been built in Sherborne Road in 1957 where regular services were held as it was more convenient than the church proper which was in Westgate. St Bartholomew's parish was united with St Paul in 1959 and the St Bartholomew's services were concentrated on the hall in Sherborne Road.[19]

The Parklands congregation was growing, so clearly something more elaborate than the hall was now required and architect Stanley Roth was instructed in July 1962 to prepare designs for a sanctuary to be added to the new hall as the first stage of conversion into a proper church. Tenders to build the sanctuary were invited in April 1964, but when they came in considerably above Roth's estimate there was much dissention in the PCC, and it was even suggested that the new Bishop Luffa School be used instead! Nevertheless work went ahead to construct what some rudely termed 'the pillbox', which was first used for the harvest festival service on 26 September 1965.

As the building was now half way to being a church it needed to be dedicated, and from the options presented to him, Bishop Wilson chose St Wilfrid.[20] The official dedication of the sanctuary was carried out by the bishop on 9 October 1966 at the end of a three-week Church Army mission in Parklands. The scale of the ministry in Parklands is indicated by the fact that the Sunday school was catering for over 100 children at this time.[21] The first stage towards St Wilfrid's independence came in 1968 when Parklands was declared a conventional district

142. St Wilfrid's church created in 1965 by adding a sanctuary to the existing 1957 hall. It was later extended again to provide a bespoke nave. (WSRO)

of St Paul's parish, with St Wilfrid's as its church. The man appointed as priest-in-charge of St Wilfrid's was Gordon Bearman, who took up his post on 31 May 1968. Gordon Bearman was the remarkable man whom we met in Chapter Five as county librarian, a post he continued to hold alongside this incumbency until 1970.

The city was well served by Nonconformist churches with Methodists (Southgate and the Hornet), Congregationalists (South Street), Calvinists (Providence Chapel, Chapel Street), Quakers (Priory Road), Plymouth Brethren (Chapel Street), Baptists (Sherborne Road) and the Salvation Army (Orchard Street). All, save the Brethren and the Quakers, worshipped in nineteenth-century buildings, but in 1958 The Baptist Church had been re-founded in new premises in Sherborne Road. The Friends' Meeting House of the Quaker congregation was a charming, characteristically simple building dating from 1700, which was demolished in 1967 and replaced by an uncompromisingly modern structure. Tragically the original building was not listed and, despite an offer to preserve it being made by a local businessman, was needlessly destroyed.

The Roman Catholics had built a new church in Market Avenue in 1958, funded by the proceeds from the sale of their Victorian pile in Southgate and gambling via their own football pools.

In the Swim – at Last

The need for a public swimming pool had been identified by Thomas Sharp in his report back in 1949, when he proposed including one in his 'City Health Centre' to be built in Basin Road, of which nothing came.[22] A swimming club, the Chichester Cormorants, had been formed in 1957 but had to hire an Everymans' coach to take its members to other towns' pools, in particular the Victoria Swimming Baths in Portsmouth. In 1958 the Cormorants entered a topical float in the gala procession which displayed a wide variety of 'Chichester baths' beneath a banner protesting about the lack of a *swimming* bath in the city.

That same year a local bank manager, David Thomas, suggested setting up a public fund to convert the static water tank in Oaklands Park* into a swimming pool, an action endorsed by the secretary of the Cormorants, W.R. Edgar.[23] However, it was not until 1960 that things really got underway when, on 23 May, the Duke of Richmond launched a £30,000 appeal under what became known as 'the Thomas Plan' for public contributions towards the £100,000 needed to

---

* This vast underground reservoir, near Oaklands Park House, had been provided as part of the war effort to provide water for fighting fires in the event of a blitz. It had been built to the dimensions of an Olympic-sized swimming pool with a view to such a subsequent use.

build a swimming pool. David Thomas was appointed honorary treasurer. The site proposed, however, was at a different location, in the East Pallant car park behind Cawley Priory, and the city council agreed to fund the £70,000 balance. Responsibility for developing the scheme was given to the council's Cemetery, Parks and Allotments Committee, known (understandably) as the 'Parks Committee' for short.

Unfortunately the appeal was launched alongside that for building the Festival Theatre, meaning that Cicestrians were being encouraged to support two major fund-raising initiatives at the same time, albeit for two very different causes. At the appeal launch it was decided that, in the event of the swimming pool project failing, the funds would not be diverted to the Festival Theatre, and a widely reported rift developed between the two projects. At a hastily convened public meeting at the Assembly Room on 27 May, attended by only fifty people, a vote was taken in which twenty-five to nineteen were in favour of omitting the Festival Theatre as a beneficiary in the event of failure[24]. The fury died down however and, in the end, both appeals succeeded.

The swimming pool appeal took the form of a 1s weekly football pool run by Robert Dearling from his house in Grove Road, and by September 1960 it had 3,331 subscribers who raised £5,600 in that first year, indicating the strong public support for the venture.

The idea of the East Pallant site was short lived, however, for the closure of the Gaumont cinema in Eastgate Square in October 1960 provided an opportunity to convert an existing building into a 100ft by 40ft swimming pool and the Corporation purchased the freehold for £35,000 in January 1962, by which time the public appeal had raised £15,000.[25]

143. A notice about the 1962 AGM of the Swimming Pool Appeal Fund which appeared in the Chichester Observer *giving the good news that the appeal had passed its half way stage. (WSRO)*

212

Sadly, in early 1963 a major disagreement erupted within the city council over the projected cost of the venture. The estimate had now risen to £120,000 but, although the county council pledged to contribute £10,000, the Rural District Council resolutely refused to contribute anything. The fact that the appeal had raised an incredible £28,717 by May of that year did little to ameliorate the situation, so the council resolved in August to reduce the scope of the Gaumont works to a budget of £89,200. Councillor Foote led a revolt for a full recon-sideration of the scheme and the editor of the *Chichester Observer* found himself deluged with letters from the public pushing for the Oaklands Park alternative to be revived as an alternative.[26]

Despite the council's resolution to stick with the Gaumont scheme, the law of delay set in and little happened during 1964 save for the momentous decision to name the venture 'The Chichester Swimming Pool'. Six tenders for the construc-tion were opened on 1 February 1965, with the lowest giving an unexpectedly high scheme total of £208,000. This brought about more agonising and so it was decided to ballot ratepayers to see whether there was still public support for a swimming pool at this price.[27] Alarmed by this news the Appeal Committee duly placed an impassioned notice in the *Chichester Observer* of 12 February:

> To all Citizens of Chichester – for your sake and your children's sake this may be the most important notice you may ever read …

It went on to urge the citizens to vote 'YES', pointing out that it would only cost ratepayers $4^{1}/_{2}d$ per week – the cost of two cigarettes – which the committee believed everyone could afford. The same issue also carried many letters deplor-ing the continuing delays to the project.

The result of the ballot was disappointing and indecisive, only 3,247 votes were cast (a poll of 48.6 per cent) of which 1,611 were for the Gaumont scheme and 1,617 against it, the remainder being undecided. Architect Stanley Roth, who was not involved with the project but no stranger to controversy, then threw a spanner into the works by suggesting that the Gaumont building was 'well on the way to falling down', an assertion which the town clerk refuted as being 'totally inaccurate'.[28]

The Parks Committee resolved at their meeting of 26 February not to res-urrect the Oaklands Park idea but instead negotiate with the lowest tenderer, C.J. Sims of London, for a reduction in scope, and that if that failed to achieve the desired savings fresh tenders would be sought. Fortunately C.J. Sims co-operated and revised their tender for the reduced scope to £159,821, which was accepted in March 1965. The council approached the Ministry of Housing and Local Government for a loan of that amount and work finally started on site in

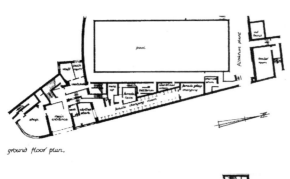

ground floor plan.

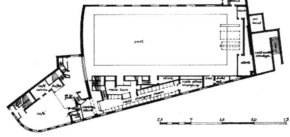

first floor plan

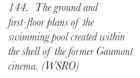

144. *The ground and first-floor plans of the swimming pool created within the shell of the former Gaumont cinema. (WSRO)*

145. *The interior of the new swimming pool on opening day, looking towards the shallow end. The large windows on the right afforded views of the swimmers from East Walls. The assembled company is listening attentively to the Duke of Richmond who is in the right-hand corner of the picture. (WSRO, Chichester Photographic Archive, CPS 3602–1)*

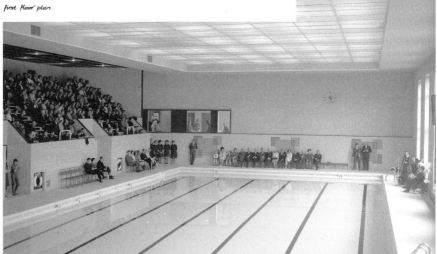

April 1965 to build the pool that would also feature seating for 250 spectators and a first-floor cafe.[29]

The economics of the pool continued to vex the council, and when in November 1966 they published their proposed charges – 3s for adults and 2s for children – there was a backlash in the *Chichester Observer* letters page to the effect that this was too high. Once again the Rural District Council, whose ratepayers would, after all, be using the pool, were approached but they, once again, unreasonably refused to contribute.

146. The Duke of Richmond opening the Chichester Swimming Pool on 29 April 1967 behind him the Mayor of Chichester, Cllr Harry Bell, watches the photographer. (WSRO, Chichester Photographic Archive CPS 4224–2)

147. The official leaflet setting out the hours of business and the charges for using the new swimming pool when it opened in April 1967. (WSRO)

The works were completed in March 1967 and the pool was officially opened by the Duke of Richmond on Saturday, 29 April following, in the presence of Mayor Cllr Harry Bell and other councillors and officers including the full Parks Committee. After his address, in which he described this as being 'a terrific day for Chichester', the Duke of Richmond unveiled two plaques in the foyer of the new swimming pool, one commemorating the occasion and the other the efforts of the Appeal Committee in raising £35,000. The first swimmer to enter the pool was 15-year-old Jennifer Lane of the Seymour Synchronised Swimming School, London, who performed a water ballet entitled 'Freedom' after which members of Chichester Cormorants dived in.[30]

215

Chichester Swimming Pool was to be a valuable and well-used asset for the city until 1986 when it closed on completion of the Westgate Leisure Centre. Once again the former Gaumont cinema lay empty (save for an Indian restaurant on the first floor) until it was finally demolished in 2007 and the site redeveloped for shops, restaurants and housing.

Notes

1   Kelly's Directories, 1964–68.
2   Hewitt, P., 'Down Memory Lane' contained a feature on Chichester Folk Club, the *Chichester Observer*, 29 March 2012.
3   *Chichester Observer*, 30 June 2005 'Remember When' by Phil Hewitt contained a feature on the fiftieth anniversary of the 12th Chichester Scouts including interviews with past and present members.
4   Chichester City District of the Girl Guider Association, Annual Report, 1962.
5   Told to the author by Allan and Pat Ware who were heavily involved with the SJAB in the 1960s.
6   *The Chi Sinjun* – the news sheet of the Chichester Division of the St John Ambulance Brigade, Vol. 2, Nos 2, 3 and 4, March–May 1960.
7   Brown, E., *Chichester in the 1950s* (EB Publications, 1996).
8   The *Chichester Observer*, 1 July 1960.
9   WSRO CG/42, Chichester City Council, minutes of the Highways Committee, 1950–68.
10   WSRO CD/3 and CD/4, Chichester City Council, minutes of the Finance and General Purposes Committee, 1959–66 and 1966–74.
11   *The Chi Sinjun* – the news sheet of the Chichester Division of the St John Ambulance Brigade, Vol. 2, No. 15, September 1962.
12   Green, Alan H.J., *Cattle, Corn and Crawfish – 900 Years of Chichester's Markets* (Phillimore, 2010).
13   The *Evening Argus*, 21 October 1963 and the *Chichester Observer*, 27 October 1963.
14   The *Chichester Observer*, 3 November 2011, 'Down Memory Lane' by Phil Hewitt contained a feature on the Rolling Stones trial.
15   Eyles, A., Grey, F. and Readman, A., *Cinema West Sussex – the First 100 Years* (Phillimore, 1996).
16   Hornsey, B., *Ninety Years of Cinema in Chichester* (Mercia Cinema Society, 1994, rev. 2007).
17   As told to the author by Pam Jones.
18   Green, Alan H.J., *St John's Chapel and the New Town, Chichester* (Phillimore, 2005).
19   WSRO Par 43/6/11, papers relating to the amalgamation of the benefices of St Paul and St Bartholomew.
20   WSRO Par 43/7/9, St Paul's Parish Newsletter, 1960–79.
21   WSRO uncatalogued St Paul's PCC Archive, AGM minute book 1959–80.
22   Sharp, T., *Georgian City – A Plan for the Preservation and Improvement of Chichester* (Southern Publishing Co. Ltd for Chichester Corporation, 1949).
23   The *Chichester Observer*, 18 December 1958.

24 The *Chichester Observer*, 23 March 1960, 27 May 1960, *Portsmouth Evening News* 18 and 25 May 1960, *Evening Argus*, 24 May 1960.

25 The *Chichester Observer*, 2 and 30 June 1961, 10 November 1961, 5 January 1962, WSRO CD/3, op. cit.

26 The *Chichester Observer*, 26 April 1963, 24 May 2 and August 1963.

27 WSRO CE/2, Chichester City Council minutes of the Cemetery, Parks and Allotments Committee 1958–74.

28 The *Chichester Observer*, 19 and 26 March 1965.

29 WSRO CE/2 op. cit. and the *Chichester Observer*, 26 February 1965.

30 WSRO MP2733, a copy of the official opening programme and report in the *Chichester Observer*, 5 May 1967.

NINE

THE NEW ARCHITECTURE

There is no getting away from the fact that 1960s architecture has, in general, an unfortunate reputation stemming from the bland, cheaply built housing estates, tower blocks of flats and faceless system-built office blocks that sprang up everywhere: indeed Chichester acquired several buildings in this idiom that it could well have done without. However, architecture, as with all the arts, has to move on, and in Chichester the new architecture was expressed in a variety of ways, which were not always bad. We have already looked at some of Chichester's new buildings during the course of this narrative, but this chapter will look at just four buildings by nationally known architects that are now widely regarded as having achieved 'landmark' status. In these four buildings materials and form were used more thoughtfully than was so often the case in the 1960s.

Lennards' Shoe Shop, No. 1 North Street/No. 88 East Street
As we saw in Chapter Three, Lennards old shoe shop, on the corner of North Street and East Street, was one of a number of elderly buildings that expressed a desire to collapse in the 1960s and was consequently demolished. The replacement building was designed by Sir Hugh Casson who, as we have seen, had become the Corporation's favourite architectural advisor in the late 1950s, which led to their persuading the owners of the site to engage him for the rebuilding.

This was a sensitive site adjacent to the Market Cross where a building that was at one with its neighbours and did not vie for attention was required. The site was also rather cramped as the frontage on to East Street was very narrow, necessitating a long and shallow sales area. Casson's successful solution to the challenge was to produce not a Georgian pastiche but a building that was honestly modern yet made a nod to the past. It was of four storeys plus basement, as was its predecessor, and its first and second floors were clad in white-painted

148. The replacement Lennards' shoe shop of 1961, designed by Sir Hugh Casson, seen when new in its setting by the Cross. On the corner its shop front has been set back and the building supported on a column to improve pedestrian circulation. (Courtesy of Ken Green)

smooth stucco whilst the fourth, clad in aluminium alloy, was set back slightly to suggest an attic. The regular window rhythm was interrupted by unexpected oriels on the first and fourth storeys whilst the ground floor contained the obligatory plate glass display windows. It was built by Jno Croad for £13,932 2s 1d and was completed in March 1962.[1] When it opened it featured a fascinating pneumatic cash carrier which took customers' remittances from the basement to the cash desk on the ground floor, and later returned the change and receipt. The building has survived in more or less original condition and is now occupied by the jeweller Gold Arts.

The Chapel of the Ascension, Bishop Otter College

Bishop Otter College in College Lane was opened in 1853 as a Church of England teacher training college and was built in the typical Victorian Gothic revival style.[2] By the end of the 1950s it had outgrown the original buildings and so the practice of Bridgewater, Shepheard and Epstein was engaged to enlarge the campus. The finest building from this era is the chapel which was completed in 1962. Peter – later Sir Peter – Shepheard who had worked on the Festival of Britain site, had been commissioned by the then principal Betty Murray who, at a meeting, challenged him to produce there and then an estimate for a new chapel. After protesting he did so and handed her a piece of paper with the figure on it. She recoiled in shock and said that it was way beyond what the college could afford. Shepheard then told Murray to write on another piece of paper what she *could* afford; this she did and when Shepheard saw the figure of £13,000 he said 'For that sum I could only design a tent.' That is what he duly

149. *The new chapel for Bishop Otter College designed by Peter Shepheard, as completed in 1962, seen from the north. The cast-aluminium sculpture on the west front is by Geoffrey Clarke and the simple colonnade affords protection to the west door and links the chapel to the dining hall. The slender flèche adds a dignified flourish. (University of Chichester Archive)*

150. *The interior of the chapel on Dedication Day, 21 March 1962. The steel roof structure provides an unencumbered and flexible floor space and the pews are moveable. The hanging seen above the altar is a temporary one made by college students as the commissioned Jean Lurçat tapestry was not ready in time. (University of Chichester Archive)*

did, designing a steel and glass structure, the final cost of which was almost spot on at £13,300.[3]

The buildings Shepheard created did not reflect the Gothic revival of the existing ones, but made their own statement. The chapel is square in plan and, above a low perimeter wall, the lofty steel-framed roof rises steeply to form Shepheard's tent-like building with four full-width gables, one to each face. The gables on the east and west sides are of brick but on the other two they are filled with textured glass which suffuse the interior with a pleasing watery light. The roof is clad in bright red pantiles and the whole is topped with a slender flèche. Inside, a gallery at the west end houses the pipe organ, but the rest of the space is open plan with no fixed seating allowing full flexibility in use.

Above the altar is a striking tapestry specially woven by Jean Lurçat in 1962 representing the Creation.[4]

The new chapel was dedicated by the Bishop of Chichester on 21 March 1962 but unfortunately the tapestry commissioned from Jean Lurçat had not been delivered in time so instead a hand-printed hanging, made by three students of the college, was provided as an interim measure.[5]

THE FESTIVAL THEATRE

Of all the buildings Chichester acquired in the 1960s, Powell & Moya's Chichester Festival Theatre, whose history we looked at in Chapter Five, is the one that receives almost universal praise, even from those who do not generally appreciate modern architecture. It is, to use the hackneyed modern phrase, *iconic*, reflected in the fact that it is one of only two twentieth-century buildings in Chichester to receive statutory listing – and Grade II* at that.

It was a most unusual building for Chichester. The form is both geometrically and structurally complex, the auditorium being a regular hexagon at the first-floor level sitting on an irregular one at ground level with the façade being set back on the three western sides so that the auditorium formed a canopy over the entrance doors*. It was also built to a strict budget which meant that the cheapest materials had to be used, especially for out-of-sight elements.

The main structure, for which the structural engineer was Charles Weiss, is of reinforced concrete comprising, on the western half of the building, three massive radial cantilever beams which carry the auditorium above the canopy. These were cast in situ and tied into ring beams at first-floor and roof levels. The clever part is that the opposite corners of the hexagon are tied together just below the roof by groups of four steel tendons, and it is this feature which makes for an auditorium free of columns. The lightweight roof structure of steel and timber was installed before the aforementioned tendons were stressed, after which the falsework was removed to reveal the building in all its glory. The visible concrete, both internally and externally, was bush-hammered in panels.

The main staircases projected from the walls below the canopy and were fully glazed in order to give an element of transparency to the building, but on completion it was found that this feature admitted too much light into the auditorium

---

* As an 11 year old I was sufficiently inspired to try to make a cardboard model of the theatre based on observation rather than drawings, and my first (natural – or perhaps naïve?) instinct was that the overhang would be the same all round which, of course it isn't. It took me a long time to get it right.

151. *The Festival Theatre from the air on completion looking south. The timber-clad stairways beneath the canopy can be clearly seen. (Author's collection)*

when the doors were open and doubtless would also have offered unintended views up the short skirts of the day. To cure this, wide vertical timber slats were fitted on the outside, a feature which Powell considered to be a weakness in the design.[6]

Inside, the roof structure was not hidden from view but flaunted, so the detail of where the three bands of tendons cross each other in the centre can be appreciated from the auditorium. Below stairs the backstage facilities were utilitarian built with walls of unlined blockwork in order to save money. Furthermore, the hexagonal form, whilst ideal for an auditorium, did not make for comfortable dressing rooms that ended up wedge-shaped – it is difficult to imagine worthies such as Sir Laurence Olivier putting up with this – but he did.

From the view in Fig. 151 above it can be seen that on completion Powell & Moya's design was pure – a free-standing hexagon unencumbered by any extensions. When the theatre first opened it was intended that the sets on the open thrust stage would be minimal, relying instead on props, but this ideal soon changed and the building was extended on the east side to provide a scenery dock, and then to the south to provide offices. The purity of the design was thus destroyed, but ironically partly by Powell & Moya themselves who designed the first extension!

In 2012, Chichester Festival Theatre, now fifty years old, underwent a major two-year renovation which both conserved the original listed structure (now showing its age and the consequences of cheap construction), swept away the later additions and updated the seating and backstage facilities.

GILLETT HOUSE, CHICHESTER THEOLOGICAL COLLEGE

In 1960 Chichester Theological College, a seat of fervent Anglo-Catholicism, was housed in Georgian houses at Nos 9–11 Westgate and St Bartholomew's church in Mount Lane, the latter serving as the chapel. South of this their playing field extended down to the banks of the River Lavant with Westgate Fields beyond.

The expansion of the college in the early 1960s called for additional premises to provide student accommodation. The building that in 1964 arose from the playing fields next to St Bartholmew's was, to say the least, controversial and certainly did not attract widespread approbation as had the Festival Theatre. Its appellation referred to Canon Charles Scott Gillett who had been principal of the college from 1933 to 1946.

The architectural practice engaged to design the new building was Ahrends, Buton and Koralek (ABK), whose partnership had been founded only a few years before in London and who were making a name for themselves in the design of innovative public and educational buildings[*]. Their design for this three- and four-storey building around a courtyard was in an idiom that was to become known as

152. A view across the Theological College playing fields with St Bartholomew's church (George Draper, 1832) on the left and the 1964 Gillett House on the right. The contrast between the two buildings is marked by the chunky nature of the new building against the classical of the old. The playing fields have since been developed as Tollhouse Close, spoiling the setting of Gillett House. (Courtesy of the late Peter Iden)

---

[*] ABK achieved a certain notoriety in 1982 when their unexecuted design for an extension to the National Gallery in London was denounced by Prince Charles as being 'a monstrous carbuncle', a jibe that was to pass into common usage, but despite this they have a large portfolio of successful schemes to their credit.

153. *Inside one of the staircases showing the rough brickwork. This was taken in 2004 by which time Gillett house had become a rest home. The Artex applied to the ceiling may well be a later addition. (Author's collection)*

'brutalism' from its strong form, assertive use of materials and the assumption that it was intended to shock. Strangely it does not seem to have shocked the Planning Committee for they granted outline permission without demur on 13 October 1961 pending submission of further details of appearance and access – and nothing further is recorded![7]

Housing thirty-five bedrooms, three staff flats, a library, lecture room and chapel, the building was in brick and concrete under flat roofs.[8] The concrete elements were set between the floors and included high-up windows set at 45 degrees to the vertical over the projecting bay to each bedroom. The concrete, instead of being fair-faced, was cast against roughly sawn boards whose impressions it bore. Inside each room had fitted furniture; the desk in the bay, top lit by the angled window, was of laminated timber whilst a shelf, intended as an altar for personal devotions, was in concrete, cast integrally with the wall. The narrow chapel rose through two floors and featured a small gallery. The internal walls were mostly either bare concrete or brick with little concession to decoration.

The first students immediately christened the building 'Colditz' on account of its severe appearance and cold, dark interior, and the name stuck. It was also unpopular because it was not connected to the other college buildings necessitating going out into the rain to get to lectures.[9] As it was so visible from Westgate Fields it also attracted public comment. Chichester Theological College closed in 1994 after which its land and buildings were sold off. The grounds were redeveloped for housing and Gillett House found itself turned into a care home, known as Marriott Lodge together with a later extension of the college called Marriott House.

Gillett House, on account of its imaginative design, became listed Grade II in 1996 which raised many eyebrows in Chichester with surprised letters to the *Chichester Observer*. However, as with so much that was once daringly modern, with the passage of time the building has become much easier on the eye.

Notes

1   *The Architect and Building News*, 13 March 1963.

2   WSRO E/351/6/1, Joseph Butler's drawings for the college.

3   This story, which has passed into folklore, was told to the author by Prof. Clive Behagg, Vice Chancellor of the University of Chichester which Bishop Otter College later became.

4   Colin Stansfield Smith, 'City Architecture', Chapter Two in *Chichester & The Arts 1944–2004*, Otter Memorial Paper 18, edited by P. Foster (University of Chichester, 2004).

5   University of Chichester Archive, Form of Dedication of Bishop Otter College Chapel, 21 March 1962.

6   Philip Powell said this at a meeting of the Institution of Structural Engineers, as reported in the September 1963 issue of *The Structural Engineer*.

7   WSRO CV/4, Chichester City Council, Town Planning Committee minute book, 1963–68.

8   English Heritage, the citation for the listing of the building, January 1996.

9   As told to the author by a former student in the early days of Gillett House.

Ten

Perils and Dangers

I n the 1960s, before the term 'global warming' had entered the vocabulary, Chichester suffered both the climatic perils of flooding and a notoriously hard winter; it also saw some devastating fires in its historic city centre. The emergency services came to the rescue, as always.

Flood

Chichester's river, the Lavant, is a winterbourne stream which these days only appears for a few months of the year, if at all, spending the rest of the time masquerading as an overgrown ditch. However, from time immemorial it has demonstrated that it is capable of flexing its muscles and inundating the city, most famously in recent times (1994 and 2000) when Herculean efforts were made to save the city centre by pumping its swollen waters round the city and into the canal using Green Goddess fire engines.

The last time prior to the 1994 event that this happened was in the autumn of 1960. On Sunday, 30 October torrential rain fell, and from 19.35 hours West Sussex Fire Brigade were inundated with calls to pump out flooded premises along the coast from Bognor to Shoreham, and later that night to a flooded house in Fishbourne. The rain continued for several weeks, coupled with exceptionally high winds and tides, and the fire brigade was kept busy with pumping-out until early December, with Bognor being the worst affected by flooding. In October rainfall in Chichester reached 7.26in (184mm) and the city first became hit by flooding on Thursday, 3 November with premises in Somerstown, Orchard Street and Westgate being particularly affected.[1]

154. Flooding in Green Lane and St Pancras, December 1960. The River Lavant has burst its banks and its swollen waters are flowing across the deck of the footbridge leading into Green Lane. A solitary road lamp on a plank serves to deter the foolhardy from attempting to cross the torrent. In the background are Shippam's fish and chip shop and the Red Lion public house both of which were inundated despite the sandbags, as was Goodacre's shop which sold prams and other accoutrements for the modern baby. Their Commer van seems to have been lifted on blocks above the floodwaters. (Courtesy of Garry Long)

There was a brief respite in the city on 5 November (Bonfire Night) but the Clerk of the Weather resumed hostilities the following day and the River Lavant began to rise to an alarming level. In St Pancras thirty Corporation and River Board workmen built up the riverbanks with sandbags as a precaution and used more sandbags to protect the doorways of adjacent houses. The West Sussex River Board and the county council held an emergency meeting at County Hall on 11 November to discuss the problem and find ways of dealing with it.

The crisis point for Chichester finally came on Saturday, 3 December when, following a night of gales and torrential rain coinciding with a very high tide, the Lavant burst its banks and flooded St Pancras, Green Lane, the Hornet and New Park, closing roads and inundating houses and shops. The river level rose so far above the footbridge leading to Green Lane that a high-level temporary timber deck had to be installed to maintain the important communications link.[2]

I was then attending the Central Junior Boys' School in New Park Road, and the fact that we had to wade through the floodwaters to get to school brought welcome excitement to the day. One day the water in New Park Road was so deep we had to be lifted over the school fence from the adjacent Jubilee Park by staff and park keepers. Not long after this we set off for school wearing the now-customary Wellington boots only to find the water gone – the rain had ceased and a very low tide had enabled the floodwaters to trickle away into Chichester Harbour overnight. We were devastated.

Following the flooding in 2000 a new cut was made east of the city to divert some of the flow of the River Lavant into Pagham Harbour to avoid future inundations. However, although this has proved effective in curbing the river's enthusiasm, the water table is still high and in times of heavy rain flooding still occurs in exactly the same places that were affected back in 1960 – *sic transit*!

THE 'BIG FREEZE' OF 1962/63

As a small boy I well remember my parents talking of the hard winter of 1947 and the dire hardships they had to endure. Little did I realise I was soon to experience a similar thing myself in the winter of 1962/63 which, as it happened, was to be more severe than that of 1947 – the most severe of the twentieth century in fact. I have to admit though that to a 12 year old it offered more by way of amusement than hardship.

On Boxing Day 1962 it snowed heavily, bringing the novelty of a Bing Crosby *White Christmas* to Chichester. The novelty was soon to wear off though for the

155. *Deep and crisp and uneven. St Martin's Square on 30 December 1962 after a fresh fall of snow.* (*Courtesy of John Templeton*)

following weekend, on 29 December, a blizzard lasting for twelve hours brought 9in of snow to the city centre and 6ft drifts on country roads. Milk had to be delivered in the city centre by farmers using tractors and trailers since the regular milk collection lorries could not run.[3]

Nationally the temperature plummeted, marking the beginning of the legendary 'Big Freeze' that caused two months of national chaos and suffering, particularly for transport, farmers and the elderly. With temperatures well below zero every night of January and February, accompanied by a penetrating east wind of a Siberian calibre, the sea froze and even the fast-flowing River Arun froze from its estuary up as far as the railway bridge at Ford. The east wind finally dropped on 26 January when daytime temperatures rose to around 5°C allowing a thaw to begin, but another (the final) blizzard followed on 6 February which lasted for around two hours. The snow lingered on all through February but warm rain on 8 March finally dispatched all but the most persistent accretions.[4]

Much of the snow that was cleared from the streets of Chichester was piled up into a mountain in the new car park at Northgate (some of it was still there in April), providing local children a unique chance to play in an authentic Siberian landscape.

Curiously there is next to nothing about the calamity in the city council minute books, the Corporation obviously thinking that there was no crisis, but the secretary of the South Ward Ratepayers' Association did not agree. He criticised the £500 snow clearance bill saying that with better arrangements the streets could have been cleared properly at the beginning, but that instead too much time was wasted on planning and other matters so that when a real emergency arose there were no preparations and a state of near chaos prevailed.[5] The *Chichester Observer* though revelled in it, featuring the weather for several consecutive weeks with evocative photographs of the arctic conditions.

156. A view along snowbound East Street on 30 December 1962. There are few people about as this was a Sunday and the Christmas lights, somewhat sparse by today's standards, do little to cheer the bleak scene. (Courtesy of John Templeton)

157. A new sewer was being laid in Orchard Street in January 1963 when the works halted for two months owing to frozen ground. In the background can be seen the house of the Lancastrian Schools' caretaker. This house was demolished when Orchard Street was widened. (Courtesy of Daphne Browning)

At this time few houses in Chichester had central heating, so families had to huddle around a fire in the living room and retire to, and arise from, freezing bedrooms; the fire brigade were constantly being called to deal with floodings arising from burst pipes. Getting about on the icy pavements was also hazardous. The vicar of St Paul's church, the Revd John Jackson, expressed his sympathy for those who were suffering from frozen pipes and the lack of coal and urged his parishioners to rally round and help the housebound – which they duly did.[6] In these times the Dunkerque spirit was revived (in 1962 the war had, after all, ended only seventeen years earlier) and citizens duly sought to help those who were less able to cope with the conditions.

One Chichester construction project that was disrupted by the Big Freeze was the laying of a new trunk sewer along Orchard Street from Northgate to Westgate. The work had commenced in August 1962, under the local contractor Bridgwater Bros, and involved deep trenching, laying concrete pipes and connecting all the houses to the new sewer.[7] The works had stopped for the Christmas holiday but were not to resume for two months afterwards owing to the ground becoming frozen and impossible to excavate. The works had halted right outside our house at No. 140 Orchard Street and the poorly protected trench constituted an obstruction to road users but provided a valued diversion for we boys.

During the Big Freeze all aspects of life were disrupted to a degree, but Chichester schools continued to function albeit sport was cancelled owing to playing fields being deeply covered with snow, making the pitch markings some-what difficult to see. At the Prebendal School exercise was taken in the cathedral cloisters, probably the first time they had been used for this purpose in 600 years. The boys improvised games to suit these constraints and, perhaps miraculously, only one pane of ancient glass in the cloister windows got broken and injuries were but few.[8] At Chichester High School for Boys the spring term edition of the school magazine *The Martlet* did not appear since, with virtually all sporting fixtures cancelled, it would have had little by way of content. This was the only time in its long history that an issue was missed.

On the morning of Friday, 8 February 1963 dense fog was adding to the dif-ficult icy conditions of getting to work, and trains were being delayed. The 0813 to Bognor left Chichester late and was followed into the platform by the late-running 0820 to Brighton. When the Bognor train got to Drayton the signalman there held it at his home signal awaiting a clear path to Woodgate. The Brighton train then left Chichester and after it did so the Whyke Road and Drayton signal-men jointly committed a block working irregularity, allowing the former to pull off his signals and let the Brighton train enter the section already occupied by the Bognor train, into the back of which it ran a few minutes later. The Bognor train had just started from rest at Drayton when the collision occurred.[9]

Fortunately, owing to the dense fog, the second train had been travelling very slowly (about 25mph) and as the first had just started from rest at Drayton the relative velocity of the collision was low, which prevented any fatalities occurring. However, the driver of the second train, seeing the first one looming up out of the fog, managed to jump clear before the collision otherwise he would most certainly have been killed. The colliding ends of the rolling stock were badly damaged; the motor coach of the first train rode up over the headstock of that of the second, demolishing its driver's cab and the guard's van. Both trains were formed of pre-war '4COR' electric stock* having timber-framed bodies that offered little by way of collision resistance; had the speed been much higher the destruction would have been extensive and loss of life inevitable.

The fire brigade were called at 0859 and five appliances and twenty-five firemen attended the scene and released the seventeen injured passengers. The St John Ambulance Brigade were also called and first on the scene was ambulance man Allan Ware who had been told that the incident was a colli-sion involving a car on Drayton Crossing and hence was somewhat surprised at the extent of what he found in the fog. The ambulances took all the injured to

---

* The Bognor train, the 0737 ex Portsmouth and Southsea, was formed of two electric '4COR' sets, with No. 3139 at the rear, whilst the Brighton train, the 0750 ex Portsmouth Harbour, was a single '4COR', No. 3134.

158. The collision between two electric trains at Drayton on 8 February 1963. Although the relative velocity of the collision was low, the damage to the coaches at the colliding ends was severe. A fireman is seen passing a carry-chair to his colleague on the train who has broken a window to give better access. Snow from the blizzard two days earlier can be seen on the track. (WSRO, Chichester Photographic Archive – CPS 1621/8)

159. Later in the day the Brighton breakdown crane was used to re-rail the damaged vehicles. It can be seen how the last coach of the first (Bognor) train has overridden the leading one of the second (Brighton) train, demolishing its driver's cab and guard's van. Amazingly the coach on the left (S 11195 S) was repaired and re-entered service, but the other one was broken up, being deemed beyond economic repair. (WSRO ,Chichester Photographic Archive – CPS 1621/3)

St Richard's Hospital, and most were discharged that same day after treatment. Occurring when it did there were many schoolchildren on the train and the worst injury occurred to one such, 12-year-old Christopher Ward of Graydon Avenue, who suffered a broken pelvis. Also in hospital was a French onion seller, Francois Craignon.[10]

The trains were re-railed by the Brighton breakdown crane and hauled dead to Chichester, and the line was reopened to traffic at 1630 that same day.[11] This last fact seems amazing today – in a similar accident now the line would be closed for several days, being declared a 'scene of crime' whilst the cause was exhaustively investigated, even though the root cause of railway accidents is invariably established within the first half hour.

FIRE

One of the hazards of ancient towns is the ease with which fires can spread to adjacent buildings; buildings constructed when little or no thought was given to fire prevention. Chichester's fire brigade has long been accustomed to tackling such fires in an almost surgical manner to prevent a spread which could quickly engulf the whole side of a street.

The majority of calls to the fire brigade in the 1960s were to chimney fires as most houses in the city still had solid fuel open fires for heating, but whose owners evidently did not pay enough attention to sweeping their flues. However, the decade saw two major fires in the city centre, both in commercial premises and both, as it happened, in the same street.

The premises of the Chichester Press were at No. 14 St Martin's Street, opposite the Hole in the Wall public house, and at 2000 hours on Wednesday, 23 March 1960, West Sussex Fire Brigade were called there to attend a fierce fire. The engines did not have far to travel from their station in Market Road and were quickly on the scene and a total of nine appliances soon crammed into the narrow street.[12]

The blaze was so fierce the premises were gutted and lay open to the sky, with almost all the printing presses and stores lost. Fortunately the firemen were able to save a small extension to the rear of the works where the firm recommenced operations two days later. Chichester Press did not rebuild in St Martin's Street, however, but moved to new purpose-built premises on the Terminus Road Industrial Estate.[13] The site of the original building is now occupied by the rear extension of Marks and Spencer.

Almost opposite the Chichester Press was the premises of Jay's Marine, the yacht chandlers that was all that remained of the once-mighty Jay's ironmonger's empire which traded from Nos 7/8 East Street (see Chapter Three).

160. Firemen tackling the blaze at the Chichester Press on 23 March 1960. The Hole in the Wall public house can be seen on the right and beyond it the dolphin sculpture marks the premises of Jay's Marine which were to be gutted by fire four years later. The difficulties in fighting a major fire in such a narrow street can be appreciated. (Author's collection)

The two-storey shop was an Aladdin's cave for the sailing fraternity, and Jay's was also the principal stockist in the City of Calor gas. The front of the building was graced by an attractive sculpture of a dolphin made by John Skelton.

At 0045 on 25 January 1964 Chichester firemen were called by a policeman on beat duty to a fire at Jay's Marine and two appliances attended. The premises were found to be well alight, so at 0058 two more pumps were called for and at 0110 the number on site was made six. By 0350 nine appliances and five senior officers from Bognor, East Wittering, Bosham and Littlehampton as well as Chichester were on the scene, where once again the cramped conditions of the narrow street made tackling such a serious blaze very difficult.

Fear of explosions from the thirty gas cylinders in the premises caused the family of the landlord of the next door Hole in the Wall and other nearby residents to be evacuated, but the firemen managed to move all the cylinders out of harm's way, thus preventing destruction of adjacent properties.[14]

The shop was completely gutted and its roof lost, with damage estimated at £25,000. However, the shell of the building stood with Skelton's dolphin still

234

161. Jay's Marine shop in St Martin's Street newly rebuilt after the fire. The dolphin, by John Skelton, survived the blaze. Externally the shop looked little different from before. (Courtesy of Ken Green)

adorning it, a little scorched but otherwise unscathed. The internal structure was rebuilt and Jay's continued to trade there for many years after the fire. The building still exists and is used as a shop but sadly no longer graced by Skelton's dolphin.

Notes

1   WSRO WDC/FB16/1/6, West Sussex Fire Brigade, Fire Register, 1/4/1960 to 31/3/1961.
2   The *Chichester Observer*, 4, 11, 18 November and 9, 16 December 1960.
3   The *Chichester Observer*, 4 January 1963.
4   Say, J.R. and Sterry, N., *The Winter of 1962–63* (a contemporary account published in *The Martlet*, the magazine of Chichester High School for Boys, Summer Term, 1963).
5   The *Chichester Observer*, 25 January 1963.
6   WSRO Par 43/7/9, St Paul's parish newsletters, 1960–79.
7   WSRO CG/2, minutes of Chichester City Council Highway Committee, 1950–68.
8   Ollerenshaw, N., *A History of the Prebendal School* (Phillimore, 1984).
9   HMSO Report by Col. W.P. Reed of HM Railway Inspectorate into the Drayton Accident (19 June 1963).

10 WSRO WDC/FB16/1/8, West Sussex Fire Brigade, Fire Register 1/4/1962 to 31/3/1963, the *Chichester Observer*, 15 February 1963 and reminiscence of ambulance man Allan Ware.

11 HMSO, op. cit.

12 WSRO WDC/FB16/1/5, West Sussex Fire Brigade, Fire Register 1/4/1959 to 31/3/1960.

13 Anon., *The Chichester Phoenix – the Cautionary Story* (Chichester Press Ltd, 1961).

14 WSRO WDC/FB16/1/9, West Sussex Fire Brigade, Fire Register October 1963 to December 1964, and the *Chichester Observer*, 31 January 1964.

Eleven

From Cradle to Grave: Provision for Healthcare – and Beyond

F or a town of its size, 1960s Chichester was very well provided for in terms of hospitals, GP surgeries, dentists, pharmacies and – finally – undertakers. The fact that there are more undertakers now is a sign of the demographic shift in Chichester's population that has occurred in the last forty years or so!

Hospitals

In 1960 there were no fewer than four hospitals serving the city. The oldest of these was the **Royal West Sussex Hospital** (known simply as 'The Royal West') in Broyle Road that had opened in 1826 as an independent charitable institution and was regarded with great pride by Cicestrians. Another hospital, **St Richard's** in Spitalfields Lane, was opened by the county council in 1939 providing services supported by rates rather than charity, and known, particularly to its detractors, as 'Dirty Dick's'. Amongst its facilities was a maternity unit where, from the 1950s onwards, most Cicestrians uttered their first cries on entering the world.

Both institutions came under the umbrella of the National Heath Service in April 1948, and the new management quickly saw that having two fully equipped hospitals in one small town was not justified and set about integrating the services they provided. In the 1950s the Regional Health Board decided that the St Richard's site would be developed to provide the principal facility with more ward blocks, new operating theatres, improved outpatient and better accident and emergency facilities. This work began in 1962.[1] Thereafter The Royal West declined in its importance and was finally closed in 1994 after which the building and its site was sold.

162. The Royal West Sussex Hospital in Broyle Road. The massive wisteria that spread along the entire frontage became its trademark. The building still survives, having been converted into apartments after closure. (Courtesy of Ken Green)

Another hospital which closed under the 1960s expansion of St Richard's was the **Isolation Hospital**, also in Spitalfield Lane. This institution had opened in 1888 in an era when treatment of infectious diseases required victims to be cut off from society. The hospital was built on the top part of the Michaelmas Fair Field and consisted of two single-storey wings of one-patient wards, separated from the road by a high wall. Little used after 1960, it closed when the system of barrier nursing was introduced, and the nursing school in its grounds expanded into the redundant buildings. The training school continued for several years afterwards* but Bishopsgate Walk now occupies the site. Although the original buildings have gone, much of the high wall in Spitalfield Lane remains as a reminder of those isolationist times.

Independent of the other three hospitals was Graylingwell, the area psychiatric hospital which was opened by West Sussex County Council as **The West Sussex County Asylum** in 1897 in handsome buildings in Summersdale.

---

* I unexpectedly became an inmate of the Isolation Hospital in the summer of 1958 when, as a result of an observational stay in The Royal West, it was discovered that I was suffering from a highly contagious form of salmonella. The transfer was swiftly effected. I rather enjoyed my stay there; having my own room instead of being on a noisy communal ward seemed the height of luxury.

Successive superintendents had adopted progressive ideas about the treatment of mental illness and central to this was the provision of recreation. To this end a large recreation hall was provided in the centre of the complex which included a proscenium-arch stage with six flies and an orchestra pit. A projection box was soon added and so recreation included film shows, plays and musical entertainments. By 1960 the range of entertainments provided consisted of weekly dances and socials, films, whist drives, community singing, a Darby and Joan Club, visiting concert parties and monthly classical concerts. The CinemaScope wide-screen system had been installed in 1957 only two years after it had been installed at The Granada.[2] Entertainment was available every night of the week, and not solely for the patients since the public were encouraged to come to events there, and in the 1960s the well-attended dances and socials helped to dispel the fear and misunderstanding about mental illness.[3] Indeed, in 1968, when the electrical installation in the hall was renewed, state-of-the-art stage lighting was provided along with reflective mirrorballs in the ceiling to enhance the facilities.[4]

Graylingwell Hospital closed in 2002 and the site was later redeveloped for housing. Many of the original buildings were retained but sadly the recreation hall, so beloved of past generations of Cicestrians, was demolished to make way for thirty-two homes. Now, of the city's four hospitals, only St Richard's survives with the epithet 'Dirty Dick's' largely forgotten.

Just as most Chichester babies emerged at St Richard's in the 1960s, so most received their early healthcare treatment at the County Council Health Centre, universally known as 'The Clinic', in Chapel Street. Here, in this single-storey 1930s building, children would be weighed, receive inoculations, have ears and eyes tested, teeth examined and have any disorders monitored.

163. The Health Centre, known as 'The Clinic', in Chapel Street, a building familiar to several generations of Chichester children and their mothers. It was recently rebuilt to much larger proportions. (Courtesy of Ken Green)

THE AMBULANCE SERVICE

When the National Health Service was set up in 1948 hospitals in the Chichester area used the St John Ambulance Brigade to provide the emergency service as there was no provision made for this by the county council. During the daytime ambulance crews were paid, but, perhaps bizarrely, the out of hours service was provided by volunteers who would camp out at the Brigade's Barford House HQ in the Hornet in order to be able to make a rapid response.[5]

In addition to this call out service, the St John Ambulance Brigade provided volunteer cover for major events including the Goodwood horse and motor racing meetings. On Easter Monday 1960, fifty casualties were treated on site from a crowd of 60,000 that had gathered for the motor racing, whilst during the 1962 Goodwood week 240 cases were treated amongst the racing fraternity. Also in 1962 the Brigade provided the first-aid cover for the ten-week first season at the new Festival Theatre.[6]

In April 1963 West Sussex County Council set up its own ambulance service to provide the front-line response, using fully paid crews with new vehicles operating, from 1964, out of a new ambulance station in Summersdale Road. The handover of the front line service from the St John Ambulance Brigade to the county took place at a Sunday parade in front of County Hall, at which

164. A line up of vehicles of the Chichester Division of the St John Ambulance Brigade seen at their HQ, Barford House in the Hornet, in 1963. The consecutive numbering of the local registrations of the two Bedfords and the Land Rover will be noted. Next to them is an elderly Austin Civil Defence rescue vehicle whose 'XH' registration shows it originally hailed from London. (Courtesy of Allan and Pat Ware)

several St John members transferred across to the new service.[7] One of those who transferred was Fanny Silverlock, the remarkable ambulance woman we met in Chapter Eight.

Thereafter the St John Ambulance Brigade in Chichester became an auxiliary, and now totally voluntary, service but continued to equip itself with new vehicles and appliances in order to provide first aid cover for local events, including the gala when they were kept particularly busy dealing with the bloodied knees of soapbox derby entrants. They continue to provide event cover to this day.

General Medical Practice

The new National Health Service also saw the services of the family doctor being provided free, and in 1968 there were seven practices listed in Kelly's Directory. The largest of these was at Langley House, a Georgian house in West Street, where Drs Collins, Lacy, Denman and Milligan were to be found. They also had an outpost at Bosham. Dr Denman was one of the few lady GPs in the city at the time and Dr Martin Collins, who had a keen interest in the arts, hung his abstract paintings in the waiting room[*]. Dr Milligan was my doctor from a very early age and was highly respected at the hospitals; any referral by him seemed to accelerate to the top of the list. Both he and Dr Collins had a penchant for fast sports cars and always had the registrations '5000 PO' and '6000 PO' transferred to their latest chariots.

Summersdale was served by the Lavant Road Surgery where Drs Pailthorpe, Coltart, Shaw and Willatt were in residence. Dr M.A. Bernays still had the surgery at No. 2 Basin Road serving some 1,300 patients that we encountered in Chapter Three, but he also had another surgery in Parklands that was soon to expand in order to serve the new East Broyle Estate.

At No. 8 St John's Street, another large Georgian House, was the surgery of Dr J.H.H. Gough. Dr Gough, another highly respected GP, had been practicing in the city since the 1930s and was also a surgeon at The Royal West where, traditionally, he would have been known as 'Mr' rather than 'Doctor'. In the war he had been medical officer to all the local army and RAF camps. The surgery and waiting room occupied part of the ground floor of No. 8 St John's Street and patients entered using the side entrance accessed through a door in the adjoining garage. He owned the house, where the family lived 'over the shop', and

---

[*] He later became one of the founder members of the Friends of Pallant House Gallery when it opened in 1982.

165. Dr John Gough, with his dog Bracken, in the garden of his surgery in St John's Street. He retired in 1968. (Courtesy of Mary Hill)

remained there until he retired in 1968. It is now a private house. Dr Gough was granted the title 'Surgeon Emeritus' by The Royal West, where a seat dedicated to his memory was provided.[8]

Other doctors' surgeries were to be found at No. 2 North Pallant (Drs Kennedy, Neasham, Palmer and Foister) and No. 24 West Street (Drs Stanley, Sears, Mickerson and Coltart).

A TRIP TO THE DENTIST

There were few things in the 1960s that instilled more fear in a child than a trip to the dentist. In those days, when we paid less attention to the effects of sweet eating than we ought, having fillings was one of life's little hazards. Most terrifying was the dentist's drill, a contraption resembling an overgrown and animated Anglepoise lamp, driven by exposed belts whose menacing whirring accompanied the high-pitched scream of the drill bit. Injections to obviate the pain were an option but as it meant losing one side of your face for an hour or so it was best to grin and bear it.

The 1968 Kelly's Directory lists seven dental practices, the best known of which was Boutwood and Wilson at No. 31 Little London which still exists in the same premises, albeit under new partners, as the Little London Dental Centre. At Richmond House, No. 47 South Street, was Fleetwood and Partners, another practice which survived, now known as the Richmond House Dental Surgery. Our family dentist was Mr Farwell at No. 50 West Street, a gentle practitioner under whom injections for fillings were never necessary as he instinctively knew when to stop drilling in order to avoid hitting the raw nerve.

The other practices were Douglas Robertson-Richie in Market Avenue, Mr Craig at No. 6 East Pallant, Mr Francis at No. 14 North Pallant and Mr Grainger at No. 30 West Street. At that time all these dentists offered free treatment under the NHS but sadly, although the number of dental practices is far higher now, ones taking NHS patients are as rare as hens' teeth – so to speak.

PILLS AND POTIONS

A visit to the doctor usually resulted in a prescription, and six pharmacies – or dispensing chemists as they were known – existed to supply the necessary pills and potions. One chemist would always stay open late, on a weekly cycle, for those attending evening surgery.

Two of these were branches of the obligatory chains, Timothy Whites in East Street and Boots in South Street. Boots moved from No. 11 South Street into brand new premises across the road at Nos 62–3 in 1964, but the legendary Boots Lending Library, which had occupied an upper floor of the old shop, did not transfer. Boots' new premises were on the opposite corner of Cooper Street to another, much smaller, chemist, Savory and Moore, but the two managed to coexist quite happily. Neither premises are chemist's shops now.

The rest of the chemists were independent family businesses. S.W. Bastow occupied a shop at No. 9 North Street, just up from the Cross, and in the 1960s it was run by the second and third generations of the family, Bill and his son Tim. The shop ran back a long way from its frontage and, as well as the usual medicines, carried a wide stock of toiletries and photographic equipment. Another attraction for schoolboys was the fact that you could obtain replacement chemicals and additional apparatus for your chemistry set, the only chemist in Chichester who catered for this particular market.

Bill Bastow was a prominent figure in the life of the city and was for many years churchwarden at St Peter the Great. His son Tim[*] took on the business but moved it in 1985 to the former fish and chip shop at No. 50 North Street. Sussex Stationers now occupies the old shop at No. 9.

---

[*] Sadly Tim Bastow died in 2012.

166. The interior of Bastow's shop at No. 9 North Street, typical of pharmacies of the period. Note the chairs for elderly customers to rest upon whilst awaiting their prescriptions. The gas light has been retained for emergency back-up purposes. (Courtesy of Ken Green)

Another old established chemist was G.F. Bevis at No. 15 Eastgate Square which, in the 1960s, was run by the second generation George Bevis. They too specialised in photographic equipment as George was president of the Chichester Camera Club, but he was also a member of Chichester Amateur Operatic Society alongside Tim Bastow – art knew no rivalry! The Eastgate Pharmacy still exists, but under new ownership, and has moved to smaller premises next door at No. 14.[9]

Another small chemist was J.T.W. Binns, at No. 49 North Street on the corner of North Walls. This was the closest chemist to where we lived in Orchard Street and I was impressed as a boy by the ranks of polished mahogany drawers behind the counter marked with the Latin names of myriad concoctions. It was to Binns that I took my first film (from a Kodak Brownie 127) to be processed and anxiously awaited the results. I proved to be no Lord Snowdon.

THE FINAL JOURNEY

When it came time for that final 1960s journey there were three long-established undertakers (or funeral directors as they preferred to be called) who would make the necessary arrangements. The oldest of these was Edward White & Son at Nos 5–7 South Pallant with their chapel of rest opposite at No. 16. F.A. Holland & Son had taken over the business of F.G. Shepherd in New Park Road and provided the principal rival service and, curiously, had their memorial showrooms in South Pallant, just up the road from White's. The third firm was Lewis & Co., who operated out of premises at the bottom of South Street, one of which was the Old Theatre. As Lewis & Co. also sold prams and furniture they could literally provide a cradle-to-grave service! They closed in 1967. All still operated Rolls-Royce hearses in the 1960s; the idea of making your last journey in a Ford was unheard of – but was only just around the corner.

The option of cremation rather than burial was being taken up increasingly in the 1960s, but the nearest crematoria were at Portchester or Brighton, neither of which was particularly convenient. Chichester City Council considered building their own in 1964 and commissioned the architect Brian Tyler to come up with a suitable scheme. On 11 May that year he presented two designs for an 'original' and a 'revised' cremato-rium, of which the 'revised' (cheaper) scheme was approved. The treasurer's report on the matter estimated that there would be 1,100 cremations per annum but the Medical Officer of Health challenged this figure opining, hopefully oblivious to his irony, that with the planned extensions to local hospitals, 'the number would be higher'. The overall cost of the revised scheme was £71,535 which allowed for a twin gas-fired system and a house for the superintendent. The treasurer tabled his estimated running costs of £13,475 which would be offset by income of

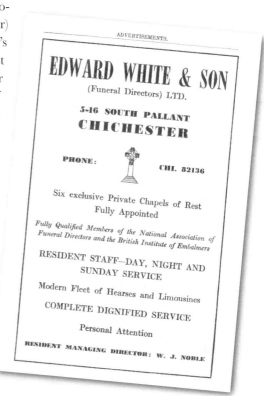

ADVERTISEMENTS.

EDWARD WHITE & SON
(Funeral Directors) LTD.

5-16 SOUTH PALLANT
CHICHESTER

PHONE: CHI. 82136

Six exclusive Private Chapels of Rest
Fully Appointed

Fully Qualified Members of the National Association of
Funeral Directors and the British Institute of Embalmers

RESIDENT STAFF—DAY, NIGHT AND
SUNDAY SERVICE

Modern Fleet of Hearses and Limousines

COMPLETE DIGNIFIED SERVICE

Personal Attention

RESIDENT MANAGING DIRECTOR: W. J. NOBLE

167. An advertisement for Edward White & Son, funeral directors of South Pallant from 1968. (Author's collection)

£10,600 derived from fees and the sale of urns and memorials. The remaining £2,875 would be borne by the ratepayers.[10]

Despite this initial enthusiasm the idea quickly petered out, perhaps the plans to build a crematorium at Worthing, which opened in 1968, reduced the pressure. Chichester did not get its crematorium until 1971.

By 1961 all the churchyards in the city centre had been closed* to new burials, so all such had to take place at the City Cemetery in Westhampnett. The clerk to the Burial Board was Eric Banks, the town clerk.

Notes

1 Cooke, M., *The Royal West Sussex Hospital 1784–1995* New Chichester Paper, No. 3 (Chichester Local History Society and The University of Chichester, 2012).

2 West Sussex Library Services S/300063156 (Graylingwell Hospital Annual Reports, 1954–61).

3 Brenda Wild (as related to Paddy Welsh) *Forty Four Years a Nurse at Graylingwell*, an article in *Chichester History No. 18*, Chichester Local History Society, 2002 (Brenda Wild commenced her training at Graylingwell in 1958).

4 WSRO – an uncatalogued collection of contract drawings relating to Graylingwell Hospital.

5 Told to the author by Allan and Pat Ware who were prominent members of the ambulance service in the 1960s.

6 *The Chi Sinjun* The news sheet of the Chichester Division of the St John Ambulance Brigade Vol. 2, No. 3 (April 1960) and Vol. 2, No. 15 (September 1962).

7 The *Chichester Observer*, 12 April 1963.

8 Information supplied by Mary Hill, Dr Gough's daughter.

9 Foster, P., *Pills and Potions*, Chapter 13 of *A Baker's Dozen*, Otter Memorial Paper No. 29 (University of Chichester, 2011).

10 WSRO C/32, Chichester Common Council minute book, 1954–65.

---

* Those in the outlying villages were still open however, and relatives of mine were buried in the 1960s at Donnington and Fishbourne.

Envoi

The main streets of so many towns I visit* shout 'Vic-Sixties' at me, an unflattering term I have coined for those places that lost half of their ancient buildings in Victorian times and most of the remainder in the 1960s, leaving little to delight my particular eye.

Chichester is very lucky to have got off lightly in the Victorian era – not being an industrial town undoubtedly helped – so the essential character of the main streets remained Georgian into the twentieth century. But what of the 1960s? Chichester did suffer some indignity and, as we have seen, 1964 was particularly bleak in this respect seeing, *inter alia*, the infamous destruction of the east side of Somerstown and the needless loss of Sharp Garland's historic grocer's shop. However, all was not as bad as it might have been, for the sad destruction of Somerstown served as a wakeup call; the brakes were applied – and sharply. One result of this is that the city still does not have any highrise buildings** to mar its skyline, and it can still be classed as unspoilt. Contrast this with poor Portsmouth where what the Luftwaffe failed to flatten in the 1940s, the developers 'got' in the 1960s. In Portsmouth you have interpretation boards telling you not what you are looking at *now*, but what *used* to be there. Sadly in the 1960s more cities went the way of Portsmouth than of Chichester.

The conservation study of 1967 was to prove the turning point in the development of Chichester; things were to be subjected to much greater scrutiny from then on. This is not to imply, however, that Chichester thereby became frozen in

---

* No names, no pack drill, as my old boss used to say!
** The new museum, built in Tower Street in 2011/12 is uncomfortably lofty for Chichester and can be seen from the Trundle, but it does not class as 'high rise' in the strictest sense of the word.

the eighteenth century – preserved in aspic so to speak – for it didn't; that is not what conservation is about. It acquired, and is still acquiring, new buildings to sit alongside the old. Some of those 1960s acquisitions are worthy of acclaim, and the prize must surely go to Powell & Moya's Festival Theatre of 1962, a design that, fifty years on, still looks fresh and interesting. For all the shock it caused in 1964, ABK's Gillett House ('Colditz'), although typifying the brutalist 1960s, is none the less a quality building, and we should not be surprised at its listing. The ingenious – even if unintended – circular form of the 1967 library still looks good, and the external lift shaft recently added to its exterior is sympathetic and does not detract from the pleasing design.

Contrast these three buildings though with the sprawl of bland 1960s housing that made up the East Broyle and Little Breach developments, and the tacky, system-built office blocks around County Hall and at Northgate. Another such office block, Stocklund House in East and St John's streets, has recently been given a facelift – or rather a new face – which, the owners claim, 'Georgianises' it; whilst the result will clearly not fool anyone into thinking it is an eighteenth-century building, its new appearance is an improvement over the 1966 original.

The guiding hand in the fortunes of the city in the 1960s was the Corporation – *aka* Chichester City Council – a body of *local* people who took decisions on *local* issues. Although, as we have seen, local scandals could arise, the Corporation was a body that cared about the city in its charge because its members lived there. At the local government reorganisation of 1974 this municipal Corporation was swept away and most of its powers – including all-important planning – were given to a new, and very much larger body, a *district* council covering an area stretching north from the coast to the border with Surrey. Members of the new Chichester District Council were now making decisions about a city in which most of them did not live – and therefore could not understand. After a struggle, Chichester City Council was allowed to live on, but essentially only in name for it was reduced to parish council status with few powers. However, it was allowed to keep its mayor and insignia and its meetings continue in Roger Morris's Council House, built with great civic pride back in 1731. Arguably that was small consolation for a city that was used to governing its own affairs, but the spirit of Cicestrian civic pride, that has existed for centuries, thereby still flourishes.

The affairs of the city and its environs were reported on by a range of local newspapers whose pronouncements have been widely quoted in this work. Principal of these was the *Chichester Observer*, a weekly organ published from its premises in Little London. Its day of publication has moved around during its long career, but in the 1960s it was every Friday. The editor from 1961 was Graham Brooks who remained in harness until 1992. From the same stable (Portsmouth and Sunderland Newspapers) came another weekly organ, the *West*

Sussex Gazette which reported on issues over a much wider area. There were also two evening papers available every day except Sunday. The first of these was the *Evening Argus,* a Brighton-based paper that had a Chichester office at No. 56 South Street. The *Argus* covered the whole of Sussex and so had several area editions giving differing geographical emphases to the main stories of the day. The other evening paper was *Portsmouth Evening News* whose coverage had a Hampshire rather than a Sussex bias, and it too was part of the Portsmouth and Sunderland empire. Its title was shortened to *The Evening News* and then later to simply *The News,* a singularly uninformative title if ever there was one. All four papers are still going today but the *Chichester Observer* has recently changed to a tabloid format, a change that has not met with universal approval as one might expect of Chichester.

Chichester will, of necessity, continue to grow, but its relative inaccessibility makes growth much slower than in, say, Winchester, another Romano-Georgian cathedral city a similar distance from London. Lucky Winchester has, despite its growth, managed to retain the water meadows which so enhance its setting whereas Chichester's water meadows are now but a fond and fleeting memory of the lost Westgate Fields where cattle grazed right up to the city wall until that fateful year of 1964.

Chichester's small size is just one of its many attractive qualities, qualities that make it the ideal place to live and work. It has everything one could possibly wish for: fine buildings, an active cultural life including a nationally renowned theatre, and an ancient cathedral, all within walking distance of both the sea and the Downs. I have never felt the need to move away – and probably never will.

Suggestions for Further Reading

Burrows, G.S., *Chichester, A Study in Conservation* (London: HMSO, 1968)

Evershed-Martin, Leslie, *The Impossible Theatre* (Phillimore, 1971)

Eyles, Allen, Frank Grey and Alan Readman, *Cinema West Sussex – the first 100 years* (Phillimore, 1996)

Foster, Paul (ed.), *Chichester and the Arts 1944–2004* (Otter Memorial Paper 18, University of Chichester, 2004)

Foster, Paul and Sheila Hale (eds), *A Baker's Dozen* (Otter Memorial Paper 29, University of Chichester, 2011)

Green, Alan H.J., *Cattle Corn and Crawfish – 900 Years of Chichester's Markets* (Phillimore, 2011)

Hewitt, Phil, *Chichester Remembered* (Phillimore, 2004)

Hussey, Walter, *Patron of Art – The Revival of a Great Tradition Among Modern Artists* (Weidenfeld and Nicholson, 1985)

McKensie, Joyce, *Memories of Somerstown – A Tribute to a Community* (Purbeck Books, 2008)

INDEX

Visit our website and discover thousands of other History Press books.

www.thehistorypress.co.uk